ROUTLEDGE
HUMAN RESO

Volume 12

WORK REVOLUTION

WORK REVOLUTION

PAUL DICKSON

LONDON AND NEW YORK

First published in 1977 by George Allen & Unwin

This edition first published in 2017
by Routledge
2 Park Square, Milton Park, Abingdon, Oxon OX14 4RN

and by Routledge
711 Third Avenue, New York, NY 10017

Routledge is an imprint of the Taylor & Francis Group, an informa business

© 1975 Paul Dickson

All rights reserved. No part of this book may be reprinted or reproduced or utilised in any form or by any electronic, mechanical, or other means, now known or hereafter invented, including photocopying and recording, or in any information storage or retrieval system, without permission in writing from the publishers.

Trademark notice: Product or corporate names may be trademarks or registered trademarks, and are used only for identification and explanation without intent to infringe.

British Library Cataloguing in Publication Data
A catalogue record for this book is available from the British Library

ISBN: 978-1-138-80870-6 (Set)
ISBN: 978-1-315-18006-9 (Set) (ebk)
ISBN: 978-1-138-28856-0 (Volume 12) (hbk)
ISBN: 978-1-138-28859-1 (Volume 12) (pbk)
ISBN: 978-1-315-26780-7 (Volume 12) (ebk)

Publisher's Note
The publisher has gone to great lengths to ensure the quality of this reprint but points out that some imperfections in the original copies may be apparent.

Disclaimer
The publisher has made every effort to trace copyright holders and would welcome correspondence from those they have been unable to trace.

Work Revolution

by Paul Dickson

Foreword by
JACK JONES

London
GEORGE ALLEN & UNWIN
Boston　　　　Sydney

To my parents

First published in Great Britain 1977
Copyright © 1975 by Paul Dickson
Originally published in USA as *The Future of the Workplace*
American spelling and usage have been retained
ISBN 0 04 331071 0

Printed in Great Britain by Biddles Ltd., Guildford, Surrey

Contents

Foreword by Jack Jones — vii

I. *Working Alternatives*
   1. Standards — 3
   2. The Human Touch — 9
   3. Up from Lordstown — 13
   4. "Work in America" — 20
   5. A Better Idea—Not by Ford — 24
   6. The Organic Organization — 33

II. *Job Enrichment*
   1. Opening Salvo in the War on Dumb Jobs — 41
   2. The Process — 43
   3. Easing the Pain with the Job Doctor — 56
   4. Unfinished Business — 69
   5. Moving up the Job Ladder — 78

III. *Scandinavian Industrial Democracy*
   1. Up to the Boards — 85
   2. The Norwegian Experiments — 88
   3. Equality at Work in Sweden — 102
   4. A Slow, Small, but Sure Start in Department 698 — 111
   5. The Arvika Experiment — 115
   6. Industrial Freedom in Denmark — 122

IV. *Democratic Designs in America*
   1. Show and Tell — 139
   2. American Velvet: "That Crazy Place in Connecticut" — 141
   3. General Foods: Gaines in Topeka — 155
   4. More Designs on People — 166

V. *Support Systems*
   1. The Customizers — 177
   2. General Electric's Columbia Experiments — 178
   3. Edwin H. Land and His Polarized Family — 188
   4. The Deal at the Dairy — 202

VI. *Breaking the Time Barriers*
   1. Dogmatic Days   209
   2. The Compressed Workweek   214
   3. The Flexible Day   228
   4. Pairing, Sharing, and Splitting—Bringing on the Permanent Part-timer   243
   5. The Sabbatical (Not for Professors Only)   257
   6. Time Off for Good Works   266
   7. Other Timely Options   271

VII. *The Democratic Office, the Do-it-yourself Factory*
   1. The Environmental Prerogative   281
   2. McDonald's: The Unwalled Corporation   286
   3. "The Social Waterhole": An Office Built Around Individual Needs   295
   4. The Place Where They Let the Workers Design a Factory   304

VIII. *To Thine Own Self Be Boss*
   1. The Self-employment Alternative   313
   2. Striking Out on Your Own—A Personal Observation   317
   3. Rescuing an Anachronism   333

IX. *Brave New Work*
   1. Portents of the Future   345
   2. The Bolivar Project   356
   3. The Bottom Line   363

Acknowledgments   365
Chapter Notes   366
Index   371

Foreword

by Jack Jones

General Secretary, Transport and General Workers' Union

Given the inadequate performance of the British economy in recent years, all concerned with industry in this country have a pressing need to look critically at the organization of work, the systems of control, and the patterns of authority in our establishments.

Many have been aware of the depressing effect on the quality of life of many of our methods of production. Many bemoan the sterile attitudes generated, as they see it, by the organization of industry. And many of us in the Trade Union Movement are very critical of those out-dated authoritarian methods of management which deny any expression of the interest and abilities of the mass of workers.

But we may all of us have been insufficiently concerned to relate our critical views to the total needs of any productive process. Any genuine concern for human welfare and development must show a comprehensive appreciation of the technological and organizational limitations and potential inherent in the work.

Paul Dickson's *Work Revolution* is, therefore, a very useful stimulus to further, and clearer, thought in this area. The usefulness of the work derives from its "reference" role—it brings together detailed descriptions of several very interesting experiments in new forms of work organization and management.

The examples of various experiments in work reorganization—Job Enrichment, if you like—and worker participation in management from Norway, Sweden, Denmark, and the USA, provoke considerable thought as to the extent to which these models could be developed and applied in the UK.

In particular, those experiments which give to the workers concerned a much wider range of skills and responsibilities and enlarge their degree of control over their work situation, deserve our critical, but sympathetic appraisal. As we in the UK enlarge and extend the scope of collective negotiation and representation to give workers similarly increased control, and develop our own systems of Industrial Democracy, we should avail ourselves of any comparable experience in those fields.

Of particular significance must be the realization of increased efficiency and productivity, through the greater sharing of control achieved in some of the developments reviewed.

Both the generalization, and the specific examples, concerning more flexible approaches to the matter of working hours, seem somewhat less convincing—possibly because of the rather superficial quotes from UK newspapers covering trade union attitudes, and the author's own bald references to "Great Britain, with its hugely volatile labour situation. . . ."!

But even in this respect we must welcome any summary which directs thought to the practicability of a shorter working week, and of more varied working hours. With the unremitting advance of technological and structural unemployment throughout most of the "Western" industrial world, this matter of redistribution of work and income through a real alteration to the working week, must come close to the top of any list of social and economic priorities.

The real problems of "Job Satisfaction", "Job Enrichment", the "Quality of Life", and "Worker Participation" have been blurred and obscured by some academic sociology, and by some whose privilege stems from authoritarian forms of control.

Work Revolution brings these problems into a proper plane of consideration. Successful initiatives—and some not so successful—are sensibly discussed in readable language. Study of this book will help break down the rigidity of thought about the basic reorganization of work.

It is a useful reminder of the real problems of alienation and relationship between those who work and their means of production. Here is evidence that, given some courage, some common sense,

Foreword

and some faith in those who do the work, the process of production can be made to serve those who produce.

Personally I would wish to emphasize more than the author does the role of Trade Unionism for workers to secure satisfaction at the place of work. Defence against the adverse effects of technology upon workers by hand and by brain and a control by workers over technology so that it meets and even develops aspirations for individual and collective fulfilment are the basic twin roles of the trade union movement. It is not surprising that those who wish to constrain workers' progress invariably ascribe to the trade unions a purely defensive role. Of course we have defensive roles, but this is not, as the opposition suggests, to stop technological progress. On the contrary. The history of the trade union movement is marked by frequent interventions to shape the technological process. The extension of trade union involvement into research and development, into the working environment, into quality control, and indeed into every aspect of investment are now amongst our main goals; and the unions welcome anything that makes better pay and shorter hours and high consumption levels possible. But the changes should be mutually agreed between management and unions. Since technical changes are taking place all the time, however, this automatically means that opportunities continually occur to make advances on hours of work and environmental conditions.

Our trade unions have on the whole been flexible about the introduction of work study and other management techniques, but we are inflexible about our desire for mutual agreement when it comes to deciding how much a worker has to do for each shift he works and what the conditions of his work should be. Concentration on tasks, of itself, does nothing to increase workers' influence over the whole productive process, indeed it may well do the opposite by centering trade union attention around small isolated groups. The so-called autonomous group organizing the production of a small sub-assembly might in reality be even more alienated from the total productive process than the workers on the large assembly line. It is the job of the trade unions to use job enrichment and work organization techniques and the control aspirations they kindle, outlined so effectively in this book, to achieve real industrial democracy so that work people, collectively, get more "say" on all the issues and policies which affect them in their enterprises. This, for me, is the only real guarantee in the future of a *better* quality of life at work.

# Working Alternatives

1
STANDARDS

The Industrial Revolution turned people from handicraftsmen and unscientific subsistence farmers into machine tenders, product assemblers, and paper shufflers. With this came all the major trappings of our modern world, as the factory system, the middle class, labor as a force, engineering, communications systems, industrial capitalism, booms and depressions, and wages and salaries came into existence.

If this was the great force shaping the modern working world, there were later influences that came along to give it sophistication. The first and most important was the scientific management movement, which got going early in this century. This entire movement can be traced back to one man: Frederick Winslow Taylor—a man who has had more to do with the state of today's working world than any other individual.

Born in Germantown, Pennsylvania, in 1856, he was still a boy when he first showed a compelling interest in engineering, science, and finding new ways to do things. As a young athlete, he, with a friend, won the national doubles championship in tennis with a racket of his own design. At Exeter, he took to the mound in baseball and began pitching overhand, and has since been credited with being the first to break with the then-universal practice of underhanded pitching. Overwork at school brought on a nervous breakdown, after which Taylor decided to become a manual laborer rather than go to college. He soon became a machinist, and went to work for the Midvale Iron Works in Philadelphia, where he rose to the rank of chief engineer in six years. At Midvale, Taylor became impressed with the failure of the workers to put in a full day's work (he estimated that the average man was only putting in a third of a day's work) and with the inability of management to handle or even be fully aware of this. Taylor saw that management was not managing and that was because it had no precise idea of what constituted a day's work and how to make that day's work most efficient. From this came Taylor's concept of the duties of management, which were:

¶ To develop a science for each element of a man's work.

¶ To select and train the best worker for each task (rather than letting each worker pick his work and train himself, as was then common).

¶ To develop cooperation between workers and managers in order to enhance efficiency.

¶ To divide labor into small, equal shares.

Taylor's goal became efficiency, and to achieve it, he reorganized things at the plant so that each man's work was simplified, fragmented, and highly supervised. Saving steps was a key to his scheme, and the stopwatch the major tool. He and his assistants took workers in groups, and watched and timed them, and then rebuilt their jobs by cutting out all time-consuming wasted effort. In this way, Taylor invented the time-and-motion study still so popular in the industrial world.

From Midvale, Taylor took his emerging gospel to the Bethlehem Steel Company, where he began reorganizing shops and departments and conducting some of his most celebrated experiments. In one, which was made famous in dozens of texts in industrial management, Taylor took a dull, immigrant laborer named Schmidt, who was loading twelve and one-half tons of pig iron a day, and through time-and-motion study and close supervision was able to get the man to load forty-seven and one-half tons a day. Taylor later wrote that the success of this experiment was in part due to Schmidt's stupidity and held that men like Schmidt are best matched to such jobs. From this and similar experiments, Taylor developed a system of judging people like show cattle in order to size them up for the proper role in the organization. By his reckoning, men like Schmidt were "prize oxen" and could be found at the ratio of one to eight in the male population. Taylor developed the concept of the "well-rounded man," one with ". . . brains; education; special or technical knowledge; manual dexterity or strength; tact; energy; grit; honesty; judgment or common sense; good health." According to Taylor, a man with three of these qualities was suited to be a common laborer, with four or five, a foreman or gang boss, and with eight or nine out of nine, the well-rounded chap who should be plant superintendent.

For a while, it was as if everything Taylor touched turned into a new tenet or practice. At Bethlehem, he became fascinated by shovels, and approached that humble object through hundreds of studies which led him to conclude that a workman needs different kinds of shovels depending on what is being shoveled. He determined that the most efficient shovel-load was one weighing twenty-one pounds and because of the density of different materials this meant that a coal shovel should be smaller than one used for ashes, to allow each to handle the requisite twenty-one pounds. Out of this work came the concept of "tool standardization," which prescribed a tool for each job.

After three years at Bethlehem, a new management took over and fired Taylor—they did not understand his methods and were alarmed by the fact that he was rewarding workers with increased pay for increased efficiency. This was a blow to Taylor, who decided that, rather than work for a company again, he would head off on his own and preach and write about what he had learned. His major accomplishments during the period from 1901 to 1910 were his writings, which were to become the foundation of modern management practice and which attracted young converts who learned from him and quietly began Taylorizing the operations of factories in various parts of the country. Still, despite Taylor's missionary efforts, few had ever heard of him or "scientific management" at the beginning of 1910. A year later, Taylor was famous due entirely to a dramatic and unexpected pair of testimonials delivered in a national forum.

In late 1910, six years before his appointment to the Supreme Court, Louis D. Brandeis was arguing in the public behalf against higher railroad rates before the Interstate Commerce Commission, where he raised the point that the increase was not merited for the simple reason that, if the railroads would adopt the principles of scientific management, they would save enough so there would be no need for the hike. Supporting Brandeis' claim was the testimony of Harrison Emerson, a pioneer practitioner in the new calling of management consulting, who estimated that American railroads could collectively save $1,000,000 a day by devoting greater attention to the efficiencies of Taylorism. The claim was based on Emerson's wide experience consulting with the Santa Fe Railroad.

With so much of railroad-dependent America vitally interested in proposed rate hikes, the hearings attracted much attention and the Brandeis and Emerson statements got terrific publicity. Within weeks, most of the popular magazines of the day had devoted feature space to scientific management and the nation was discussing the promise of "efficiency," the catch-all term used by the press and public to sum up the principles of scientific management. The nation's first efficiency societies began springing up in major cities, and Taylor's writings became must reading for the captains of industry. New enterprises were generally the quickest to adopt the new philosophy, one of the first and most illustrious being the Ford Motor Company, which embraced Taylor's thinking as it built itself around such scientific practices as standardized operations, time-and-motion studies, fragmented work, and continuous assembly. Taylorism not only captivated Americans such as Ford and his capitalist counterparts in other nations but also found an eager student in Nicolai Lenin, who saw this American ism as just the thing needed to increase the efficiency of the collectivized industries of the Soviet Union. In case after case, the ideas that Taylor pioneered proved themselves in application by producing gains in productivity which made them hard to resist. Organized labor was at first antagonistic, then skeptical, and finally, friendly to scientific management, as it became evident that greater productivity and earnings meant higher wages and that scientifically managed companies tended to be less prone to layoffs and sudden failure.

Although scientific management had become very popular and broadly applied before the First World War, it became even bigger during that war as the need was felt to create efficient war industries in a hurry. Practitioners of scientific management were brought into government to serve on production boards and to beef up the agencies and bureaus which were overseeing wartime industry. To meet the demand for munitions and equipment, the government converted civilian industries into adjuncts of government and forced them out of their unproductive ruts. By war's end, not only had many industries been reshaped along scientific lines but Taylor's methods were being imposed on government itself.

Taylor's work not only resulted in new standards for work but produced what in the 1920s came to be known as the "management movement." The managerial side of enterprise now had an identity and direction and was no longer a simple matter of issuing orders and counting profits as it had been before Taylor. Management now boasted its own literature, rules, theories, research plans, and debates. Significantly, in 1915, there were less than five courses in management given in America's colleges and universities; ten years later, there were virtually no business or engineering schools without a series of such courses.

This concept of science was one which came on strong and fast, as evidenced by the new texts of the period. These read like physics books in which workers were put into formulae like so many pieces of predictable physical equipment. Though these books generally started by conceding that workers were humans and deserving of certain basic human considerations, they tended to lose sight of that contention as they got into the scientific heart of the matter. It was if everything, including being nice to people, needed a hard-nosed, empirical rationale. For example, a company cafeteria was not a service rendered as much as it was a center installed to insure that workers would toil through the afternoon hours properly fueled. Some considerations of the period could only be termed scientific extremism, as this passage from the 1923 text *Industrial Management*, on determining when a worker may be nearing the point of inefficiency, shows:

> Dr. A. H. Ryan of the Scoville Manufacturing Company, Waterbury, Connecticut, has to date made the most promising contribution toward the quantitative measurement of industrial fatigue . . . This test consists in making a stroke on the surface of the forearm of the worker with a blunt instrument so devised that the stroke can always be made with the same pressure. The white streak which results from this stroke is studied with regard to its latent period, the time required for it to reach its maximum intensity, and the time at which it begins to spread and fade.

Having established that true fatigue could be determined by a bop on the arm, the same text went on to describe rest periods which could be used to contend with it. One kind of rest period, which it felt was especially desirable for workers who stayed at one place during their labors, was to allow them to rest—not by a few minutes outdoors or moment to sit back—but by giving them a change of tasks. With zeal, it points to this model rest period:

> . . . at the Joseph and Feiss Company, in Cleveland, it has been found desirable to allow girls working on various operations in the manufacture of clothing to secure batches of material from control desks, and to deliver these batches, when finished, back to the control desk, rather than to have persons move this material to and fro for the worker.

2
THE HUMAN TOUCH

Fortunately, the stern doctrines of scientific management were offset to a degree by another movement. Just as Taylor and the management movement brought standards to bear on the work itself, the second movement—which was beginning during the same period—was to bring human standards to bear on the extrinsic side of work. It has been variously termed the human relations movement, the personnel movement, and the employee movement—all of which tend to be inadequate terms to describe a tremendous change in work-related human values.

Unions (and the fear of them), labor strife, articulate labor spokesmen, progressive legislation, economic and political pressure, forward-looking individuals in industry, reformers, and visionary academicians all worked together to create a movement toward industrial peace and social justice on the job. Unlike scientific management, it is difficult to pinpoint exactly when the human relations movement started, but an important early year was 1913. According to a book on the movement, *Human Values Where People Work*, by Thomas Spates, this was the year in which the personnel function began to take hold, when, in more progressive companies, four new positions were being added to the organizational chart: safety engineer, employment manager, training director, and medical director. It was also the year in the Progressive era when state legislatures were rapidly approving accident compensation laws for industrial workers. Prior to that time, it was uncommon to have a personnel office and only a few steps had been taken to elevate the worker from the position of a wage-earning beast whose only right or privilege was being able to quit.

The most important single influence on the human relations movement, however, was not to come until much later when a series of studies were released by the late industrial sociologist Elton Mayo. These studies, conducted between 1927 and 1932 at the Hawthorne Works of the Western Electric Company in Cicero, Illinois, quickly became world famous. The work got underway when Mayo and other researchers from Harvard were called in to decipher the perplexing results of a company experiment that had been conducted to see whether productivity would increase if there was better illumination in the plant. Western Electric had kept careful records of its experiment and was amazed to find that every group of workers who had agreed to participate showed an increase in productivity regardless of whether the lighting was brightened, dimmed, or left the same. To test the effect again, Mayo did his own experiment in which working hours and rest periods were varied and, again, productivity went up regardless of how the schedule was or was not varied. He concluded that in both experiments the rise in productivity and morale had nothing to do with lighting or hours, but resulted from singling out people for experimentation —which gave them the feeling of being important and unique.* This, coupled with a massive follow-up study in which 20,000 workers were interviewed, led Mayo to conclude that workers needed to feel important and were forming powerful, informal groups to get the importance, cooperation, and comradeship that the modern industrial organization was ignoring. His prescription for industry included improved communications to give management and labor a better understanding of one another, supervisors who were more understanding and cooperative, and greater expression of concern for the individual through better employee benefits and a fostering of team spirit. Many organizations adopted the Mayo school of thinking, despite the fact that it

---

* This has become known as the "Hawthorne Effect." Today's experimenters take considerable pains to discount it, because it is temporary and has little real impact over time.

was short on specifics. Saul Gellerman, a professional management consultant and a student of motivation theories, summed up Mayo's thrust in his book *Motivation and Productivity*: "In the final analysis it was . . . warmth, rather than any particular style of managing, that Mayo was pleading for."

Unlike Taylorism, which came on the scene quickly and with a relative degree of finality, this movement evolved over a long period and is, in fact, still evolving. It was only in 1970 that Congress got around to enacting a tough Occupational Health and Safety Act, and there are many organizations which still exude very little of the warmth that Mayo was calling for.

Overall, however, the changes which have taken place from the beginning of the century until now have been great. The workweek has been shortened and standardized, Social Security and minimum wage laws have been put into effect, child labor has been virtually eliminated, organized workers have the right to collective bargaining, and unorganized workers have the right to organize. Employee benefit packages have come into being as rich packages of vacations, group hospitalization and other insurance plans, retirement guarantees, sick pay and educational plans. Extra pay is widely guaranteed for working overtime, wages are generally good, in most quarters the doctrine of "treat 'em rough and tell 'em nothing" is out of style, and recently and belatedly enacted equal opportunity and pension reform statutes are beginning to take effect.

Many aspects of this change are taken for granted. To take one example: It is common today to think of the personnel office, with its formal policies, as rather humdrum givens, but the changes in that area have been phenomenal since the days before World War I. Some of them, as outlined in Spates' *Human Values Where People Work*, include the shift from employment by a crook of the finger to personal interviews and test batteries; from the once-over by the gang boss to medical exams to determine fitness; from indifference and discipline toward accidents to safeguards and accident prevention training; from sudden and irregular layoffs to a high degree of employment stability, and from merit rating by gossip to systematic performance reviews.

Taken together, scientific management and the human relations movement have created a standardized Western way of work. On the job, Taylorism is still very much the order of the day—and not just in heavy industry but also in offices and service industries, as anyone who has ever looked at or worked for a government agency or insurance company will agree. The cliché "doing things by the book" is ever so appropriate when applied to most work, because "the book" brings to mind the great body of literature which has been produced by the management movement. We have been standardized to the point where our workweeks are all generally forty hours long and contained in five consecutive days. Our retirement age is generally sixty-five, we have the same holidays, we get a two-week vacation if we are new to the job and three weeks if we have worked longer and, if we have worked long enough, our Social Security checks arrive on the same day. Job applications tend to look and be alike, as do the pink slips handed out to the unfortunate at the time of layoff. There are, of course, differences when it comes to wages, titles, functions, and customs; but our differences are standardized as well, and it is significant that the working population is divided in two by the color of its collar.

It would be unfair to make a devil out of Taylor. He did give the industrialized world what it wanted in terms of greater efficiency—which economically benefited both labor and management. It would also be foolish to make light of the change in personnel standards and not to appreciate the fact that the working person is no longer slaving away under sweatshop conditions for six 12-hour days with neither overtime pay nor vacation time, while being bossed about with no rights.

But all is not well. The standardization we have achieved in and around our jobs has begun to fail us and smell of anachronism. Ranging from the assembly line—the prize brainchild of scientific management which more and more looks like a numbing cruelty—to the 5-day, 40-hour week—which so many struggled so long to achieve but which is now increasingly being seen as an inflexible custom binding us all to the same hours and days—the old standards are being questioned and attacked as sources of discontent.

3

UP FROM LORDSTOWN

Enough has been written in the last few years on the subject of job boredom and worker alienation to fill a large shelf. Virtually every business and general-interest magazine has done its big story on the blue-collar blues and the tight white collar. Most major newspapers have also done their series on the workingplace blahs, replete with quote after quote from men and women who feel frustrated, rebellious, or at a dead end. Scholarly interest in the subject has become such that *Newsweek* has called alienated workers ". . . the newest darlings of the sociologists and industrial psychologists," an assertion borne out by the many recent conferences which have been held on the quality of working life. Such books as *Where Have All the Robots Gone?* by Harold L. Sheppard and Neal Q. Herrick, *The Job Revolution* by Judson Gooding, *Work in America*, produced by the US Department of Health, Education and Welfare, and Studs Terkel's *Working* have been especially important in bringing the issue into focus and prominence.

What has happened is that another major issue has crept up on us and exploded into full flower. The media, the survey takers, the pollsters, and an increasing number of academicians and politicians have discovered the fact that a lot of people actively hate their work and a lot more find it tolerable at best. Of course, many people didn't have to be told about boredom and frustration through a series in *Fortune* or the latest Gallup poll, because they themselves had been working at the bad jobs or finding less and less satisfaction in work that was once good but seemed to be losing its appeal.

While the evidence on job dissatisfaction first manifested itself as a blue-collar phenomenon, it was quickly apparent that this was something which went beyond the hourly worker trapped in an assembly-line nightmare. It is as if the worst blue-collar jobs have come to symbolize all fragmented, unimaginative work no matter where it is to be found. A critical metaphoric moment in all of this came about in 1972 when workers at the General Motors plant at Lordstown, Ohio, went on strike for twenty-two days. The issue was *not* pay, benefits, or any of the traditional reasons for going on strike. The workers had gone on strike over what amounted to the issue of dehumanizing, hard, and monotonous work; 101.6 Chevrolet Vegas were coming off the line an hour allowing each man or woman in the process only thirty-six seconds to perform the same fragmented job 101.6 times an hour.

Almost overnight, Lordstown became to the working world what My Lai was to Vietnam and Watergate has been to politics: a once-obscure place-name which quickly came to represent in one word far more than the headline-making event which took place there. Despite the fact that only about 5 percent of all working Americans find themselves actually working on an assembly line, people throughout the working world understood and appreciated what had gone on in Lordstown. An executive at the Travelers Insurance Company working on a plan to combat job boredom told me of a white-collar workforce just beginning to wake up to the fact that their clerical tasks are nothing more than stations in a paper- and punchcard-dominated assembly line. "The image of a clean, well-lit

Lordstown is current," he says, "and it grieves me to report that some of our more alert people refer to themselves as 'data coolies.'" Meeting with a manager at the Saab automotive complex outside of Stockholm, where experiments are underway which may lead to the end of the assembly line at that company, I was told, "The importance of the Lordstown strike is international. It is exactly what manufacturers all over the Western world have been fearing for some time. Now that it has happened and gotten a lot of publicity, the fear has grown." A highly paid corporation officer in Boston sits in his plush office and describes the "executive Lordstown," a state of mind stretching from coast to coast in which all but those at the very highest level share in the meaninglessness of their assembly line—albeit a sophisticated variety of assembly line. He explains, "You knock yourself out on your part of an important survey for the company—even take the work home for the weekend to make sure that it gets done on time—and then it goes down the hall for someone else to work on. You lose track of it and never see it again, not knowing if it went out with the trash or was used by the board of directors." That frustration is what makes auto workers go on strike or take unauthorized absences and causes talented executives in their prime to start dreaming about opening a ski shop in Aspen.

Despite all sorts of indications to the contrary, some of the arch defenders of the status quo claim that unhappiness with work and the spreading Lordstown syndrome has been overplayed, another overstated reaction of the press and the pop psychologist. Dr. Harold Sheppard, co-author of *Where Have All the Robots Gone?* and a fellow at the Upjohn Institute for Employment Research, points out, "We interviewed some 2,000 workers and from this sampling were able to conclude that one out of five white, male blue-collar workers under thirty was unhappy with his job. To me this was startling and a call for action, but others took it in the other direction, expressing it with the sentiment that all this statistic shows is that most young blue-collar Americans are happy with their work."

Rather than get into the debate over the extent to which working people are dissatisfied and get bogged down in philosophical discussion on the erosion of the work ethic, it is enough to say that a substantial number of employed people don't like what they are doing and a far more substantial number may not actually be unhappy but are looking for a better way to work.

All of what follows in this book is a report on the search to find such better ways of working. It concentrates on a number of diverse organizations which are finding that greater individual satisfaction and higher group productivity are the logical results of true workplace innovation—a new and vital movement now in its infancy.

The movement still lacks a proper name—or at least one which those involved can agree on as being fully descriptive of what is taking place. Regardless of which term is used—the humanization of work, job redesign, work reform, job satisfaction, the quality of work (as in the quality of life), or a half dozen other synonyms or near-synonyms—there is no question that it is gaining attention and beginning to strike a responsive chord as the positive complement to worker alienation, the blue-collar blues, and the white-collar woes.

In general terms, this movement that began to make itself felt in the United States in the early 1970s has to do with prospecting for new ways to work which break away from long-established trends not seriously questioned before. New premises are being offered that include:

¶ Treating workers as educated adults.

¶ Allowing those at all levels to have greater involvement in decision making.

¶ Increasing the opportunity for individuals to use their minds on the job.

¶ Substituting individual responsibility for heavy-handed discipline.

¶ Giving working people greater individual identity.

¶ Removing a layer or two of supervision.

¶ Giving people greater control over time.

¶ Taking jobs that have become fragmented and rebuilding them into new jobs with coherence.

Technically, such ideas are not really new; each has had its advocates for years, and a few are actually throwbacks to much earlier times. The renewed interest in giving people identity as artisans rather than as interchangeable pieces of machinery, for instance, is the modern incarnation of a way of thinking about work that predates not only the Industrial Revolution but the birth of Christ.

What is important in all of this is not just that these ideas are being discussed, but that a small but growing number of employers are testing them—and business executives, labor leaders, and government officials clearly want to hear more. And though these ideas gaining attention clearly smack of on-the-job democracy, employees' rights, and new workplace freedom, one is hard pressed to find the stereotyped traditionalist with jowls aquiver calling it all bunk. To be sure, the skeptics still vastly outnumber the converts, but the skepticism tends to be the healthy variety, expressed by those with open minds who are very, very interested in what is going on.

This interest first began to manifest itself with authority in 1972. A handful of major corporations—including General Foods, AT&T, Corning Glass, GE, and Polaroid—and a number of smaller ones had been experimenting with these new ideas for varying lengths of time; suddenly, a sizable pack was beating paths to their doors to find out what lessons they had learned. These experimental exceptions to standard rules of work not only attracted the interest of the media in forms ranging from a *Newsweek* cover story to an ABC-TV special, but also much communication and visiting within the business community. Giants like General Motors had teams of executives out looking at the likes of tiny Donnelly Mirrors of Holland, Michigan, which was having great success with a system that featured participatory management, profit sharing, and an absence of traditional bossing. Interest in Donnelly's experiences has become so keen that the company is now selling tickets to special seminars in which it spells out its plan for productivity and worker satisfaction. After word got out, via *The Wall Street Journal*, about a successful experiment in job redesign at a small Corning Glass plant in Medfield, Massachusetts, the plant manager reported that he was buried in requests from students, businessmen, reporters, and professors who wanted to stop by and see what was going on for themselves. Executives from several firms, which had converted their operations to new time arrangements like the 4-day workweek and the flexible workday, tell of having to resort to form responses to be sent out to the hundreds of other companies that want information on what they have done and to what result.

This thing has been showing up on other barometers as well:

¶ There have been more seminars and conferences on "The Humanization of Work," "The Changing Work Ethic," "The Quality of Work," and so forth in the last few years than can be easily counted and there are more to come.

¶ The Ford Foundation saw it as fresh ground to plow and has been funding study teams to look at various aspects of it and, in Washington, the National Science Foundation began dispensing study grants of its own in 1973.

¶ There has been a definite renewal of national interest in profit sharing and other "piece of the action" schemes.

¶ Predictably, this business has fostered business of its own as several dozen small consulting firms have come into being of late to help others usher in workplace reforms.

¶ College and graduate school courses have cropped up quickly to take detailed looks at "job enrichment" and other alternative schemes as have statistics-laden primers for professional managers and piles of academic papers covering the same material.

¶ *Industry Week* magazine sensed such interest in job restructuring that it sponsored a nationwide closed-circuit television conference on the subject which was seen by nearly 3,000 executives.

¶ The humanization of work is a topic that has not been missed by major politicians. Senator Charles H. Percy, for instance, has spoken often on the subject, asserting that the workplace is the "last redoubt of yesterday's values," but adding that the nation is ". . . on the brink of a major breakthrough in the effort to change our ideas about work." Senator Edward M. Kennedy has had much to say on the subject (sample quote: "We must act and act soon to restore the soul to work . . .") and officiated at a series of 1972 Senate hearings which looked into worker alienation and ways of decreasing it.

There is more, but the point is made: The external signals that indicate the start of a broad attempt to effect fundamental change in the way people work have gone up. It is far too early to predict how far it will go or how fast change will occur, but it is obvious that significant momentum for change is building.

Why is the business community adding to this momentum? Because carefully considered and executed workplace reform can allow an employer to couple humanitarian and hard-nosed business goals in a single package. As scores of studies and experiments have demonstrated, an organization which changes to make people's work more interesting, meaningful, and responsible commonly makes business gains in terms of lower employee turnover and absentee rates, better quality work, and higher productivity. For leaders of industry and commerce, it provides a rare opportunity to have one's cake and eat it too—that is, to take statesmanlike action against employee alienation and malaise while improving the health, condition, productivity, and profitability of the organization. As an executive involved in a job redesign effort within a company in the Bell Telephone System put it, "The unbelievable thing is that a successful program can make a manager a hero to both the largest stockholders and the people on the lowest rung of the ladder in the company."

However, this description of what is happening makes the current turn in direction sound simpler than it is. The fact is that what is occurring is the result of a complex set of factors, forces, and influences ranging from an increasing national concern for the overall state of American productivity to a growing proclivity on the part of business organizations to experiment in an experimental age.

To best illustrate the variety and depth of influences which are at play, it is worth examining three of the most important. One is a highly readable and frank government report, the second is a daring set of experiments aimed at rendering foolish the conventional wisdom that brought us the assembly line, and the third is a new and iconoclastic way to look at organizations. Besides serving as a sampling of the kind of developments which will be reported on in the rest of the book, they are specific sparks which have helped touch off the beginning of what some have termed the "third work revolution," in a series which began with the Industrial Revolution and continued with the revolution of scientific management.

4
"Work in America"

Late in 1971, at the age of 26, Dr. James O'Toole was hired by the Department of Health, Education and Welfare as a "policy planner"—the indefinite kind of title which government agencies use when they hire bright young aides. O'Toole had just the credentials which big Federal agencies like for their resident pools of whiz kids. He was a self-confessed Republican with a doctorate in social anthropology from Oxford University, where he was a Rhodes scholar, and he had formerly served as co-coordinator of field investigations for President Nixon's Commission on Campus Unrest.

The well-paying job that O'Toole took didn't quite work out the way it was supposed to. He had been hired as an aide to one of then-HEW Secretary Elliot L. Richardson's top aides, but there was sudden shift in the organization just as O'Toole came in, and because of the shift he was left with literally nothing to do.

"For two months I sat around trying to find out where I fit in and what I was supposed to do," says O'Toole. "I was bored and extremely unhappy. All I had was a desk and a check at payday and I felt denigrated. I was starting to drink more than I should and was beginning to fight with my wife. I hated myself."

O'Toole's frustration in bureaucratic limbo led him to two conclusions. First, that he had to take his plight to the top and get it resolved and, second, that he would like to get into the business of finding out to what extent others are denigrated by employment.

Fortunately, when O'Toole got to the top, Elliot Richardson was harboring a frustration of his own: namely, that the research and reports coming out of his department and out of government in general tended to be narrow and academic. Richardson wanted a seminal document—a rich summary of research and new findings that would cross-cut a major section of American life and give Americans something worth pondering.

The outcome of the O'Toole-Richardson meeting was fruitful. O'Toole was taken out of mothballs and given the title of Task Force Director, and given time and money to pursue the topic of Work in America. "The report could have as easily been about the American family or the American community," says O'Toole, explaining. "Richardson believes that government has been busy fragmenting its concerns into hundreds of different categories and programs and there is a need for major policy studies which ask if these hundreds of individual policies have one direction and relate to each other."

The task force was officially appointed on December 29, 1971. The final task force report was released on December 23, 1972. A total of ten participants sat on the task force, and some fifty consultants were brought in to write papers, each on a single aspect of work in America. The project research was administered by an outside agent, the W. E. Upjohn Institute for Employment Research.

Richardson gave the report its sendoff as a report that "literally takes on everyone, not excluding some of the thinking of the present Administration" and one which was more "doughy, controversial and yet responsible" than any other government report he could remember. Save for Richardson's comments, the report was greeted with stony silence from the White House and other cabinet members. Then-Labor Secretary James D. Hodgson did express displeasure with the report privately, but this was largely a territorial matter, as it was no secret that the Labor Department felt that it should have been the organization to produce the study.

The Nixon Administration's track record on its own commission reports had often been to disown them outright; the final report of the President's Commission on Campus Unrest, for example, is perhaps best remembered because it prompted former Vice-President Agnew's label of "pablum for permissivists." In this light, the silent treatment the O'Toole report was accorded constituted a kind of tacit approval for an extremely forthright and jarring work which challenged some of the Administration's policies and cherished beliefs. Among other things, it presented a mass of evidence leading to the conclusion that satisfying work is a basic human need which gives identity, self-respect, and order to the life of the individual. This was in direct conflict with former President Nixon's repeated assertion that the "welfare ethic" was replacing the "work ethic" in America (because of his belief that many aren't willing to work).

Because the report was so widely read and reported on, there is no need to report on it in detail. However, its major points bear reviewing.

It concluded that American working people at all levels are

Working Alternatives 23

becoming more and more dissatisfied with the quality of their working lives and that this is sapping the economic and social strength of the nation. Furthermore, in addition to such widely acknowledged problems as boredom and absenteeism, there is much evidence to show that a decline in physical and mental health, decreased family and community stability, increased drug and alcohol abuse, less "balanced" political ideas and certain forms of adult delinquency are also work related. After examining this situation, the task force concluded that there are two main causes for the problem: the diminishing opportunity to become one's own boss (as more and more corporations organize work to minimize the independence of individuals), and the outmoded faith in and application of scientific management. Finally, the report offered a number of courses of action to be taken to reverse the trend, which include: overhauling jobs at all levels to give greater responsibility, challenge, and autonomy to the people in them; giving people a greater share in the profits and decisions of the organizations they work for; setting up a "renewal" mechanism in which any worker who wants to improve his job or change careers can have access to retraining; and creating employer tax incentives for hiring, training, and upgrading workers from traditionally low-employment groups.

Work in America became a hot item overnight. Not only did the government print and sell it but the MIT Press published its own edition with a first printing of 25,000 copies, of which 2,000 sold the first day it was offered. The report quickly became must reading for employers, Congressmen, and labor leaders, and has prompted continuing and mostly favorable press and scholarly comment.

Its importance is not just what it says, but that people seem to have listened. It serves as an official handbook on work, spelling out what is wrong and offering possible remedies. The report is, at once, ammunition in the hands of the reform-minded, a persuasive influence for those on the fence, and a challenge to the established order that it criticizes. For instance, by accusing organized labor of only bargaining for the extrinsic rewards of work while completely neglecting job content, it has, by their own admission, given some of the major trade unions added reason to reexamine their policies. And while there are a number of critics of the report—they have charged it with everything from having some "economically naive" suggestions to containing assertions derived from "a faded neo-Marxism"—few have disagreed with its basic plea for reform and renewal.

Unlike the vast majority of government task force reports, this one is having an impact and is not going to be forgotten quickly or easily—which makes it fortunate that James O'Toole got stuck with a lousy job in 1971.

5

A BETTER IDEA
—NOT BY FORD

In 1972, the Ford Motor Company announced that it would close its Highland Park, Michigan, plant within two years. This was the same plant where Henry Ford set up his first assembly line in 1909, thereby changing the face of industrial production and giving those on the line about as much variety in their work as he gave his customers (who were offered a Ford car in any color as long as it was black). While Detroit's color options were long ago liberalized to embrace peach melba and tangerine, the assembly line has remained as an industry-wide article of faith. Indeed, the Highland Park closing is only a historical footnote, not something indicating more fundamental change—since bigger, faster, and more modern versions of Henry, Sr.'s original are still being planned and built.

The year 1972 also brought two far more important developments in the normally news-poor world of the automobile

Working Alternatives 25

assembly line. The first was the aforementioned and internationally famous labor revolt in Lordstown, Ohio, at what General Motors had proclaimed to be the fastest and most efficient assembly line in the world. The second event was a set of announcements from Sweden, where SAAB and Volvo announced independently of each other that they were breaking with automotive tradition to launch major experimental programs posing alternatives to the assembly line. Both companies were quick to point out that they had not done away with the line, nor were they sure that they would ever totally abandon the principle, but rather they chose to think of themselves as determined experimenters trying to develop alternatives.

The importance of these decisions by Sweden's two automobile manufacturers was that neither limited itself to minor experiments in isolated corners of their operations. These decisions involved major production areas. What is more, both have made strides in humanizing and de-monotonizing existing assembly lines and have pushed their alternative-seeking to what some would call extremes. Volvo, for instance, has gone so far as to see what would happen if it let one man put a whole car together by himself. (Although this one-man/one-car idea proved to be far too costly to be practical, just the fact that they tried it was delightful heresy to the spirit of mass production, and no doubt caused considerable spinning in the better graveyards around Detroit.)

These two established competitors in the production and sale of cars and trucks have locked horns in a new form of competition to see which will outdo the other in such areas as self-managing work groups, job rotation, "industrial democracy," and a generally improved working environment. When SAAB lets it be known that it has decided to improve the level and intensity of its on-the-job-training effort, Volvo announces that it is doing the same thing but going further by starting a system in which experienced workers are given a small extra fee for training others. True to form, in the summer of 1972, Volvo led off with a major press conference in which it outlined its plans for its first nonassembly-line plant which was to open in 1974; shortly thereafter, SAAB called the press in to see its new engine plant where a limited version of such a system was already in operation.

The SAAB engine plant is conventional to a point, as the engine block, crankshaft, cylinder heads, and connecting rods are machined and fit together on an assembly-line basis. The special area is the one where the rough engine is finished and all external pieces are fitted. The rough engine is carried mechanically on a dolly to the group assembly area. There, there are six regular work stations (a seventh is for training) to which groups of workers, mostly women, are assigned. At full strength, there are four in each group. Each team chooses the way it nts to divide the work and can change the arrangement anytime it chooses. If, for example, two workers want to work alone on a given day, each will normally take about 30 minutes to finish an engine. Should the other two members of the team decide to work together, they will then divide the tasks giving each a work cycle of 15 minutes. The next day, all four may decide to work as a team, spending 7.5 minutes on an engine or, if one is absent, they become a three-person team with a 10-minute cycle. Even the groups themselves are flexible; there is nothing to prevent workers from trading themselves from group to group, or for two groups to merge for the day. (If the job were done on a conventional assembly line, each worker would be locked into an inflexible 1.8-minute work cycle of a single repetitive task.)

On a visit to SAAB shortly after the experiment began, I was told by company officials that it would take awhile before the extent of its success or failure would be evident, but they had come up with a list of expectations based on their limited experience. On the positive side, seven benefits were expected: reduced absenteeism and turnover; an assembly area much easier to keep in "balance" (one foul-up on a conventional line can stop it); a higher overall quality of work resulting in fewer rejects and refitting jobs; a better and more cooperative attitude among workers; greater worker responsibility and initiative; greater ease in recruiting new workers; and better public relations. Four negative aspects to the new way of working were identified: the parts and distribution process becomes more complex; the new system takes up more floor space than a conventional line; the conveyor system used to move the engines out of the work area is more expensive to build than expected; and the time to complete each engine takes "a bit" longer than it would the old way.

Apparently, the pluses overshadow the minuses because in mid-1974—almost two years after the engine operation began—the plant was meeting its production output targets, and an official of the company told *Business Week*, "We would never build another engine plant using a conventional system."

While the Swedish assembly-line alternatives have made all the news, the two companies have also gone a long way to try to alleviate conditions on existing lines. A good case in point is the half-kilometer-long line in the large SAAB automotive complex near Stockholm where its trucks are assembled. This was where SAAB's experimentation began in 1968.

Physically, the large 445,000-square-foot plant is a refreshing oddity. Clean and quiet, it offers such amenities as a bright color scheme and indoor tropical gardens which get their light from skylights. These incongruous, well-tended, and bench-lined oases are used as rest areas to which workers can come during their breaks. All heavy moving and large-parts handling jobs have been automated.

Job innovation in the plant has been the province of a special factory-wide board composed of representatives of management, the workforce, and its local union leadership. This board, called the "reference group," is free to set up and oversee any new procedures in the factory in any area (except for wages and benefits, which are handled through traditional collective-bargaining channels). The major accomplishment of the reference group has been to create a system for open communications and continuing change. The system involves workers at every level and is composed of two basic units. The first comprises production groups each of which is made up of a team of workers who perform one complete operation (such as the production of an axle) in a limited geographic area of the line. Each production group is semi-selfgoverning and free to tinker with such things as its own work layout and job assignments. Should a production group of seven wish to adopt an arrangement in which each rotates through all seven jobs, it is up to the group to initiate it.

On a higher level is the second element of the system, the development group, which is made up of representatives from several production groups (serving in rotation, so that every worker spends time in the development group), foremen, and industrial engineers. This group serves as the agent for change in such areas as job satisfaction, product quality, and overall working conditions. They meet on company time every second week to discuss such topics as the need for new tools, improving job safety, sources of employee dissatisfaction, and production problems.

Beyond these basic units, there is still another part of the system: the temporary project group, which is formed from development groups to work on major jobs for the whole plant (such as a new layout, or a system for handling parts).*

The manager of the truck plant, Nils Nystrom, strongly believes that the system is a vast improvement over the norm in the worldwide automotive industry and points out that its success has been such that there are now over one hundred production groups and forty development groups covering not only the truck plant where they were first tried but other company plants as well. Nystrom says,

* As if this weren't enough, the complex of plants of which this one is a part has started a broad array of special groups, councils, and boards which involve workers in decisions on such complex-wide issues as employee parking, environmental protection, amounts paid to workers for money-saving suggestions, and personnel policies.

I feel we have created a much better relationship between workers, their foremen and the company as a result. Now a worker who is unhappy with some part of his job knows that he can make an issue of it in the development group where the foreman must listen and discuss the problem seriously. Another benefit is the improved attitudes of the production workers towards each other which is important here because we have workers of twelve different nationalities.

Still another advantage he lists is that the system has sharply increased the quantity and quality of physical improvements suggested by the people on the line. "It is far superior to the normal suggestion-box system, because now the worker can present his idea in the development group on a face-to-face basis with the people who can put it into practice." On a tour of the plant, Nystrom pointed to one improvement after another which has emerged from the development groups. A typical one is an air-hose apparatus which a worker on the line devised to replace an arduous manual process for coating an inner surface of an axle. Finally, Nystrom says that the overall degree of worker satisfaction has improved. "Not only have the workers themselves told us this but it shows up in lower absentee and turnover rates."

Meanwhile, Volvo's plunge into experimentation and work reform has been intense. So intense, in fact, that between the spring of 1971, when it took the plunge in earnest, and a year later, it had involved a sizable portion of its workforce in one or more experimental plans. While much of this takes the form of job rotation, work teams with a new degree of autonomy and other concepts being tried at SAAB and elsewhere, it has introduced some novel twists of its own. For example, it is pioneering the idea of the internal employment agency, a scheme to help people move out of a disliked job or to move to another plant in the Volvo system.

The most important and impressive aspect of the Volvo plunge is that it is so committed to developing alternatives to the norm that it is building new plants around what are basically experimental concepts. In 1974, a new $20-million plant opened in Kalmar, Sweden: the world's first large-scale automotive assembly plant without an assembly line.

Key elements of the Kalmar plant—which make it so different—are electrically powered wagons which move the car bodies in lieu of an assembly line, and the unique team-oriented design of the plant itself. The aluminum wagons move automatically from one work station to another as ordered by a computer. At first, this may sound like an assembly line on wheels, but the critical difference is that the wagons are ultimately controlled by the twenty-five work teams in the plant. The team can stop them to work on them, stand on them and work as they move, or stop a number of them if the whole team wants to take its coffee break together.

The plant has been designed to create a small workshop atmosphere within a big factory. Each team is treated as a separate group of craftsmen responsible for a different system, such as steering and controls, safety (interior padding and seat belts), or the electrical system. Each inspects its own work and is free to parcel out work as it sees fit within its department. To support this "workshop feeling" every team has its own section of the plant, replete with its own locker room, rest areas, and saunas. The plant is set up so that most work areas are near large windows looking out into natural settings. Considerable effort has been made to keep noise levels to a minimum.

As the Kalmar plant was going into operation in 1974, Volvo admitted that this $20-million plant had cost about $2 million more than it would have had it been built along conventional lines; however, it felt that this amount would be quickly recovered through the decreased turnover and absenteeism it forecasts.

Volvo appears to be quite confident that it has found the answer to work dissatisfaction; an engine plant built along similar lines opened elsewhere in Sweden later in the year, and the company has announced that its mammoth assembly facility —planned to open in late 1976 in Chesapeake, Virginia—will employ the same basic philosophy.

Complementing the new plants and the experiments it has going on elsewhere in the company are a series of new company-wide, worker-oriented policies, like the one which promises, "All new projects started within the Volvo group will include consultation with the employees."

Like SAAB, Volvo believes it is taking the right step at the right time. Some early signs seem to confirm that belief. Attitude surveys conducted among workers in experimental groups have been generally positive. The rejection rate of substandard items has dropped. However, there is still very much of a gamble in all of this, or, as Volvo managing director Pehr Gyllenhammer put it when the plans for the Kalmar plant were announced, "This is an experiment—we have no proof that it's going to be profitable." Indeed, some of the early gambles have not paid off. Volvo invested considerable time and money in rebuilding its fitting shops, where castings are cleaned and fitted with chisel and grinding stone. The company scrapped the continuous line and replaced it with a system in which each worker was responsible for a whole casting and could work at his own pace. The desired result of reduced turnover and better attitudes did not follow and Volvo concluded that the task itself—no matter how configured —was so tiresome and tedious that the only answer was to automate the worst parts of it out of existence.

These efforts by SAAB and Volvo have not been prompted as much by corporate derring-do and idealism (although these are definite factors) as by a variety of strong pressures, the strongest of which have been astronomical turnover and absenteeism rates. At both companies, annual turnover has been running at an overall annual rate of 30 to 40 percent and much higher on assembly lines. In 1966, when jobs were especially plentiful in Sweden, SAAB reported that it had to replace 100 percent of its assembly line jobs annually. In 1972, Volvo admitted that it was recruiting a third of its workforce annually and that, at the same time, it was forced to keep one-seventh of its workers in reserve to fill in for others who did not show up. Both companies have had to rely heavily on imported labor, as they have been unable to attract young Swedes; today, nearly half of each company's production workers come from other countries.

Along with the rest of Swedish industry, both have long felt the pressure of the trade unions, which have pushed for an end to meaningless and monotonous work. For its part, the Social Democrat government of Prime Minister Olof Palme has been actively plumping for greater democracy in the workplace. Also, there is the pressure resulting from what the Swedes call their "education explosion," which has not only brought a dramatic increase in the educational level of the young but has created a situation in which an estimated 1.5 million people are participating in adult education—an awesome total for a nation of 8 million. As with others, SAAB and Volvo fear that they will be unable to attract new workers and keep their increasingly well-educated older workers for the robotlike jobs traditionally associated with automotive production. Considering the fact that both companies already rely so heavily on workers from points ranging from Finland to Turkey, it would seem that they are a bit late in their attempt to make work palatable to home-grown talent.

The importance of what is going on at these two Swedish companies, however, goes beyond the particulars of Swedish society. For one thing, rising educational levels and high absenteeism also exist to varying degrees in the United States and other Western nations. What interests us here is what is being done in the face of job dissatisfaction. At one level, SAAB and Volvo have performed important experiments in pioneering the workplace of the future.

On another and much more significant level, monkeying with and subverting the assembly line has a tremendous symbolic impact. Like the symbol of Lordstown, which is appreciated by many who may or may not have the details on what actually happened there, SAAB and Volvo have become popularly known as two major fronts on which the assembly line is coming down. Add to this the use of the line itself as a symbol for the machine controlling man—from Charlie Chaplin in *Modern Times* to Harvey Swados' novel *On the Line* to the statements of automobile workers in Studs Terkel's *Working* to Lordstown itself—and the industrial heresy committed in Sweden takes on extra meaning.

Nor is it just one article of industrial faith that has been threatened by SAAB and Volvo. If two automobile companies can tamper with the assembly line and not only not go out of business, but improve their operations, make their workforces happier and, on the public relations front, get the image of humane innovators in the bargain, then there is less safety and sacredness for such other institutions: the time clock, the 40-hour week, the 8-hour day, the "efficient" division of tasks, the pink slip, the divine rights of bosses, the concept of the hourly worker as a "variable expense" rather than an asset, and the traditional concept of the organization. Indeed, the traditional organization which ties the other elements of work together has come under increasing attack.

6
The Organic Organization

In the course of the last twenty years, a small number of intellectuals working more or less independently of each other have been probing the basic suppositions underpinning the modern organization. They have been laying bare the anatomy of a creature first formed by the church and military as a means of gaining stability, then, with the advent of the Industrial Revolution, adapted to work needs. A key question they have grappled with has been: Whether the traditional concept of the organization is still relevant in an age when adaptability and flexibility have emerged as virtues. Their long-form answers have differed slightly, but they all boil down to an emphatic "no." Generally, what they see is that the traditional, hierarchical organization is fast becoming outmoded and inefficient. Although it served the developed world quite well in bringing it to its current level of affluence and achievement, it is being overcome by vast changes in technology, education, society, communications, the personal aspirations of the average person, and the pace of change itself.

From this point of agreement, a number of theories have emerged on what has to be done (and what will happen if nothing is done). Since they are not all that dissimilar, only a few need be summarized.

The best known of these theorists is the late Douglas McGregor, a prominent psychologist and for a while the president of Antioch College, who was in the fore of those calling for the application of the latest knowledge in the behavioral sciences to the management of organizations. In his 1960 book *The Human Side of Enterprise*, he took the position that there were two basic styles of management, each of which was based in an opposite view of humanity. To make them most graphic, he chose to illustrate them in extremes. The first is his "Theory X" style, which assumes that people basically hate work, must be coerced into doing it, and generally prefer to be bossed in order to avoid responsibility. "Theory Y," on the other hand, assumes work to be the natural pursuit of humans who will accept and even seek responsibilities under the proper circumstances. He also contended that heavy-handed X managers were not only inhibiting the potential of individuals but were actually creating the kind of person they believe populates the workplace by making them indifferent and lacking in creativity. The assumptions of X, he argued, lead inevitably to rigidity, while those of Y demand flexibility, experimentation, and innovation.

While the body of McGregor's work in this field was primarily diagnostic rather than prescribing a specific course of action, his X and Y have become food for thought for many who run organizations. A survey conducted among managers in 1969 revealed that McGregor was the behavioral scientist cited most often as an influence on them. McGregor's most famous disciple is Robert Townsend of *Up the Organization* fame, who is a self-confessed Y man.

Another key figure is behaviorist-economist Chris Argyris, who has looked at the organizational status quo in the bleakest terms. He stresses the damage wrought by the difference between the needs of the organization and those of the individual: By ignoring the social and ego needs of people—self-esteem, a sense of participation, a chance to be creative, and so on—the organization frustrates and often causes serious human problems. Argyris goes on to say that people cannot be energized, but do naturally possess a given amount of "psychological energy" which can either be used creatively when their goals and the organization's are similar, or directed into apathy, tension, and dissatisfaction when the goals are dissimilar and the organization's goals dominate. These negative results are the common "unintended consequences" of the "sick" organizations which populate industry, commerce, and government today.

To cure the sickness, Argyris insists, organizations must begin serving human as well as corporate needs. The first step involves moving away from centralized power to an equalization and balance of power throughout the organization, while simultaneously developing a climate of openness and trust. As this is being done, the organization must begin working toward cohesive groups, carefully redesigned jobs, and a new flexibility in maintaining the system.

McGregor, Argyris, and others must be seen as members of a chorus each singing different parts of the same song. Social psychologist Rensis Likert argues, among other things, that most organizations are not tapping the resources and potentials of their employees. The team of Robert Blake and Jane Mouton have created a conceptual framework called the "managerial grid," which demonstrates that the problems of production and the problems of people are complementary. Organizational psychologist Warren G. Bennis, who has forecast the death of the bureaucracy (which he predicts will be replaced by new, largely temporary systems organized around specific jobs and problems) warns organizations to be prepared for change whether they want it or not.

There is no question that these people have been and are being listened to. While it would be premature to say that they have had a major impact, their influence has begun to be felt; there is now a widely recognized increase in attention to and application of the behavioral sciences among organizations. In a sizable handful of companies, this has occurred as a formal program which has become very popular in recent years: "organizational development," or "OD." There are a host of very specific, long-winded definitions for OD, but the gist of all of them is simplicity itself: creating a permanent mechanism within the organization for organizational change and development. OD has become something of a phenomenon unto itself with its own conferences, journals, texts, and a developing set of common practices. For instance, in many organizations, a special group of internal OD consultants has been put together to act as a roaming catalytic force not tied to any specific department. The specific concerns of OD practitioners are numerous, and include team building, training to help foster individual growth, acknowledging conflict and resolving it openly, making sure that top management is in close touch with the mood and feelings of the employees, redistributing the power to make decisions, and altering structures to remove long-standing frictions between groups and individuals.

Historically, the emergence of OD represents a major step

away from the key human relations movement in which management made working conditions more tolerable by treating employees better, and over toward what has become known, perhaps awkwardly, as the "human resources approach" in which the boss becomes less of a boss and more a developer of those under him, who are given a greater opportunity to contribute and grow. It is a highly significant departure. One difference between the two: *human relations* dictates that groups of employees should be given selected information about the company and its goals through company newsletters and the like, while the *human resources* approach says that the group itself should decide what information it needs to carry out its job and reach its goals.

Although there is still more talk than action in this area, it is growing, and a few organizations have gone beyond its early stages and are now deeply involved in job experimentation and overhaul. And while the actual term organizational development and the hubbub it is creating may be a fad, it is the shift it represents that is important.

This shift from human relations to human resources is what *Work in America* has attempted to make a public concern and what SAAB and Volvo are showing at a dramatic pace. This shift is also the key to the future of the workplace and what we will look at in detail in the succeeding pages. The first stop will be made to look at "job enrichment," the best-known formula for making the shift.

Job Enrichment

1

Opening Salvo in the War on Dumb Jobs

In *Working*, Studs Terkel's excellent best seller in which people talk about their jobs, there is a statement from *New Yorker* film critic Pauline Kael, who says, "Work is rarely treated in films. It's one of the peculiarities of the movies. You hardly see a person at work." She goes on to point out that despite other trends toward realism, so far as work is concerned we are still primarily offered fantasies in films and on television, adding, "We now have conglomerate ownership of the movie industry. Are they going to show us how these industries really dehumanize their workers?"

If such films were to be made, there would be no problem finding materials and characters. These come to mind readily:

¶ A woman college graduate takes a job with a large Chicago bank. She is told it is a managerial position with training and planning functions. As she quickly finds out, the job is actually that of a senior clerk, or "checker," catching the mistakes of those below her, and a warden, whose "managerial" role includes the right to decide who can get up from their desks to get a drink of water. Many of those who must raise their hands to get permission to get water are working mothers whose three- and four-year-olds don't have to ask permission for a drink when *they* are thirsty.

¶ A woman, who takes what sounds like a nice white-collar job with responsibility and advancement potential at a Hartford insurance company, later discovers that her job is so fragmented and repetitive that there is virtually no chance to accept responsibility or show that she can perform at a higher level.

¶ A male junior-college graduate works in a Southeastern

factory where he must ask for permission to go to a men's room—in which all the toilets are in open view, making it easier for his bosses to check to see whose elimination processes are too slow for the stockholders. There is another room in the plant which bothers this man: "the office," to which he is summoned to be chewed out when he has performed badly. He notes bitterly that he is never called to the office when he prevents an accident or spots a malfunction which could necessitate stopping the line.

¶ A salesman, who entered that field because he felt that it would give him a certain degree of freedom in mapping out his time and territory and an amount of control over his economic destiny, finds—after the novelty of the job has worn off—that he does have some freedoms, but that his company shortchanges him when it comes to listening to his opinions on such matters as product improvement, sales promotion, and marketing. He begins to see himself as only a traveling order-taker working on commission. *His pet peeve:* Instead of rewarding him for outstanding performance by attempting to include his ideas in the making of policy decisions, the company gives him two tickets and a trip to the Super Bowl as "an incentive award." Besides thinking of such awards as childish and superfluous, he hates football.

These potential film characters are composites of real people who populate American industry and commerce. Their cases are not at all exceptional, either. In fact, these small sketches are derived from recent studies in which certain types of jobs have been examined in detail (and, in some cases, restructured on the basis of the findings). Significantly, a number of respondents in these studies have said that it is not inadequate pay and benefits which bother them—some actually curse good pay and full baskets of employee benefits as traps which keep them from quitting—but rather what some academicians have described as a lack of "psychic income," a catch-all term for responsibility, meaning, opportunity, and recognition.

2
THE PROCESS

Of late a process called job enrichment has begun to attract broad attention as a possible solution to the frustrations felt by people such as the ones above. Today, job enrichment is not only a term bidding to become the hottest industrial buzzword of the 1970s, but is also a process which is on its way to becoming the opening wedge in the redesign of jobs in America.

The concern which led to job enrichment began in the early 1950s, when a small number of industrial engineers and behavioral scientists began examining the possibility that the *content* of jobs was a factor in employee morale and motivation. As is still true today, but to a lesser extent, it was then axiomatic in industry that happy, well-adjusted working people were the product of a good working environment; because of this, great attention was paid to such things as bright lunchrooms, weekly company newsletters, good "employee relations" and fringe benefits. Even with all this, however, the problems of low morale and productivity remained. Those who questioned the "good environment" assumption asked whether or not the key to these problems was, instead, the high specialization of most jobs. Out of this concern emerged several theories and experimental solutions.

The solution which got the most attention at the time was a scheme called "job enlargement." It called for redesigning a job from one main job to include a number of other related tasks, thereby giving the man turning the fifth bolt from the left on the fourth subassembly the right to turn all the bolts on the subassembly, and perhaps even the privilege of being able to go to the storeroom to fetch new bolts. Although a few firms experienced limited success with "enlargement," it generally went nowhere—for two important reasons: The man with the wrench was typically given no good reason for the change and so understandably felt he was being manipulated, and, secondly, the scheme only widened the scope of the job rather than deepening responsibility. Quite simply, it was a cosmetic and timid approach to a deeper problem.

Along with such failures, the period also brought two highly significant developments, the impact of which is just now beginning to be felt.

The first initially had nothing to do with work *per se* but came out of a psychologist's general research into human motivation. In 1954, Abraham H. Maslow published his book, *Motivation and Personality*, which contained the now-famous "Hierarchy of Needs." In that book, Maslow proposed that motivation comes from within and that one's life is motivated by a progression of needs, beginning with the most basic physical ones. From bottom to top, Maslow's hierarchy looks like this:

¶ Physiological needs—food, shelter, sleep, sexual fulfillment, etc.

¶ Safety needs—both actual physical safety and the emotional feeling of being safe.

¶ Need for belonging and love—the basic social need.

¶ Need for esteem—both self-esteem and esteem in the eyes of others.

¶ Need for self-actualization—the realization of self and the freedom to become what one is capable of being.

Central to Maslow's theory is the belief that people are not concerned with the next need up until the one they are seeking to satisfy is met, and that once that need is satisfied, it no longer motivates. A person in constant physical danger is not concerned with love and belonging; but once safety is assured, this other need becomes all-important.

Gradually, Maslow's ideas came to the attention of those interested in the behavioral aspects of work. The lesson was obvious: If a satisfied need no longer motivates, then all the company newsletters and management-employee discussion

Job Enrichment 45

groups in the world would not make much difference. If Maslow was right, things had to be rearranged so that people could better strive for self-actualization.

Meanwhile, another man was doing work which was to both borrow from and contribute to Maslow's thesis. Shortly after Maslow's book came out, Frederick Herzberg, a psychologist at Case Western Reserve University, finished an analysis of all the major studies of job satisfaction. He concluded that job satisfaction and dissatisfaction are not always opposites at the poles of the same continuum, but may derive from totally different sources. To test the theory, he conducted a series of interviews with two hundred engineers and accountants to determine what they felt was exceptionally good or bad about their work. When the answers were tabulated, he found, overwhelmingly, that feelings of strong satisfaction came from the job itself (or content) while strong dissatisfaction came from the job's surroundings (or context). This validated his initial theory that there are indeed two sets of factors—one which satisfies, another which dissatisfies —and that the opposite of satisfaction was not necessarily dissatisfaction. It was often, instead, *no* satisfaction. This first study, which has been repeated over thirty times in the United States and Europe with the same basic results, led to the compilation of two summary lists:

Satisfiers (content)	*Dissatisfiers (context)*
Recognition	Organizational policy and administration
Achievement	
Work itself	Supervision
Responsibility	Interpersonal relations
Growth	Working conditions
Advancement	Status
	Salary
	Job security
	Personal life

Drawing on Maslow's conclusions, he then began to tailor his findings to use in actual working situations. He began calling his satisfiers "motivators" (because they are factors which help the person move toward self-actualization) and the dissatisfiers were relabeled "hygiene" factors (because they were essentially preventive). Positive hygienic considerations were nonetheless important, because when weak, they contributed to job dissatisfaction, and when removed entirely, would push the person down the ladder to become concerned about them and not the context of his or her work. Herzberg went on to say that Western industrial society has basically taken care of the lower needs on the scale for most of its working population through such things as workman's compensation, safety laws, trade unions, and benefit packages, but that this did not mean that hygiene was to be neglected. On the contrary, it was meant to be improved constantly as economic and social pressures demanded.

Using the motivator/hygiene concept, he developed the idea of job enrichment, which has as its core the need for increasing the challenging content of a job so that the person in it will be free to grow in responsibility, accomplishment, and skill. It was entirely unlike job enlargement, which simply added more tasks in the blind hope that a little variety would satisfy. To Herzberg and his disciples, adding more dumb tasks to a dumb job amounts to heaping insult on injury and is liable to do more harm than good. In order to differentiate enrichment from enlargement graphically, he termed the former "vertical job loading" and the latter "horizontal job loading"—one built upward and the other just contributed at the same level. Specific principles were developed for accomplishing vertical loading: removing controls, giving a person a complete natural work unit with additional authority over that unit, allowing the individual to take greater accountability over his work, and making sure that the person was given direct feedback on his performance on a routine basis. Within the context of these other changes, new and more complex tasks were to be added, not just for the sake of adding them, but as a means of stimulating growth and learning.

While Herzberg's ideas would appear to be neither radical nor even moderately iconoclastic, they constitute a dramatic departure from the conventional industrial and commercial wisdom of the twentieth century to date in that they try to show that the old principles of scientific management are serving to block people from self-actualization. It is not unreasonable to suggest that given time, the pattern of thought begun by Maslow and Herzberg and now being developed by their followers may actually have as great an impact as the one started by Frederick W. Taylor and the first generation of scientific managers.

One immediate drawback to Herzberg's work was that it was primarily theoretical and without readily applicable by-the-numbers outlines on how to go about taking a sterile job and enriching it. In the mid-1960s, however, several personnel specialists in a major corporation began the first set of major experiments in job enrichment. Led by Robert N. Ford, a manpower utilization specialist, nineteen formal field experiments were conducted within the American Telephone and Telegraph Company between 1964 and 1968. As Ford tells it, the effort was actually touched off as the result of "good-natured bantering." One of Ford's bosses and a good friend continually charged Ford, then involved with college recruiting, with hiring the wrong kind of graduate—specifically, the kind that quits in six months. This continued until one day when Ford countered with the remark, "You don't deserve the people you get, they're too good for that job." The comment touched a nerve and the banter stopped. These two were now confronted with the alternative of either hiring poorer-qualified graduates or improving the jobs they had been giving the graduates they were then hiring. They opted for the latter and chose Herzberg as their guide. This conversation about college recruits was by no means the only reason for the first experiment, but rather a final one.

There had been company-wide turnover problems for some time, and a telling one-liner had come into popular use in the Bell System: "We've lost too many good people who are still with the company"—indicating psychological as well as physical turnover. Since it was recent college-graduate turnover in a specific department which had forced the issue, it was decided that this department was a good place to begin.

The group in question was one hundred twenty women in the corporate Treasury Department who answered complaint letters and calls from AT&T's millions of shareholders. Approximately 70 percent of those in this high-turnover group were college graduates. With Herzberg's suggestions before them, a small study team chose not to change any of the hygiene factors surrounding these jobs for the duration of the test but to concentrate entirely on the job itself. The stated purpose of the trial was to see if Herzberg's theory could be applied to improve the quality of service, improve productivity, cut turnover, lower costs and—the key to the others—improve job satisfaction.

With a control group set apart for contrast, an "achieving group" was picked for vertical job loading. The test was set to last six months. Ford and his colleagues figured that was long enough to allow it to get beyond both an initial drop in productivity that might result from the changes and a possible short-term gain in productivity and attitude resulting from the novelty of change—the "Hawthorne effect." To further protect the trial against this short-lasting effect, it was decided that the women in the group as well as their immediate supervisors would not be told what was taking place.

Work began as the supervisors above the first level and the project's directors used Herzberg's general suggestions on vertical loading and came up with a list of possible changes for the group. During these sessions, a number of suggestions were made which were horizontal in nature. As it became apparent they would do nothing to challenge the employee, these were rejected. Among these rejects were suggestions to set firm work quotas, to rotate

Job Enrichment

the women through various units for variety, and to let them take on clerical functions that others were performing. Finally, out of many ideas, a cluster of seven changes were decided upon. They were:

1. Subject-matter experts were appointed for other members of the group to consult with before going to a supervisor.

2. New correspondents were to be told to sign their own letters from the first day on the job. (In the existing system, the supervisor had signed for many months.)

3. Work of the more experienced correspondents was to be looked over less frequently by the supervisors.

4. Talk from supervisors about productivity—i.e., pressure—was to be cut down and limited to general terms.

5. Outgoing work was to go directly to the mailroom without crossing the supervisor's desk.

6. All correspondents would be told that they would be held directly responsible for the quality of their work rather than sharing that responsibility with supervisors and verifiers.

7. Correspondents would be encouraged to answer letters in a less formal, more personalized, way to get away from the form-letter approach.

It was agreed by those running the experiment that the changes would be introduced at the rate of about one a week. This was done successfully and without the apparent knowledge on the part of any of the women or their immediate supervisors that a major experiment in job restructuring was underway.

After the planned six months was up and all the changes had theoretically been adjusted to, the experimental team began looking at the results. On the quantitative side, turnover was greatly reduced. Only one of the women in the achieving group left; her reason was that she did not like the added responsibilities given her and specifically complained that there was nobody verifying her work any longer. Even though absenteeism was not really a problem before the experiment began, the rate went down slightly in the experimental group and up slightly in the control group. Promotions were up in the test group because workers were better able to show their ability to accept greater responsibility. The company's index quantifying the quality of the work showed the experimental group dropping well below that of the control group in the early weeks of the experiment (reflecting readjustment) and then rising above it to sustain a higher level. Most significant were the results of a questionnaire on job satisfaction given to both groups before and after the experiment. Each question had five answers with values ranging from zero to five. For instance, the answer to the question, "As you see it, how many opportunities do you feel you have in your job for making worthwhile contributions?" ranged from zero for the answer "almost none" to the five-point answer of "unlimited." The possible score extremes ran from zero to eighty. Before the experiment, the mean score for both groups was around forty. After the six months, the control group's score had dropped four points (perhaps because its members heard of changes in the other group), while the activity group posted a sixteen-point gain. The final report on the experiment commented, "There is less than one chance per thousand that this is merely a sampling fluctuation."

Looking at more subjective results, supervisors noted a number of improvements: The test group showed higher overall morale, was more enthusiastic about tackling problems, and was talking more about job responsibilities than hygiene. Two "problem" employees had come out of the experiment transformed. It was also observed that the overall level of "small, annoying personnel problems" had gone down. The experiment's subjects, still unaware that they had been in a major job-enrichment effort, had favorable comments on the new procedures (which showed up on the second questionnaire in a space provided for spontaneous remarks). Not only did they generally note greater satisfaction, opportunity, and learning, but some pointed out that the company was still not fully recognizing their talents and were asking for still more responsibility.

Job Enrichment

After this trial ended in late 1965, an eighteen-month program was instituted to bring job enrichment to the total population of the two hundred fifty managers and nine hundred employees in the division in which the original experiment had been conducted. The same kinds of impressive gains were noted. In addition, on this scale, the economic advantages of the idea became apparent. A decrease in turnover of 27 percent was realized, which was estimated to have been worth $245,000 in saved recruiting and training costs.

Meanwhile, eighteen new controlled experiments, involving a variety of jobs including phone installers, keypunchers, equipment engineers, service representatives, and information operators, had gotten started in Bell locations across the US and Canada. By design, the more than 1,000 employees involved in these tests, and a like number in the control groups, encompassed people with different ages, education levels, and job responsibilities. The question implicit was whether or not the all-female, predominantly young and highly educated workforce in the first experiment was typical of other telephone workers in their dramatic response to job enrichment. The answer was no. Large gains, like those achieved in the first test, were posted in eight of the eighteen, another was adjudged a "visible and consistent" gain, eight more were considered "modest" and one trial group showed no difference over the control group. Collectively, these results were not as impressive as the first, but they were good and clearly showed that the effort had been worth it. A degree of measurable improvement had been made in all but one situation, and even this one showed promise. In the "no difference" trial, the main improving idea had been to give each installer his own section of the city as his territory of responsibility, replacing the old system of day-to-day assignments—and the men liked and wanted to continue the new system.

In early 1968, AT&T's top management reviewed the results and decided to let company managers introduce job enrichment —or the Work Itself Program as it had come to be called in the

Bell System—on a permanent nonexperimental basis at their discretion. Within a year, seventy-seven new programs were underway and another forty-six were slated to begin early in 1969.

Besides proving Herzberg's theories and prompting the Bell System to follow a course in job reform, Ford's experiments also provided a set of insights about work itself. Looking at the issue of hygiene in real situations, Ford saw that bad hygiene will render job-enrichment attempts useless, or, as he put it in his book, *Motivation Through the Work Itself*, "Employees leave for maintenance reasons too."

However, he did find exceptions to the theories of Herzberg. For example, a bad context *could* add meaning to content. It had long been recognized in the phone company that nothing improved employee performance better than a snowstorm—it was said that when morale went sour, managers prayed for snow—and, remarkably, it was found that such emergencies often prompted a drop rather than a rise in employee accident rates. Ford believes that a blizzard, flood, or other context emergency actually makes the content of the job more meaningful, because the community comes to depend on the individual employee. This, among other reasons, led Ford to conclude that the distinction between a content and hygiene factor was not always distinct, and urged job reformers to look at the total job.

Ford also gave thought to how jobs got "denuded" in the first place, and came up with three basic reasons. One lies in the natural history of many jobs as they moved from one technological era to another. The example of this that he often uses is the elevator operator.

Early elevators were operated by "stationary engineers" who ran complex power hoists from the ground by responding to hand signals from above. Then came the first major advance, which was putting the man on the hoist (as the elevators became safer and more reliable). This still required a resourceful person, because he was still working with a difficult piece of steam or hydraulic machinery. Electricity came next and wiped out almost all of the skill and decision making associated with the job. When all the gadgets were added to the modern elevator, the operator no longer even had to be able to remember the floors that were buzzing or be able to jockey the vehicle into position at the floor. Many of these jobs have been automated out of existence, and those that remain are bound to be boring and unchallenging. Denuding of this type is the inevitable result of technical and economic imperatives and, as Ford sees it, such jobs come to a point where so few fragments of the original job are left that it should either be eliminated through automation or, if that is not possible, somehow be given back some of its original meaning.

A second form of denuding—with much more promise of salvation—is the case of the job which has been simplified and partitioned by management over the years for short-term productivity gains or through an effort to save on training costs. One of his nineteen experiments was a case in point. "Framemen" working in a large urban telephone center to cross-connect wires for customers needing new permanent circuits were having problems. These forty men, who referred to themselves as "frame apes," were known in the local company for their high-error rates, low quality of work, low productivity, and high rate of grievances. As the jobs were examined in planning sessions for the experiment, it was seen that neither individuals nor the teams of three they were assigned to had full assignments—or, in the job-enrichment jargon, complete modules of work. One kind of team, for example, contained one man at either end of a wire making the connections and a third, in the middle, who ran the wire back and forth. Commonly, these men had no idea if they had done the job correctly because their connections were usually not checked until the next shift, when another kind of team came on duty. Nor did the connecting team have any sense of "customer" in their work, because it was still another kind of team that had the job of handling the order and finding out the purpose of the connection. In this situation, the major element of the enriching process was putting the jobs back together in meaningful units. Instead of three types of teams, each handling a few specific tasks, new teams were created and trained to do all the work on a single order, from writing it up to turning over a working connection to the customer. The results of this experiment were excellent; a difference was shown in all the problem areas, ranging from the number of errors (which had been cut to one quarter of their original level) to the formal grievances (which went from a rate of one per week to none at all during the period of the experiment). What is more, the group gained a sense of client and total job, and began using terms like "my circuit" and "my customer."

The final form of denuding is the one Ford calls "tightening up": the process by which management takes responsibility from one job and moves it to a higher level. This commonly begins as an employee makes a mistake, say, in a transaction with a customer. The customer complains, with the result that management decides that a supervisor must now okay all transactions. Then an overworked supervisor misses several mistakes in a bad week and another policy decision is made to move the responsibility for the transaction up the ladder one more rung. This process is repeated until responsibility rests at a level high above the person actually conducting the transaction; when a mistake comes to the attention of this higher-up, any reprimand forthcoming must travel back down the ladder. In the AT&T experiments, where many examples of this type were uncovered, Ford observed that tightening up will not end occasional errors but will add to costs, slow service, and take responsibility out of the hands of the people who should have it. In many of the experiments, responsibilities which had crept up the line over the years were pushed back to their lowest level—with success. Ford

Job Enrichment

contends that the answer to the person who makes more than occasional errors is to retrain that one person, and not to take responsibility away from everyone at that level.

Another observation which Ford brought out of the nineteen trials sounds almost too simple to be called an "insight," but it is so often forgotten or not fully appreciated that it deserves mention. As Ford puts it, "Corporate purpose is not individual purpose." More fully explained, the individual is looking for responsibility, growth, and meaning, and the task that the company has given that person—installing phones or whatever—is incidental to these other goals. No threat, pep talk, or training film can change this. The lesson is clear: Good jobs must be a corporate objective and satisfying employees must rank with satisfying shareholders and customers.

Since the original AT&T work, Ford's experiments have become the most talked about in the world of organizations since those of Taylor and Elton Mayo. Job enrichment has become something of a phenomenon in that world—albeit, more talked about than applied—but nonetheless, attracting much attention. Most trade magazines and business journals in America have carried articles on it and most business schools now either offer a course in it or have introduced it into an existing course. Several dozen companies and banks are deeply into the enrichment process and have created special groups to act as missionaries carrying job enrichment from department to department. Many more organizations, ranging from the Air Force to the Canadian civil service, are in the early phases of testing the idea with an eye to further application for their employees. In short, it is growing, and shows signs of becoming much bigger in the mid- and late-1970s. One reason for this momentum is a former AT&T man who is doing a very effective job of promoting and selling the idea.

3

EASING THE PAIN
WITH THE
JOB DOCTOR

Roy Walters is a tall, gray-bearded man in his early fifties who generates that special enthusiasm that comes naturally to a person on top of a good exploitable idea. It is immediately obvious that he enjoys what he is doing, which is serving as the leading private consultant and public advocate in what he terms "the business of easing the pain of painful jobs." He is a graduate of the University of Pittsburgh who spent most of his working life as a manager for the Bell Telephone Company of Pennsylvania. In 1960, he went to AT&T, where he later became a member of the team doing the Ford experiments. In 1967, he left to open a one-man consulting firm devoted to helping others with job enrichment; since then he has established for himself the third starring role in the job-enrichment story, following Herzberg, the theorist, and Ford, the experimenter, as the practitioner and popularizer.

Today, his firm, Roy Walters Associates, is made up of Walters and eight enrichment specialists. They work out of a small, cluttered office in Glen Rock, New Jersey, which is home base for their highly mobile operation—as a group they have been running up airline ticket tabs of over $100,000 a year for the last few years.

There is a special style to this operation set by Walters himself. Unlike the more academic advocates of job enrichment, who write chart-and-statistics-heavy papers on the subject, and the quiet specialists in industry, Walters is an active practitioner and promoter who does things such as getting himself invited onto late night radio talk shows to talk about job discontent, and issuing press releases in which he does things like list the "Ten Worst Jobs in America." His style is a mixture: He consults

Job Enrichment

discreetly over long periods with those who hire him as their work doctor, but he is out to popularize the issues at hand and to raise the consciousnesses of the bossed and their bosses nationwide. If releasing a "Ten Worst" list or distributing a packaged job-boredom test to the newspapers for people to administer to themselves is gimmickry, as some of his colleagues in the job-enrichment field privately charge, it is effective gimmickry and a needed breakaway from the jargon-laden journal articles on work which seldom get read by line managers or workers.

The "Ten Worst Jobs" list is an interesting case in point. In no special order, Walters tagged these as the most boring, and therefore the worst:

assembly-line worker
highway toll collector
car-watcher in a tunnel
pool typist
bank guard
copy-machine operator
bogus typesetter (those who set type that is not to be used)
computer-tape librarian (a fancy title for a person whose job is rolling up spools of tape all day)
housewife (not to be confused with mother)
automatic-elevator operator

In treating jobs the way one would handle the listing of the ten best-dressed women or the ten worst movies, Walters has taken some heartfelt observations on the way people are treated and has packaged them in a form which can be picked up readily by the media—and has been. And while you might disagree with his choices, they are heartfelt. Walters can go on at length about the tunnelmen who sit in their glass booths breathing fumes and watching cars with the indignation others save for war atrocities. Nor did he put housewife on the list just to be provocative and get his name in the papers; he is firmly convinced that that job is "one of the worst, most boring, unrewarding, and unrewarded" that has ever been created. Or: "To me the ultimate inanity of the age is to go into a brand-new New York City office building and find a human being working eight hours a day pushing an automatic elevator button so that others don't have to push it."

Like any other group of consultants, Walters and his crew are out to make a buck and a name for themselves. But this is not to say that they are not legitimate, thoughtful reformers with a potential impact on the way Americans work and think about work, which is far greater than their number would suggest. They are serving as both consultants to their clients and consultants to the whole country, and in the latter role of national gadflies are not reluctant to issue the relevant zingers that occur to them in their work. For example, an air-clearing zinger which has attracted a lot of attention was issued by senior associate Robert Janson, who discovered in a national survey of salesmen that one of the things bothering them most were all those sales contests which so many companies feel are essential to keeping their sales forces happy and on their toes. "Manipulation—not motivation—is behind many contests, resort trips, and special citations," says Janson, "and a lot of salesmen politely refer to them as 'dum dum awards.'"

Walters and his co-workers are quite open about the fact that they intend to make job enrichment into a major movement, but concede that they have a long way to go. "Relatively speaking, it is still a very minor movement," says Walters, who estimates that there are still less than sixty companies in the United States and Canada that are serious about it and have actually implemented a job-enrichment program as a matter of policy.

"The gestation period in this field is amazingly long," he says. "Many companies are looking at it, but most of them are going to spend the next few years appointing task forces and holding special seminars to decide how to approach it. Then maybe—and only maybe—they will muster the guts to do something."

He says there are other organizations which think they can attend a seminar on the subject, make a cosmetic change or two

Job Enrichment

in one or two departments, and then proclaim they are part of the job-enrichment movement. These are the people who are looking for a teaspoon of job enrichment to give their company the reputation of being forward-looking and progressive. Still others fall into the category of one-shot miracle workers who, says Walters, ". . . try it out for a short period of time in one department and drop it when there is no quick evidence that productivity has zoomed and the company is realizing savings."

Walters understands some of the reluctance because he feels that starting a program calls for a definite commitment, and that job enrichment is not suited to dabbling because the dabblers tend to raise expectations and then dash them when the dabbling is done. Such one-shot deals, he contends, have been responsible for a good share of whatever bad reputation job enrichment has had to share with its success stories.

In his role as the leading enricher-for-hire, Walters' point of view is direct and simple, overwhelmingly committed to the Herzberg-Ford idea that changing the job itself is essential to true reform. Hygienic innovations are very important—in many cases, long overdue—but peripheral to his crusade. "Sure I can see the advantage in the four-day week," he says. "Four days in a lousy job is better than five." The flexible workday? "Fantastic! It means that an employer has begun to treat you like a big boy." Again and again, he comes back to the same point: that such things are sweeteners, and no matter how many we throw at people, or how much we pay them, if the job is lousy, the job is lousy. It is as if the man who watches cars in the Lincoln Tunnel has become Walters' personal touchstone to whom he must return time and again. "We now have to pay these men over $12,000 a year and will continue to have to keep buying them off with more money and more benefits. Unless the job changes radically, we can only hope to pay them for their pain."

The jobs which the Walters group does are generated, for the most part, by a series of six two-day seminars a year held in major cities, to which he attracts a group of representatives of major companies who are curious enough to pay up to $250 a head to come and hear Walters interpret and explain the gospel of job enrichment, and to hear testimonials from clients who have successfully applied it. These seminars are intended to serve as crash courses on the subject and as a meeting ground from which Walters attracts new clients.

Thus far, about one out of each hundred companies that have attended a seminar have come back to Walters and established a long-term working arrangement. "Some come back but can't make that final commitment," says Walters, "and others are willing to hire me but are not sure if they want to make any serious changes. If they aren't serious, I want no part of them." Even so, he has been able to attract a sizable clientele of about thirty, which includes Bankers Trust of New York, the Borg-Warner Corporation, Travelers Insurance, and the Indiana National Bank.

Once a serious client decides to go ahead with job enrichment and hires Walters, there is a general procedure beginning with Walters and his associates coming in and "taking the temperature" of the group to be enriched by finding out how its members feel about their jobs. This is done through questionnaires and in-depth taped interviews, in which workers are asked to talk about their work and their feelings toward it. At the same time, measurements are taken of a number of variables such as absenteeism, productivity, turnover, and error rates. These measurements change, depending on the situation. For instance, in nonclerical situations, job safety is measured, because dulled workers are more liable to have accidents. In extreme cases, incidents of theft and even sabotage are used. This part of the process usually takes several months.

Next, a series of four- or five-day sessions are scheduled with the three levels of management immediately above the group to be enriched. In these, they are given what Walters calls "a concentrated dose of new learning." He says, "We not only tell them about job enrichment and what it can do, but also give

Job Enrichment 61

them an idea of the troubles they will have if nothing is done. Playing the tapes we have made of people talking about their jobs is a very effective way of making this point."

These sessions are also used to wrestle with the inevitable roadblocks which are thrown up by those who claim it would never work or insist that the workers would not stand for it. Gradually, the sessions move toward "green lighting"—the process of coming up with specific changes in the job in question. The term green lighting is used because the person running the session gives a green light for all the managers and supervisors in the room to start coming up with changes as fast as they can think of them. These ideas are written down on easels at the front of the room for later evaluation in the red-light sessions when each point is discussed in detail. Evaluation at the green-light sessions is forestalled so that ideas will flow freely and quickly, and so that those in the group are not hindered in their creativity by discussion and disagreement. Once people run out of ideas, the list is examined and the process of rejecting them by consensus begins. First to go are those which are relatively poor in contrast to the others, and those which were initially offered in jest or to shock. With the aid of the workshop director, the group pares the list to a dozen or so changes which are purposely spread out through the following categories of reform: changing the work module, granting new responsibility, creating new forms of recognition and feedback, initiating growth potential, and the elimination of old rules which are serving as roadblocks. While there are no hard rules or quotas involved, it is important to get a balance between these categories to give dimension to the enrichment.

Walters sees these sessions as more than just a time for education and planning; they serve to begin the enrichment process in an indirect manner. Because they always take place away from the workers for a number of days at a time—often, in fact, they are held out of the plant in a hotel conference room—the process starts immediately because the workers are left unbossed, giving them a taste of new responsibility. Correspondingly, getting away gives the supervisors a chance to see that their working world will not collapse into anarchy when their people are not constantly monitored and bossed.

Next comes the process of slowly introducing change—typically, two to three months to fully insert the first item. At this point, the process is best described by example. To show how it works and how it moves into other parts of an organization, Walters points to one of the many enrichments which he helped perform.

Like many other employers, the Bankers Trust Company of New York had long brandished the motto that its most valuable asset is its human resources; but it had become increasingly apparent from high turnover and low-quality work that this resource was dissatisfied. In 1969, the bank's top management had become sufficiently alarmed that it decided to experiment with the new concept of job enrichment. Walters, who was working with several other banks, including the Chase Manhattan and the Bank of New York, was hired to get the ball rolling.

Illustrating his point that the best place to start is the place where conditions are the worst, the division picked was the one that handled stock-transfer operations. By all accounts, it represented the worst kind of routine, repetitive and intrinsically meaningless "grunt" work which yielded predictably bad morale and performance. Bickering was common in a workforce where adults were treated like children: They were told exactly when they could go to lunch, and were taken to the rest room under supervision. The specific job targeted for enrichment was that of production typist: two shifts of approximately one hundred people whose job boiled down to typing and recording stock-transfer data, transferring the information from one piece of paper to other pieces of paper and onto computer tape. They could not, and did not, identify with their work, because they performed only a small fragment of it. Due to the costly nature of errors which could cause lost certificates, improper registration, stray dividends, and unlimited customer irritation, the bank had assigned one checker to each typist. When an error was detected, it was forwarded to a special unit for correction and then checked again by another checker. Once verified, the information was put on tape and fed into the computer.

Walters describes the first item introduced from the final selection of twelve winnowed from the fifty-two new ideas generated during the green-lighting workshop:

> One of the limits of the job was that a typist was not allowed to change her computer-input tape, and in order to get one changed she had to raise her hand and get the supervisor to come over and do it for her. I don't know where the procedure came from or why, but it probably dated back to a day when one of the typists had screwed up and it was ordered that only supervisors could handle the job. What we did was to start letting a few of the typists start changing their own tapes, and we waited for the reaction.

The reaction was fast. Those who had been given the "privilege" held that it was about time they could be trusted with this simple task, and the others started asking that they be allowed to do the same. This was the desired result. By letting the first few change tapes, the supervisors had more time to coach the others in the process, and by the time that most everyone was changing their own tapes, it was time to move on to other changes. Within six months, a dozen changes had been introduced. A sampling:

¶ Work that had been normally assigned randomly by the supervisors was replaced with a system based on customer territory, in which typists were given permanent responsibility for the clients whose names began with a certain portion of the alphabet.

¶ Typists were given the right to check their own work and correct their own errors. Once detected, an error was immediately fed back to the person who had made it.

¶ "Specials," or those transfers involving difficult and complicated entries, which had been performed only by those few deemed most experienced, were now given to the rest of the typists. The most experienced women were used as teachers.

Certain typists could take total responsibility for their clientele, while others who were less accurate in their work were still given added responsibility by being assigned to teams with total responsibility. These teams scheduled their own work, corrected their own errors and their own quality records.

The results were good. Greater productivity, higher quality work, lower absenteeism and turnover, and an improvement in attitude were all shown. Some measures showed higher degrees of success than others. Error rates only went down "slightly" but the improvement in attitude was adjudged "significant" as measured by questionnaires and interviews given both before and after the work change. Over the six-month period, common comments changed from ones like "I have five bosses to account to. It is ridiculous, I like to be treated like an adult," and "The same sheeting every day. You don't even know when you make errors," to this kind of reaction to work: "I feel I am responsible for something. I know if anything happens it's going to come back to me and I'm going to feel bad about it."

In purely economic terms, the bank's biggest payoff from the project was that, because of it, many of the checkers could be taken out of the group and reassigned to other jobs in the bank, cutting the cost of running the stock-transfer typing operation by $300,000 a year. Not all of the economic benefit went to the bank, because a number of typists were able to get better pay, having improved their job classifications through what they learned in the process. A few were spotted for clear promotion to other jobs.

Job Enrichment

Not all the improvements were noted in statistics and dollars. As Walters points out,

> An important repercussion in this case and many others like it was that it changed the people who were managing the typists. Before job enrichment, the supervisors were essentially rated by how busy they were. As became apparent during the process, much of their busy-ness was really production work and much of what remained was nickel-and-dime decision making, like deciding if someone could go to the bathroom, which left little time for developing the people under them. They were really senior workers rather than supervisors or managers. As they gave these production tasks and lower-level decision rights to the people under them, most began to develop into real managers in the best sense of the word. Rather than merely doing their employees' harder tasks, they became consultants who helped them deal with tough jobs; they began to anticipate problems and steer their people around them, rather than spending much of their time solving problems that had been created *because* they weren't managing. So in truth the people doing the enriching were also enriched.

Walters concedes that a few of the supervisors found this change in their own roles hard to adjust to especially at first, but most had no trouble and some flourished because of it. One woman who was serving at the lowest level of supervision did so well that she made two quick jumps to become the first woman ever promoted to the position of section head in the history of the department. A report on what went on in this department, which was co-authored by an officer of the bank and one of the consultants from the Walters group, says of her, "Prior to her involvement in job enrichment she had been considered a good 'technician' but 'a little too outspoken' for future consideration.

She has since taken pride in being called upon to make presentations to officials of the bank, including the president, with great success."

The management of the bank was impressed with the results of the demonstration, and, after due deliberation, decided to move it into other parts of the bank. The commitment from the top was clear and, as is far from common, public. Chairman of the board W. H. Moore wrote of the bank's experience in *Financial Executive* magazine, "We are continuing the enrichment program and expanding it as rapidly as possible. It's difficult to administer, since it involves management practices that are completely different from the ones we have used in the past. But we are determined to enhance individual growth among our employees to prevent them from stagnating or reaching a plateau. We don't want this to be just another management promise that went nowhere."

As is usually the case, Walters' role as prime mover in the work diminished after the first demonstration. While he has continued to consult with the bank on job-enrichment issues, the day-to-day job of enrichment has become the task of a group within the bank led by Kathleen Williams, a young assistant treasurer. Although she has not been formally trained in job enrichment (her background is in computers), she has worked closely with specialists from Walters' group and now enjoys a reputation as a top specialist in her own right. Among other things, she has worked with other banks on their problems and has appeared as a spokeswoman for job enrichment at several conferences. Her role in the bank is that of an "internal consultant" who is "hired" by departments in the bank as they decide to try the enrichment process. Williams has moved into other areas in the bank to continue the process, and though the number of the bank's 11,000 jobs which have been treated are still far in the minority (at the time of our conversation), others were in the process or about to start. The results of the continued effort varied from group to group, but have been generally good. One major effort has been to enlarge the enrichment in the original stock-transfer operation through five additional projects—with much the same results as in the original group. "We've taken the pressure off in that department," says Williams, who points out that more than a half of the 1,000 jobs in that area have been restructured so far. Not all of them will be touched by the process, as some of the jobs were complete and relatively meaningful to begin with.

While the basic concepts of greater responsibility, regular feedback, and more complete jobs have been at the heart of the expanded redesign effort, specific changes have differed considerably. For example, in one area, a prime element of the enrichment was to give people greater financial responsibility. Employees in the deposit accounting group, whose work included verifying the authenticity of checks, making payment stops on checks, and filing checks to be included with statements, could not handle problems or questions about checks over $500. These had to be turned over to supervisors. As part of the enrichment process, these employees were gradually given the responsibility for checks up to $10,000—although they were still trained to go for help when a question remained about, say, a possible forgery. These people were also given a phone so that they could contact branch offices to work out problems, a right that had previously only been given to higher-ups. Accomplishing these and similar changes occasioned special methods such as an exhibit on spotting forgeries which was put together by one of the supervisors.

While there are still years of work to be done in enriching the total organization, it is already apparent to those running it that the program will not be able to end with initial reforms in each department. Williams says, "We're finding that there is a bottom line to all of this, which is that you have to keep presenting change, reinforcing what has been done already and reselling the idea."

The Bankers Trust case is neither unique nor special among

companies which have adopted job enrichment. Its experiences are paralleled closely elsewhere, such as at the Travelers Insurance Companies, which began experimenting in the same year; the reforms got good results, attracted the commitment of top management and are now moving through the company at deliberate speed. Actually, the initial trial at the Travelers had more impressive results than the one at the bank—or in most other situations, for that matter. Here a group of keypunch operators were used, says Norman Edmonds, a company official spearheading the job-enrichment effort, "because it was probably the most difficult job in the company to enrich. Once a person learns to keypunch, that's it as far as learning. Also, keypunchers are tied to machines and this distinctly limits the opportunities for varying that relationship." After a year, in which twenty-five changes were introduced in the test group, the results were compared to a control group. The enriched group had increased its capacity to process work by almost 40 percent, established a favorable difference of absence rate of 53 percent over the control group, and dropped its error rate from 1.53 percent to .99 percent. By standards established by the company an error rate of less than 1 percent gives a keypunch operator a rating of "outstanding." *

* For Travelers, this contrasted dramatically with another experiment it had performed a little earlier. In an attempt to improve the efficiency of offices where policy-holder claims are settled, it took one office as a test and broke down the old system in which teams of clerks had been responsible for specific groups of clients. It was felt that lumping them together in a pool from which they could be drawn for assignments would improve things. Instead, response time lagged, errors increased, and there was a noticeable rise in employee dissatisfaction. Travelers' President, M. H. Beach, recalls, "We almost had a walkout."

4
Unfinished Business

Early success in the application of job enrichment has led to the understandable situation in which a number of theorists, converts, and progressive industrial types have become so excited by it that their statements in its behalf have taken on religious overtones. This zeal is normally well intentioned, but risks overselling and thereby ultimately damaging the idea. There are a number of stories of cases that are making the rounds which are factual but which, when taken alone, give job enrichment the hocus-pocus aura of an industrial magic show in which worker happiness, labor peace, and better profits seem to be automatic. Such an example is a recent development at the Southern Central Bell Telephone Company where employees compiling telephone directories were given the right to establish their own cut-off dates for the sale of Yellow Pages advertisements as part of their job enrichment. On their own, the employees consistently set later deadlines than management had previously allowed. In one year, this ended up giving the company a total of three weeks' extra sales time, in which $100,000 extra in advertising was sold. The effect of a dozen or so cases like this told at one sitting can be quite compelling.

Zeal and awe-inspiring examples aside, job enrichment has its drawbacks. Because of its significance as an icebreaker in job overhaul in America, the most important of these deserve attention.

One drawback, often stated but apparently overlooked by some, is that the process can damage an organization when turned on and off like some sort of executive toy. Attesting to this is a young personnel specialist who started a job-enrichment experiment in one department at a large Midwestern bank. As he tells it, the experiment was going quite well when the top leadership of the bank decided to cancel it and go back to the old procedures. The reasons given were that it smacked of gimmickry, violated the principles of scientific management, and would probably cost the bank money in the long run. The specialist argued that the experiment was on the verge of saving money, but to no avail. Understandably, he left for another position (where he is now in charge of a large enrichment effort), but he did check back to see what had happened in the experimental group. "Close to half the employees in the experiment left within a year and the supervisor in charge claimed that most of those who left were the best workers. Many of them said they were leaving because they were neither trusted nor respected."

This drawback is seen as an advantage by many in the field because it acts as a deterrent to dabblers who like to play around with a new idea just to say that they have tried it.

Of course, some sincere attempts fail, too. There have been several such failures which have come to light, and undoubtedly more which have not. One that has been made public is the case of the Weyerhaeuser Company, where 70 percent of the twenty-three plants that adopted enrichment dropped it to start again. As an official of the company told *The Wall Street Journal*, "Where we made our mistake was in bypassing some of the managerial levels and work-force leadership; now we get them in on the early stages." Another failure which has been made public was an attempt to enrich certain jobs within the Internal Revenue Service (detailed in a report from the Industrial Conference Board entitled *Job Design for Motivation*). According to the formal report, which was prepared by the Board's Hal Rush, the effort had "limited success," which he terms an understatement when interviewed in person. The reasons for the failure, according to Rush, include hygiene needs which were not adequately met and generally superficial job changes. Significantly, this experience neither soured the IRS or the Federal Government on the idea.

IRS officials told Rush they would try again, and several agencies, the Social Security Administration among them, launched their own job-enrichment efforts late in 1974. Among these failures, however, none has yet come to light which has significantly tarnished the basic idea.

Beyond its actual application, an important hurdle the idea faces is the opposition it has attracted from key individuals in organized labor. The most vocal opponent has been William W. Winpisinger, Vice-President of the International Association of Machinists (AFL-CIO), who has variously called it "a stopwatch in sheep's clothing," "a trick to force higher productivity," and "a speed-up in the guise of concern for workers." He contends that if you want to enrich the job, you enrich the paycheck, begin to decrease hours, and improve the physical environment. Looking a little deeper, however, one finds that the feelings of this union are not as strong as these public statements would seem to indicate. Albert S. Epstein, the Machinists' research director, says that the union is actually neither for nor against the idea at present and that Winpisinger's statements represent an admittedly "extreme position" taken to force attention to the union position that changing jobs will not be accepted as an alternative to better pay, hours, and working conditions. While other union leaders have not been as outspoken, many are quite stand-offish to the idea.

There are several good reasons for this. One is that, by all accounts, most job enrichment is taking place in nonunion job situations, which is interpreted by unions as a possible ploy for improving jobs so that the urge to unionize is lessened. Enrichment that is taking place in unionized locations is seldom done with union collaboration either in planning or application, let alone being done after giving the local union a full briefing on the process. Many in the labor movement, including those at the Machinists', point out that the unions will remain cool to the idea until this situation changes. If one can say that there is a job-enrichment "movement," one of its most serious shortcomings has been leaving the unions out of the picture. A few, like AT&T and the Communications Workers of America, have begun talking with each other on the subject, but they are still the rare exception.

One does not have to be an expert in management-labor relations to see the potential problem here: Union coolness could easily turn to open hostility if communications on the subject do not improve. Meanwhile, it seems reasonable to surmise that part of the reason why the unions are being left out in the cold is that one of the goals of job enrichment is greater productivity, which, if realized, gives the unions one of their best cases for wage increases. And if a union was a participant in this, the case would be even stronger. Eventually, this could prompt the unions to demand a role in job enrichment by making it a matter for collective bargaining.

Another job-enrichment problem—and another reason for union involvement—is the use to which it can be put as a sophisticated tool for getting rid of people. This is the skeleton in the closet for those in the job-enrichment field, who never mention it in their articles and papers on the subject. Many of those enrichers that I asked about it acknowledged the problem, opposed the practice, firmly maintained that it would not happen as a result of one of their projects, and pointed out that as soon as the employees began to believe such a thing, the whole effort would fall apart. A typical response to this issue comes from Charles V. Pfautz, a job-enrichment supervisor for the Chesapeake and Potomac Telephone Companies, who says, "It's inconceivable that this could happen in the Bell System. If any jobs do get eliminated through the process the people in them are invariably transferred to other jobs." One place where this is not so is at the large brokerage firm of Merrill Lynch, Pierce, Fenner and Smith, Inc. where Gary Lungen, skills training manager, freely admits to "casualties"—supervisors let go because they couldn't perform under the system, and clerks whose employment was terminated when their jobs were eliminated and there was no spot open for them elsewhere in the organization. While it must be emphasized that this kind of behavior is uncommon, it will not take too many similar situations to give the idea a bad reputation, which will eventually reach those whose jobs are ripe for enrichment. Naturally, these job holders would be very suspicious of any changes in the way they work and might actively resist them.

An entirely different kind of threat to job enrichment arises when any work idea—good or bad, old or new—adopted by a company or advocated publicly by someone is reported on as part of the job-enrichment movement. Even though the term has a very specific meaning, it apparently has broad appeal because it has become a catchall for a great number of ideas, ranging from the four-day workweek to sensitivity training, none of which bears any relationship whatsoever to the preachings of Herzberg, Ford et al. This mistake is being compounded by more than a few journalists, politicians, labor leaders, and businessmen. This might seem to be a minor problem of definition, but it is more, because the impression being rendered is that job enrichment consists of radical changes in everything from benefits to working hours—a much larger dose for a captain of industry to swallow. For example, in late 1973, Senator Charles Percy introduced into the Congressional Record a report which primarily concerned itself with moves in such places as Peru, Chile, and Sweden to put workers on company boards as directors. Senator Percy had this report labeled "Foreign Experiments in Job Enrichment," fostering the impression that job enrichment includes putting hourly workers in the boardroom. It doesn't.

Still another problem, and the most important criticism that can be made of the enriching process, is that a major element of it is almost as paternalistic and nondemocratic as the system it replaces. To date, without exception, the process of coming up with job improvements and their implementation has been done without the participation of those on the lowest rungs. Nor, for that matter, are workers commonly told what is happening during the enrichment process. In some cases, they are *never* told what has been done to them, or why—that is, unless they happen to read about one of the top bosses of their company bragging about turnover rates and productivity in *Business Week* or the *Harvard Business Review*.

The major practitioners since Ford, who first established the practice of nonparticipation, each have a collection of reasons why worker involvement in the process would not work. David Whitsett, who, as a consultant, has worked with a number of companies, says:

> Bringing the workers into the act would only screw things up. They aren't prepared to design their own jobs. For one thing, using them might quickly turn into a hygiene fight with the employee, using the planning sessions to take up causes like higher pay and longer vacations. Also, when you invite a worker into a planning session in which he is asked what should be included in his job, he will come up with all sorts of ideas which may be unfeasible, not fit in with other jobs or be too grandiose for the plan—but which may be very exciting and appealing. Sometimes a green-lighting session will generate one hundred fifty ideas of which ten or twenty actually survive. If the worker was a part of this he would see his ideas dropped and perhaps feel angry about it. You know, there is a common myth which says that the person in a job actually knows that job best. The man in the job is actually in a bubble and can't see beyond it, so it takes management to see how that job fits in. This is not to say that the man in the job lacks imagination about what could be done with that job, but this imagination presents a problem because it will generate a host of ideas which for one reason or another may not fit into the enrichment plan.

Job Enrichment

Others add different reasons. An economic argument commonly made is that it would cost too much to take a large number of workers off their jobs and into a series of long redesign sessions. The point is also made that it is better to make the supervisors the architects of the plan because it enlists their support in an effort which would be doomed without their enthusiasm and cooperation. There is even a humane reason offered, which says that it would be cruel to bring a person in to work on a job which may be so fragmented that it cannot be improved. Some, but not all, have worked out a rationale for never telling their people why things have changed, which boils down to the fear of rising expectations and demands for greater change before it is due. Increasingly, practitioners of the art are explaining enrichment to the enrichees either just after it has started or after the first set of motivators has been added. On this, Whitsett says:

> I tell the companies I work with to tell their enrichment clients the whole story at the beginning and to ask them for their advice along the way. Some organizations still keep their people in the dark, because this is what Ford did at first, but what they forget is that Ford was trying to get pure experimental results and so had to prevent the Hawthorne effect. Today there is really no reason for it because Ford proved his point.

While a number of the points made against worker participation in the design process seem to have some validity, they have not been tested. Walters, Whitsett, and others in a position to know are unaware of anyone attempting enrichment with nonmanagerial job designers, which means that, until someone has the courage to try it, there will be a definite hollowness to the many arguments against it. As will be shown in the following chapters, this timidity about using employees as reformers is not evident among pioneering efforts outside of job enrichment. Some in the field of work reform think much less of enrichment for just this reason. For instance, James O'Toole who headed the HEW *Work in America* task force, says, "Job enrichment is better than nothing, but not as good as those plans which provide for worker participation."

On the other hand, there are those who question its underlying premise—and, by logical extension, most other attempts to reshape jobs. Charles L. Hulin, a University of Illinois psychologist, has written, "The assumption behind job enrichment is that everyone can be made to think that his job is his life. That simply isn't always the case." He believes that it makes the same mistakes as Taylorism, in that it assumes the working community is a less complex group than it really is, and views all workers as people who share the enricher's middle-class concern with self-actualization. James Windle, a professor of management supervision at Purdue, has collected evidence to support his thesis that the issue of "worker alienation" has been vastly overplayed and that most workers don't want their jobs changed. He has said, ". . . repetitive and monotonous factory jobs may be a cause of concern to some sociologists and managers, but they apparently don't bother the workers." Based on this, he concludes that job enrichment will be ineffective. Windle also contends that the issue of worker dissatisfaction is either a fad or a "cover" by unions that want to eliminate overtime and are using the issue to make the point that having to spend extra time in boring jobs is cruel.

Only the future success or failure of job enrichment will fully determine the worth of these criticisms; however, there have already been enough successful starts to weaken their arguments. Since they assume an American workforce which is, in large part, content with spending its days at dull and monotonous jobs, they are arguing for the *status quo*—specifically, for the continuation of the worker-as-oaf premise behind scientific management—in the face of a great deal of contrary evidence. Their contentions sound too much like an excuse for doing nothing. Hulin's comment that work enrichment is based on middle-class values is probably true,

Job Enrichment 77

but that seems to be a strength rather than a weakness in a country where there are not many working people who do not see themselves as present or future members of the middle class. And as for Windle's suggestion that the worker alienation issue is a union ploy, it would seem that he has not bothered to listen to union leaders, who are of many different minds on the extent of the problem. A few are not even sure there is a problem. In fact, there have been as many or more business leaders as union leaders who have gone to the podium and worried aloud about dissatisfied workers, which would imply that such figures as the heads of General Electric and AT&T are collaborating in an organized-labor machination.

Even after taking all the drawbacks, criticisms, and problems into account, job enrichment must still be termed a major, positive development in the world of work—albeit with bugs still to be worked out. Opinions vary as to whether job enrichment itself will emerge as the dominant blueprint for more widespread job reform. Even if it does not, it has already made its mark by creating two distinct legacies.

The first is as a general model for theory and experimentation in the working environment. Of course, there have been scores of theorists besides Herzberg, and many experimenters besides Ford, but these two in tandem have been able to foster an experimental momentum which makes it easier for other new ideas to get tested in the workplace. Many of those running alternative working schemes reported elsewhere in this book make the point that Ford's AT&T work made it easier for them to start their experiments.

The second legacy is that job enrichment has opened people's minds to alternative thinking on the structure of jobs, just as the four-day workweek has opened people's minds to thinking about alternative working schedules. The fact that job enrichment has gotten as far as it has means, at least, that it is now very hard for anyone to say that the old way is the only way.

Meanwhile, it is becoming apparent that while some look

upon job enrichment as a rigid process with rules that are not to be broken, a few have begun to vary the format. New experimentation aimed at determining the strength, flexibility, and varied applicability of the basic notion is essential; one such example is worth looking at before moving on.

5

Moving up the Job Ladder

Bert Brosius is a middle-aged middle manager working in the Bell System for the Chesapeake and Potomac Telephone Companies as a job-enrichment specialist with a subspecialty: enriching supervisory and managerial jobs. As this system of companies has done more to pioneer and apply job enrichment than any other group (one knowledgeable Bell System source estimates there are now more than 100,000 enriched jobs in the organization), it is not too surprising that the idea is making its first major leap to higher echelons here. Brosius and others are escorting the idea several rungs up the ladder for the simple reasons that the jobs of people with authority are as much in need of enrichment as any other, and that foremen and those above them will be better able to reform the jobs of those below them after they have benefited from the process themselves.

This type of enrichment works differently than it does at a lower level. For one thing, those whose jobs are involved do their own green lighting, and though the items themselves are divided into motivator and hygiene categories, both are acted upon and, within reason, each item that the group lists is studied, evaluated, and, if approved, implemented by the group. What is more, the process has no scheduled end—the group keeps meeting for as long as it wants—and the green light is always on to provide for the addition of more items.

When a given item is brought up in a group of, say, twenty supervisors who have decided that the item is not trivial and bears further investigation, it is turned over to a small group of volunteers to study and report back on at regular intervals. At any given time, eight to ten items are under investigation. The questions to be resolved by each study group are: what roadblocks stand in its way, how would they be resolved, what level of approval within the company would be necessary to get it approved, and what are its advantages and disadvantages to the company as a whole, the employee, and the customer? Often the ability to approve an item rests within the group, but in other cases, it must go to a higher authority. Once a group of items is resolved—that is, adopted or dropped by consensus—a new group is taken up and assigned to study groups.

Brosius, whose role in this is to act as a consultant to such groups, says that his experience with this kind of enrichment has been very good, and reports that it generally leads to orderly but rapid change. He adds that the people he has observed in such sessions take the business of restructuring their own jobs "with deadly seriousness," generally steering clear of both far-out and superficial reforms, and, when it comes down to the economics of what they are doing, are as cost conscious as those in top managerial posts. To show me the kind of reform that gets enacted, Brosius offered to assemble a small group of participants to talk about their experiences. I spent a morning with four supervisors from various managerial levels and found an overwhelmingly positive consensus. Each individual could see that jobs were improving, that frustrations were being eliminated, and that attitudes were getting better. In addition to these hoped-for results, there were also by-products that had not been predicted.

One of these was that there was great misunderstanding among people with authority as to just what authority they and others had. Often, items were thrown out as possible reforms which were really long-established rights and procedures. Typically, a man or woman would suggest that people at their level be given the right to sign important letters rather than having to have them signed by a higher-up. It was quickly revealed that the higher-up (often part of the group) was signing the letters for the simple reason that they were being sent to him to sign, not because they had to be sent to him. Ross Campbell, a plant supervisor, summed it up: "The biggest advantage I've seen in this is that we found we weren't communicating with each other. This has been quite a revelation to me, because I thought we'd been doing quite well in this department."

A similarly important development reported on was that the freedom to green light anything you want led to unexpected but important areas for change. In one group, for instance, the matter of race and sex was raised when a man admitted that he was upset because he felt that whites were expected to do more than blacks and males more than females. This prompted further investigation in which it was found that there was truth to the allegation, and that the problem was in fact bothering all parties. For example, a higher-level manager working with the group admitted that he was not allowing women to get into situations where they would have to confront nonsupervisory employees with evidence that they were goofing off or not doing their jobs correctly. He was afraid that they might get into unfriendly arguments replete with verbal abuse. As it turned out, both the men (who always got this work) and the women (who never got it) resented the situation and a pledge was made to give both sexes the job.

Also, despite fears to the contrary, matters of hygiene did not present problems, but resulted instead both in a better understanding of the system in cases where study showed that changes could not be made, and in rapid change in areas where it was feasible. A staff supervisor reported that a group wanted to change a policy by which each person was allowed a flat fifteen dollars in toll-free calls per month by the company. The feeling in the group was that it would be better to allow ninety dollars for each six-month period to cover a situation in which an emergency would require many long-distance calls to be made at one time. Once the group decided it wanted the change, it was accomplished with one phone call to a higher authority. There were other positive developments reported on at this meeting, but these few are enough to show that this and future variations on the basic job-enrichment formula can be rich indeed.

The immediate prospects for job enrichment are good: The recession that took shape in early 1975 has spawned new converts. In fact, the early evidence suggests that the recession encouraged some who viewed job enrichment as the path to greater productivity and economy at a time when they are most welcome.

Meanwhile, as this predominant form of workplace reform continues to grow in the United States, another type is ascending in Northern Europe. Called "industrial democracy," it differs in many respects from American job enrichment. Most notably, the reforms it aims to achieve are broader and deeper, and workers at all levels are involved directly in the redesign process.

❖ III ❖
Scandinavian Industrial Democracy

1
Up to the Boards

The long-standing Scandinavian urge to experiment with social institutions is now so intensely focused on the workplace that, once again and in still another area, that part of the world has become a laboratory for the testing of new ideas. The rubric under which the trial-and-error process is being conducted is industrial democracy. Unlike job enrichment, there is no single, precise definition or formula for industrial democracy. The term describes a societal goal rather than a process per se and, for this reason, is best described by examples and boundaries. The SAAB and Volvo experiments are by far the best-known examples but there are many more.

At one extreme, industrial democracy is changing corporate structures. On the first of April 1973, for instance, a Swedish law went into effect which gave the employees of every firm in the nation with more than one hundred on the payroll the right to begin electing two of their own to the company's board of directors. This idea had been hotly debated for several years, with much opposition shown by powerful people in industry, but the idea gradually lost its sting, and well before it was voted on in Parliament several large companies—including Volvo and a large mining and steel combine—had voluntarily set up the system. When it came to a show of hands, the only political faction in the country to oppose it was the Communist Party, which felt it signified a regrettable step in the direction of labor-and-capital collaboration. Earlier, a similar law to put workers at the top had been passed in Norway, and in late 1972, the Danish Prime Minister proposed a similar law for his country whereby two workers would be placed on the boards of all Danish companies with over fifty employees.

At the other extreme are the many changes which have been

made on a smaller, but no less significant, scale. One such Swedish development which probably has had an even more direct effect on the daily life of the working man or woman than having a vote to put a co-worker on the board is the metamorphosis of company-produced employee publications into true vehicles for reporting what is going on at work.

Interestingly, this movement toward honest internal house organs has been led by management—in the form of the Employer's Federation, a national management group which has sponsored contests for employee publications; awards go to the corporate editors who encourage the greatest debate and capture the *real* feeling within the company. While the norm for such employee handouts in the industrialized world is usually a mixture of corporate propaganda, trivia, and "good news" from the top, the Swedish internal papers and magazines are beginning to act more like daily newspapers. It is now common to report such things as plant accidents—complete with quotes from the injured party blaming the company—attacks on layoff policies, and letters rebutting new policies. In a departure from the common custom of announcing a new product or expansion plan in the daily papers and the trade press, such news is increasingly broken first in Swedish internal house organs. This unusual frankness is beginning to attract wide attention. Recently, *Business Week* covered it, pointing to such choice examples as the employee newspaper of Stockholm's largest department store, which commissioned an outside freelance writer to come in and rip into the store and its practices in print, and an article in the publication of a company which makes pollution control equipment which reported on complaints of pollution in its own plant.

The significant difference between these two developments is that the election of workers to boards of directors came about primarily because of the push of the trade unions while the reform in employee publications was primarily management's doing. Both sides have become deeply involved in the movement to democratize the workplace. There is, of course, considerable disagreement as to how this working democracy is to be realized, but both sides are responding and advances are being made.

The really important story which is emerging from the Scandinavian workplace is neither the ability to elect one's co-workers to boards nor the new breed of hard-hitting company newspapers—these are symbolically important reflections of a desire to change things, but are not the true liberators which will change one's day-to-day working life. The real story lies in the changes which are being made at the shop-floor level, changes which are affecting the way the average man or woman thinks and acts. This is industrial democracy in the most direct, fundamental sense of the term.

The term "industrial democracy" has been kicking around for a long, long time, and has been applied to all manner of things. Managers have used it to describe such diverse practices as profit sharing and the suggestion box. Before World War I, when American corporation heads and mine owners were trying to kill national trade unions, they set up weak company unions and shop councils which they termed "industrial democracy in action." Unions, on the other hand, have used the term to describe *their* programs, and when collective bargaining was a new idea, it was used to label that process.*

---

* One of the minor movements under the banner of industrial democracy appeared in the United States in the 1920s. This particular system, which was installed in about forty mostly small companies at its peak of popularity, aped the form of the United States Government, with a House composed of elected workers, a Senate of foremen and department heads, and Cabinet of major executives. Either house was empowered to bring up a change in policy or procedures in the form of a bill, which had to be passed by both houses before it was sent to the Cabinet for acceptance or veto. Despite its democratic shortcomings— e.g., a veto could not be overridden—the idea was an interesting one for its time. It never really caught on, and was lost sometime in the Depression.

With industrial democracy having enjoyed all of these and many more uses, it would seem hard to say what it really means. Yet a young Norwegian psychologist named Einar Thorsrud, with the aid of others, has, over the last ten years, developed an operating definition which may prove to be the final word.

2

THE NORWEGIAN EXPERIMENTS

In the early 1960s, the nature of work emerged as a major topic for debate and discussion in Norway. The concern was with those same facets of national worklife that came alive in the United States and other Western nations a decade later. Under scrutiny in Norway were such now-familiar themes as blue- and white-collar alienation, the national ability to be productive yet satisfied, and the assembly line and other "scientific" advances which turn people into work zombies for eight hours a day.

Rather than let this concern continue as nothing more substantial than lively debate, a plan was framed to seek alternatives to the predominant Norwegian way of work which, needless to say, varied little from the way of work in France or the United States. The Central Trade Union Council and National Confederation of Employers met and agreed to finance and cooperate in a series of experiments. They were later joined by a third party, the government. Called the "Industrial Democracy Project," it got under way in 1962, with Oslo's Work Research Institute acting as overall director. The Institute is an independent, nonprofit operation which relies on a combination of government support and private contracts and grants to support research into such areas as work organization and industrial safety. Einar Thorsrud, who was then directing the

Scandinavian Industrial Democracy

Institute, was put in charge; he, in turn, invited London's Tavistock Institute of Human Relations to join in. The Tavistock Institute, which had been long active in exploring new work structures, was looking for a place to help launch advanced experiments.

The first task the Oslo Institute took on as part of the national Industrial Democracy Project was a study of worker representation on company boards of directors. In the early 1950s, Norway had begun to experiment with one type of industrial democracy by allowing workers at five state-owned companies to elect representatives to their respective boards. At the time this was done, it was somehow felt that this would lead to radical changes in the attitudes of workers, but little hard evidence had come forth to indicate that much, if anything, had changed. The Institute not only interviewed those concerned at the Norwegian companies but also those in similar arrangements that had been going on for ten years or more in England, Poland, Yugoslavia, and West Germany. The results were discouraging. The problem was that considerable pressure was put on the worker representatives to act as "regular" members who just happened to have more information on the temper of the workers; the nearest most of them could come to really helping their fellow worker was to cooperate with the regulars on the board and hope that such behavior would lead to increased company prosperity, thereby resulting in greater job security. At best, it was concluded, the practice was an amenity with little or no meaning to the worker on the factory floor or in the office.

After this survey, the main thrust of the project began with a series of experiments which attempted to democratize the job itself. In all, four experiments were tried in four cooperating companies in the metal and chemical industries. These areas were picked because they were felt to be most strategic to the economy and because they were at the forefront of modern technology. For these reasons, the experiments could not be later termed as being of secondary importance. While the setting and direction of each experiment was clearly distinct, they all had the same basic elements, and all four sought to test the basic hypothesis that workers who were allowed to develop naturally into semiautonomous groups would create jobs which were more satisfying, meaningful, and productive.

From the outset, it was agreed that in each experiment specific changes would be dictated by the workers themselves rather than have them imposed from above. And in each experimental situation, the attempt would be made to meet a set of "basic needs" which were developed by the Tavistock Institute and adopted by Thorsrud as an operational definition of industrial democracy. These six needs are: the ability to learn on the job and keep on learning; some minimal area of decision making; job content that is reasonably demanding in terms other than sheer endurance; a degree of social support and recognition; the feeling that the job leads to some sort of desirable future; and the ability to relate one's job to one's outside social life. In practice, this meant getting away from the one-person, one-skill tradition, originating new incentive schemes, insuring the constant feedback of information to workers on their performances, concentrating to a high degree on learning, and training and encouraging workers to meet on their own to plan their work. It also called for the difficult task of helping foremen and supervisors assume new roles as they shifted from being bosses in the traditional sense to acting as resident consultants and coordinators for the work groups.

The first experiment got underway in 1964, when the team entered a large company making steel, wire, and other finished metal products. They looked for and found the worst situation—a wire-drawing mill where the operators' days were spent silently watching wire come off their machines, an activity interrupted only when an occasional wire broke and had to be mended. A new scheme of things was devised to get the wire tenders to work in groups, do simple maintenance, and generally move about more and make their own day-to-day decisions. It did not work.

Scandinavian Industrial Democracy

The workers never overcame their initial suspicion that the experiment would somehow cut or limit their pay, and neither management or the local union ever really got behind the effort. Looking back, Thorsrud believes that inexperienced researchers zealously approaching the worst case they could find as a starting point was a mistake.

A second experiment was launched the next year in cooperation with Hunsfos Fabrikker, a paper and pulp corporation in southern Norway. It was decided that the place to start was in the department where chemicals were produced from pulp, as this was a problem area where many batches of chemicals were not passing company quality standards. "This situation was much more promising than the first," says Thorsrud, "because quality was falling off in a company in a small town where the whole local economy depended on that company. Both labor and management knew that the whole town would be in trouble if the company went under, and so there was a will to experiment with anything that could improve working conditions and the company's product."

The major actions taken to set up the experimental situation involved cutting the supervisory staff in half. Many supervisors were moved into laboratory, planning, and other jobs, while the workers were taught to take charge of their own quality control. The laboratory equipment needed to test samples was actually put on the factory floor, and the workers were given instruction in quality analysis. Each shift was offered greater autonomy and, by means of wage incentives, encouraged to learn each others' jobs. Although it was over a year before it took hold, Thorsrud says that the "breakthrough" he had been waiting for came quickly thereafter. The breakthrough took the form of an "action group" formed by the workers on their own initiative to take over the management of the experiment. After the researchers left, the workers showed increasing autonomy, coupled with: a doubling of productivity per man hour; much higher product quality; and an annual turnover rate which tumbled from 25 to 6 percent.

Thorsrud feels that this experiment proved three major points: Workers generally want to take on more responsibility; the motivation exists in workers to design their own jobs; and high technology provides the means for giving relatively unsophisticated workers sophisticated jobs such as quality analysis, which is normally thought to require specialists. Outside the formal framework of the experiment, it had the "chain reaction" the research team was hoping for, as the whole company is now involved in organizational change. "Even the board of directors got the message," he says. "If a business is to stay alive, it must realize that human resources are the only true resources and it has to be willing to reshape itself to keep its people happy, interested and productive."

As with other experiments of this type, some had a hard time warming up to it. As put by the company's managing director in an article on the experiment in *International Management* magazine, "We met plenty of resistance from foremen and middle managers. Naturally, they were afraid they were losing not only their authority, but maybe their jobs. In fact, they were trained for higher responsibilities."

A third experiment with a number of differences from the second began in late 1965 at a plant near Trondheim, which produces electric heaters. The plant belongs to Nobø Fabrikker A/S, a diversified manufacturing concern which had reconsidered after declining a request to be the site for the first experiment. The heater plant was picked because it was a classic example of scientific management, in which jobs were highly specialized and narrow and without allowances for variation, decision making, or cooperation. Though the work was boring and uninspiring, the general situation in the plant was good. The company paid higher wages than average, offered liberal benefits, and provided a high level of job security. Management-labor relations at the plant were described by the research team as being "cordial."

In the first twelve weeks of the experimental period of thirty weeks, a new way of working was developed jointly by the research team, plant management, and the three groups of workers to be involved. The major points agreed upon were: training workers for more than one job, self-regulation of day-to-day work variations, the election and training of one "contact person" in each group to help plan production, bonuses based on the number of heaters produced per day, decentralization of simple maintenance tasks to further vary work, and a new and rapid feedback system on performance.

The next eight weeks were spent changing over to the new system. Once it was set in motion, almost immediate changes took place. Within the ten weeks in which the research team stayed on to observe, production and wages jumped noticeably higher, and the workers showed both the ability and desire to rotate between jobs and handle the internal coordination of the workday. Early problems resolved themselves without outside coaching or coaxing. For instance, most of the women employees remained passive and outwardly disinterested at first—a condition Thorsrud attributes both to the fact that the men were generally more experienced, and to traditional sex roles—but this changed quickly when one of the women emerged as a forceful and competent coordinator and others followed her assertive lead.

Follow-up studies showed even more impressive results. Not only did the first groups not revert to the old system, but they continued to improve on the new one. Groups which had not been included in the experiment petitioned for and got permission to switch over. The 20 percent boost in productivity scored during the first ten weeks was followed by gains of 10 percent per annum for the next three years and, owing to production bonuses, worker earnings soared at a rapid rate. Local management reported that it had pretty much withdrawn from routine factory matters and now felt secure in leaving the premises for a day or two en masse any time it wanted to without worry. A development which Thorsrud considers very critical was that the time perspectives of workers changed radically. The average worker, who had only thought ahead three hours on the eve of the experiment, had increased that perspective to three months and was now taking such variables as seasonal product demand and holiday periods into account in planning his daily activities. As for psychological attitudes, a study conducted a year after the experiment began showed that an overwhelming number felt it had achieved its stated goals (improving variation, learning, responsibility, decision making, relations with co-workers, and relations with the company) and that their individual jobs now contained the seeds of personal development and advancement.

By 1970, according to the study team, the scientific workstyle of the plant had completely disappeared. Worker initiative, flexibility, and self-management had become the new order. The number of workers able to do *all* the jobs in the plant rose rapidly. As a group, the workforce asked for and got training in the theoretical side of manufacturing. Also, the system of awarding prizes for usable suggestions was dropped through worker initiative; it was their contention that new ideas were now an integral part of their jobs and, if a new idea showed promise, they would try it. If it proved to be a good one, it would increase productivity and everyone would share through bonuses. Meanwhile, the traditional role of the plant supervisor had virtually disappeared, to be replaced with one of combined technical advisor, training consultant, and troubleshooter—when, for example, raw materials were delayed in delivery, a supervisor would intervene.

In 1971, the company completed a new, larger factory because the market for its heaters was growing and the technology of the old plant had become obsolete. A total of three hundred workers—the force at the old factory, plus two hundred others—were assigned. The joint management-union decision was to continue the course of development begun in the 1965 experiment. As implemented, the setup at the new factory was one of

Scandinavian Industrial Democracy

much larger self-managing groups (containing as many as eighty people) with *no* supervisors on the floor. One very uncommon innovation installed in the plant is a computer system to help the workers plan production and answer questions posed by others. With the aid of the computer, the workers can deal directly with a salesman, to tell him, for example, when a rush order can be completed, and how much it will cost.

Although the final word on the new factory will be some time in coming, the situation after a year, when I met with Thorsrud, was far from stable. He was frankly worried about the large size of the groups, and felt that some of the advances had come too quickly, especially for the two hundred new workers who were thrown right into a radically new environment. He termed the first six months there as a time of "uninterrupted crisis," citing such problems as an unresolved ambivalence about calling in management to help with a problem, and an inability to come to grips with certain responsibilities. "Without anyone to tell them to do so, they have found it difficult to determine how to assign their peers to do things like clean up the canteen. The result was that the canteen area became extremely dirty."

The location selected for the fourth experimental variation was a new fertilizer plant then nearing completion by Norsk Hydro A/S, Norway's largest industrial combine. Unlike the other experiments, this one involved volunteers who were invited to join from an existing fertilizer plant belonging to the company. According to Thorsrud, the traditional shopping list for such a factory would have been:

Twelve unskilled workers for cleaning and transport duties —or "slaves," as he calls them;

Twelve maintenance people;

Forty-eight production workers split into four shifts of twelve;

Twelve working foremen—three for each shift;

Eighty-four workers in all.

The major object of this experiment was to get away from this formula by reducing the number of jobs while creating an active, productive, satisfied, and involved workforce. A major specific goal was to despecialize jobs and thereby eliminate all slave jobs and—through sharing—much of the maintenance work. He says, "The slaves in a plant infect other workers with their despair. The best alternative is to get the others to share the work traditionally done by slaves and train the slaves for skilled jobs." Two years after the volunteers entered the new plant, the following line-up had developed:

Zero slaves
Eight maintenance people
Forty-four shift workers
Zero working foremen
───
Fifty-two workers in all

The trimmed-down factory has done well and, by Thorsrud's reckoning, much better than a factory with a full force of thirty-two more people. All indications have been that the workers have attained a high degree of satisfaction and involvement. Turnover rates have been near zero, absenteeism very low, and individuals are spending about ten times as many hours in training as they had before. What is more, the new system has been so popular that it quickly began to transfer itself to the nearby old plant as that workforce copied it.

What happened to bring this about? Thorsrud cities four key factors:

¶ First, the conditions for change were excellent—and were meant to be. There was an eager volunteer force moving into a new plant with the latest equipment and technology.

¶ Second, there was intense training: Each worker was first given a two-hundred-hour regime in such areas as elementary chemistry, quality control, and simple maintenance.

¶ Third, the workers developed their own job designs.

Scandinavian Industrial Democracy

¶ Finally, there was the new pay and bonus system which evolved with the experiment—perhaps the most interesting aspect of the experiment.

Under the new system, everybody is paid on the basis of broad competence rather than for what they are doing as specialists for a given day or week. People are put into wage classes based on the number of skills they master and on their theoretical knowledge about chemical processing. A person who has mastered all eight basic skills in the plant and completed eighty hours of theoretical training is placed in the top wage group. After two years, the average worker has conquered five skills and most have completed their eighty hours of special training. In addition, a collective bonus system was developed which can add as much as 10 percent to an individual's basic pay. The factors dictating the amount of the bonus are a variety of cost, production, and quality considerations, all directly controlled by the workforce. For example, the bonus increases as the workers cut the need for outside maintenance, the amount of chemical balancing agents needed to offset mixing errors, and the chemicals lost by discharge (which constitute not only money lost but are a source of pollution).

Together, these four experiments have taken on increasing influence, ranging from their impact on the companies where they took place—even the company where the one failure took place is now involved in broad experimentation on its own—to the growing attention they are getting from other countries.

In the original companies, the new systems are growing, and it is easy to see why: Greater satisfaction and opportunity accrue to the worker—along with a more equitable and lucrative wage system—while management gets a more stable, happy, and productive workforce.

An example from the fertilizer plant experience shows why such systems can be very endearing to management. In this plant, the workers suggested that the company start producing and selling a special fertilizer (at a higher price) which would meet optimum quality standards rather than the minimum set for the regular product. The idea was accepted and the workers agreed to maintain the rigid specifications for the new product, which became a profitable item for the company. Such corporate windfalls are not all that common, but enough do come along to constitute a special bonus for management.

On the national level, the experiments have had a clear and sustained impact. A National Council on Participation in Industry was formed by the original labor and management sponsors to instruct others in the lessons learned and to foster new experiments in other industries. Inspired to large degree by the Industrial Democracy Project, experiments and restructured jobs are popping up all over Norway. Some are directly patterned after the originals, while others have been tailored to fit other situations. A large hotel, for instance, is democratizing its restaurant operation with a mixture of old and new concepts, such as a pool for tips and a revolving maître d'-ship shared by the waiters. Another influence has been a perceptible shift in national industrial values: a growth in fixed salary as opposed to piecework pay rates; group bonus systems; increased emphasis on training and education; and an emerging skepticism toward scientific management and its rigid job specifications.

An example of a company which is trying to achieve its own brand of industrial democracy without trying to replicate the experiments is Nylands Verkstad in Oslo, a ship- and engine-building firm. Here industrial democracy has come to mean shared power. B. Sørlie, the company's director of industrial engineering, says, "We've come to the point in collaborative management where something like going abroad to buy a new machine or type of tool is now a matter for a delegation to accomplish. Such delegations are naturally made up of equal numbers of management and the men who will actually use the new equipment." This company has pushed the idea of committees in which management and workers share powers to the level

Scandinavian Industrial Democracy

where the head of the personnel department estimates that five hundred of its seventeen hundred employees are now involved in some sort of collaborative committee on such issues as production, company products, safety and work practices, and adds that more could be involved. According to Willie Hansen, a metalworkers' union shop steward, the growth of collaborative committees works well for the workers: "It gives us a chance to have a voice in improving our working situation on a direct basis. It also lets us put something back into the company, which is good, because if we can make this company as productive as it can be, that is to our advantage."

Another effect has been the new interest that trade unions have begun to take in such issues as the right to learn and train and the concept of bargaining for new work systems. Thorsrud sees a significant development signaled in the fact that the new contract at Norsk Hydro, the site of the fourth experiment, now has a "right to learn" clause in it, guaranteeing training for all workers. "I think trade unions here and elsewhere are doomed unless they can learn to go beyond salary and benefits as their major areas of influence. All too often, organized labor charges that management is not progressive, yet labor is often surprised when it is suggested that it take an active role in job design, job enlargement and worker satisfaction."

In the decade since the original experiments began, the work situation in Norway has definitely changed. However, one much-heralded advance in industrial democracy was not the result of the efforts of the Work Research Institute. Despite the results of the 1962 survey, which held that electing workers to company boards was relatively meaningless in terms of grass-roots change, Norway passed its 1972 law requiring 30 percent worker representation on the boards of large companies. Thorsrud, an outspoken advocate of direct and fundamental democratization at the workbench level, calls the law "silly," as he believes that it is a flashy practice with no democratic relevance to the average worker. He explains that this form of industrial democracy is usually prompted by political rather than humanitarian or reform instincts. He says:

> I don't think that this was done in Norway to change things. Rather, it was an easy way for the trade unions to pass a progressive-sounding law to show that they were not losing power. In Yugoslavia, Tito did the same thing as a symbolic gesture to show the masses that he respected workers, and in West Germany the practice was really started by the Allies as a means of keeping company boards diverse to thwart the reemergence of people like the Krupps as industrial-political superpowers.

Meanwhile, on the international level, the Norwegian experiments are well known in the rest of Scandinavia and are commonly cited, especially in Sweden, as either the inspiration for or a factor contributing to the launching of a wide variety of novel experiments. Thorsrud and his colleagues have had their results published and distributed widely. Delegations from organizations as diverse as the Ford Foundation, the United Nations' Office of Economic Cooperation and Development and national trade union groups have come to see what application these experiments have for the rest of the world. While it is fair to assume that the full impact of the Institute's experiments has yet to be felt, their international significance is already well established.

The broad and quick diffusion of results and rush to experiment which has occurred in Norway is, in Thorsrud's opinion, abnormal and not to be expected in other industrialized nations. He says:

> Ours is a small homogeneous nation with a close, relatively simple influence structure. Our class differences are remarkably weak and we think of ourselves as being the only people to come out of World War II with less of a class structure than existed when it started. We still have a

network of managers and laborers who were in concentration camps together and who worked side by side to rebuild after the Germans left. This has helped create the atmosphere for Norway's well-known modern history of labor peace and makes it easier for new ideas to be developed by labor and management as joint sponsors. The importance of the fact that labor and management got this project started together is that it prevented it from being co-opted by either of them.

The role of the Work Institute and its British confederates through all of this has been that of active participants in framing new programs, thereby rejecting the traditional social scientist's role of purely academic researcher and aloof consultant. As a prime mover, Thorsrud does not hide his involvement or his fear that the impact of his very visible experimentation may get ahead of itself. "I'm scared by much of this," he says. "I fear that it may get moving too fast and go faster than the workers at the grass-roots level can handle it. I'm also concerned that as this begins to break out and move beyond a few penned-up little experiments in Norway, it may frighten the old power structure to the point of reacting against it."

Despite these fears, Thorsrud and his team are moving into new areas of experimentation in order to push the concept of industrial democracy into somewhat unexpected realms. One series of experiments is concerned with removing hierarchies in education. Thorsrud sees this as the next logical step, since he sees education as Norway's largest industry. A second and somewhat more startling attempt is being made to see if the conspicuously nondemocratic organization and hierarchy aboard ships can be democratized. These new experiments, which had just gotten underway at the time of the author's visit, are an attempt to test the idea that the general concepts of democratization can be fit to situations outside the factory.

Across the border in Sweden, the industrial democracy

movement now in progress began later than Norway's, and shows a clear debt to the style developed there, complete with national experiments under joint labor-management-government sponsorship. Unlike Norway, the movement in Sweden is tied to a larger movement aimed at reshaping all of society.

3

EQUALITY AT WORK IN SWEDEN

Clichés to the contrary, Sweden is no utopia. However, as a nation, it has come to grips with the fundamental problems of domestic unemployment, hunger, and poverty, and offers its populace a rare level of security through a set of social systems and sweeteners ranging from day care for infants to an almost perfectly functioning national pension system. Long termed an "experimental" society because of its proclivity for trial-and-error departures from the traditional, over forty years of Social Democratic rule has fashioned a highly sophisticated state which has mixed socialism and capitalism to a prosperous blend; in terms of relative GNP it is now the second-richest nation in the world, with a standard of living to match.

Having gotten so far without relying totally on any ism, the modern Swedish state finds itself cast in a singular national role that is hard to live up to. It has been called a model, a utopia, a state without parallel, and what-have-you for so long that its problems take on a special significance. That the Sweden of the early seventies was not a utopia became news, prompting a rush of articles like "Troubles in Paradise" *(Forbes)*, "Paradise Lost" *(Newsweek)*, and "Model Welfare State Runs into Trouble" *(US News and World Report)*, which announce that Sweden is not perfect, but rather a complex society grappling with inflation, high and rising taxes, an unemployment rate of about 3 percent (since reduced to 1.2 percent), and strikes.

The important news from Sweden is not that it is a prospering but imperfect Western society, but that it is attempting new solutions to its problems—in short, that this experimental society is continuing to experiment.

The latest and perhaps most exciting development in the course of the Swedish Social Democratic experiment is an attempt to enact a series of reforms which fall under the banner of greater equality. Compared with other Swedish reforms such as the national pension system, educational reform, and national health insurance, it is a more difficult task which, among other things, means reforming and rethinking those earlier reforms. To illustrate: Sweden's detonation of an education explosion over the last two decades had advanced the opportunities and skills of the young but left those of the older generation lagging behind. Under the banner of equality, Sweden is now priming a similar explosion in adult education. Needless to say, the equality question has brought with it more than a little anguish as the nation confronts the question of how equal do you have to become to have an equal society, and what is the cost of that equality.

Today, Sweden is struggling to find the proper mix of programs, reforms, laws, ideas, and attitudes which will bring that equality to functioning reality. The search for a solution touches upon virtually every aspect of Swedish life. It is as if the premise behind just about everything is being questioned anew. The breadth of what is envisioned was brought home when, in 1971, Swedish Prime Minister Olof Palme listed the top priority measures needed to realize his party's call for greater equality. He ticked off 24 items including: greater equality for women; abolishing differences in social treatment between white- and blue-collar employees; preschooling for all; diminishing of income differences, primarily by helping low-income groups; reforms for the handicapped and other special groups; extension of the concept of industrial democracy and better planning of land resources and measures against land speculation.

In attempting to create a new popular movement based on the goal of equality in a nation where class differences have been blurred (but by no means eradicated) and where social programs have been the order of the day for over forty years, Palme's government has chosen an important and difficult course.

The Swedish drive to industrial democracy is unique because it is part of this larger overall effort to overhaul almost every aspect of Swedish life under the banner of greater equality. Aside from Prime Minister Palme himself, the person most closely associated with the issue of the new Swedish equality has been Alva Myrdal, the wife of economist Gunnar Myrdal, whose somewhat cumbersome official title was Minister Without Portfolio for Disarmament and Ecclesiastical Affairs. Among the several important roles she played was to officially head the Swedish delegation to the Geneva Conference on Disarmament and, unofficially, to act as a leading theoretician of the Swedish Social Democratic Party. As of this writing she was chairwoman of the Party's Working Group on Equality, the group appointed to search for the means to greater equality in Swedish life. Its first report, *Towards Equality* (it is also called the "Alva Myrdal Report") has, since it appeared in 1969, become the widely and sometimes hotly discussed working plan for the next stage in Swedish social development.

When I met with Alva Myrdal, late in 1972, in her office in the ornate Old Parliament Building in Stockholm, she was quick to point out that there has been some confusion as to what is meant by equality in the modern Swedish context.

> It is a rejection of the traditional liberal idea of equality of opportunity which is based on the assumption that we are all equal at the outset. Our concept goes further because we say that there are certain people who must be compensated for in a systematic manner, such as a person with a physical

handicap. Traditional equal opportunity means that the strongest will always come out on top and get more. We are talking about a systematic rectification of social situations. We maintain that society's responsibility for creating equal opportunity applies throughout life, not just at the beginning.

Explaining how the issue of equality and the decision to create a new climate to foster it came about, Alva Myrdal says:

> We had believed that with socialism, strong trade unions and the Swedish cooperative movement, we were working toward a social order which would automatically give us greater equality. We knew that we had a kind of floor of social security and other institutions which would not let people fall through, but then in the late 1960s we began to realize that these institutions were not promoting equality per se. This made us begin to examine every aspect of Swedish life and to begin to discover the real inequality which our society still tolerated.

This determination to find out where inequality lurked resulted in the Alva Myrdal Report, a broad summons for one of the most progressive societies in the world to reform itself. The report opens by pointing to a long list of prior advances, but moves quickly to the "great inequalities" which still exist between such groups as the young and the old, men and women, and those of low and high income. (It is interesting to note that many of these great inequalities are situations which most Western nations find quite tolerable.)

While it would be too long a digression to list most of the proposals contained in the report, it is worthwhile summarizing the direction it advocates for some aspects of Swedish life. Under education, for example, the top priority is assigned to breaking the cycle whereby the most advantaged get the most advanced education, and to setting greater emphasis on preschool and adult education. Other important educational advances include: a total system of recurrent education in which the boundaries between study and work are relaxed, greater integration of the handicapped into the educational mainstream, and gradual replacement of the traditional grading system with individual reports and a broadening of the student sphere of influence, even at the primary school level.

In another area, the housing reforms called for concentration on the equal right to good housing, with compensatory attention being paid to those most in need of it, such as the person just out of prison. Equality in housing also demands a policy of encouraging socially differentiated, nonsegregated housing, in which separate middle-class, working-class, and pensioner sections are not acceptable. Still another housing reform is the call for greater citizen participation in community residential planning.

Of all the realms studied in the original report, Alva Myrdal feels that the top priority must be assigned to equality in work, which means restructuring the workplace. "Why," she asks, "if you are an industrial worker, should you be content to be a part of a hierarchy which is military in nature? The young Swedish worker realizes this and is now growing impatient with the factory and workplace—after all, these are the people who have gone through schools where they have been treated as equals and they are then sent out to a factory where they are ordered about like slaves."

The chapter of the Myrdal Report on work comes on with the authority of a karate chop—demanding that Sweden shuck many of the most dearly held tenets of the Western way of work. For openers, it finds the average individual's limited control over work itself to be an intolerable situation, and says, *"Industrial democracy must be created in private and governmental, municipal and cooperative enterprises."* The point is clearly made that the report is not just attacking the hierarchy of private capitalism, but is just as solidly against those hierarchies in schools, hospitals, and government offices which were created by over forty years of Social Democratic reign.

In order to reorder the nation's worklife (which it tags as the most unequal side of Swedish life), the Myrdal group maintains that it is a matter of the "first priority" to follow the Norwegian lead and replace hierarchical systems with democratic ones; to ensure that employees gain influence over decisions made at various levels of the firm's organization up to and including boards of directors; to enable workers to participate in decisions, especially about company management (requiring greater opportunities for training in such areas as business economics and industrial psychology); and to gear working life to the objective of stimulation and meaning for the individual.

It specifically calls for a program of experimental activity, and suggests a list of new ideas to be tested. Among the items on this list are: participation in the appointment of foremen, personnel staff, job-study men, and other key positions; letting workers have influence over personnel policies; utilizing an employee-elected auditor to give workers better insight into the financial condition of the company they work for (an agreement providing for this has since been reached by central labor and employer groups); participation of workers in long-range planning and new projects; and greater influence in such areas as work organization, techniques, and environment. It suggests putting workers on boards (which has since been accomplished), and two other measures which have become law as this was being written: to plow a fifth of all companies' 1974 profits back into improving the working environment and to give employees the legal right to leaves of absence to go back to school.

Restructuring the workplace and work traditions has become so important to those in power in Sweden that they have programed the 1970s as the decade in which the major arena for reform will be work, as contrasted with the fifties and sixties, when the concentration was on health, pension, education, and housing reforms. Of more than passing significance is the fact that the major ad hoc Swedish contribution to the UN Conference on the Human Environment in 1972 was a report advancing the idea that the work environment is as important an aspect of the human environment as air and water. The concern of the report ranges from eliminating health risks to recognizing the growing desire on the part of the employee for independence, participation, decision making, and the upgrading of skills. In effect, the Swedes have asked the world to join them in a search for a more humane and democratic work environment. The UN report was produced and sanctioned by Swedish organized labor, government, and management groups—truly a national statement.

Steps which have been taken in Sweden to realize the goal of industrial democracy have been varied and taken at various levels. With the election of workers to company boards having been accomplished, both blue- and white-collar unions have taken new initiatives in demanding greater worker control. Jan Erik Moreau, an official of the Trade Union Confederation, listed some of the specific items on his organization's shopping list of demands:

> In the future we are committed to gaining worker participation in such areas as budgeting, planning, and personnel policies. We want our own auditor, to give the workers better financial and economic information about the company and not have to rely only on public information as we do today. In the area of personnel policy, we feel that we must move quickly to a situation where such policies will be determined by councils which will be made up of an equal number of managers and workers. We also see that training and education at work are important parts of the democratic ideal, and we want to see more of this.

In 1971, the Trade Union Confederation also let it be known that it was opposed to the employer's sole right to manage and organize work, and is now looking toward the employee's right to joint decision making over all matters which effect their employment and working conditions in the broadest sense.

Management has responded with solutions of its own. The Swedish Employers' Federation has come out strongly, albeit not as strongly as the unions, in favor of greater collaboration between managers and workers, advances the goal of enabling the individual to have more control over his or her work, and has been encouraging its members to experiment toward this end. This central representative of management interests predictably stops short of the trade unions' desire to give workers and their unions control over hiring and firing, but it does, however, see a role for employee "consultants" in hiring and firing. And while it was basically opposed to giving workers full rights on company boards, it did not oppose the idea of sending worker representatives to board meetings to be heard. Considering the fact that this is a management group, it is relatively quite progressive when judged by international standards, and has become a true advocate of democracy at the shop-floor level while reserving major policy-making roles as a managerial prerogative.

On still another level, a number of individual companies have independently come up with their own democratic systems tailored to their own operations and problems. Certainly, one of the most radical is the Grängesberg Company, a large steel and mining combine, which has adopted a list of reforms including the very uncommon one of not firing anyone for any reason. The company now assumes that it no longer has that right and must learn to live with its own recruiting errors. Kockums Shipyard, the largest in Europe, hit on a novel approach to solve its turnover and absenteeism rates, which were the highest in the country. The company worked with its trade union to compile a massive, no-holds-barred study on what was bothering workers. The resulting encyclopedia of irritations was published openly for all to see, and the company and union have been rapidly moving toward greater democratization, more equitable wages, better training, and a totally new safety system. Today, the company has become something of a model for high productivity and employee satisfaction.

The most important step that has been taken in Sweden to advance industrial democracy has been the joint movement of the Employers' Confederation, the Central Organization for Salaried Employees, and the Confederation of Trade Unions. These three dominant forces in the labor market formed the Development Council for Collaboration Questions in 1966 to study industrial democracy. Since 1969, the Council has taken on a much more active role as the major initiator and monitor of new experiments. Its policy is now to test various democratic alternatives and new ideas in field trials around the country. The agreed-upon goal of this alliance between forces often opposed on matters of labor policy is *"increased productivity and greater worker satisfaction"*—a crowd pleaser which implies that these two items are not mutually exclusive.

Following the Norwegian lead by ten years, by mid-1972, the Development Council had launched ten experiments in voluntary partnerships, with firms in areas ranging from insurance to iron mining, and was busy looking for openings for other experiments. The Council is now dealing in a half-dozen experimental realms, including worker influence over personnel policies, worker production planning, and worker design of their own jobs. While the larger proportion of its tests are being run among blue-collar workers, it is making a determined attempt to democratize the lot of the garden-variety white-collar worker as well. One experiment now underway in an insurance company is trying out the idea of "policy codetermination," or permitting employees to participate with management in the formerly lofty realm of financial policy making.

By starting, supporting, and following the course of different experiences in deepening democracy and inspired in large part by the Norwegian Industrial Democracy Project, the Swedes now have what the resident expert on industrial democracy at the

Employers' Confederation calls "the largest coordinated research project in the field of workplace redesign in the world." The remarkable thing about the Council is that it is operating in the midst of some strong differences of opinion between labor and management as to how industrial democracy will take shape. Such differences aside, however, both sides feel that the field trials will show what is feasible, and both expect them to create a large and usable body of knowledge on the subject.

It will probably not be until the late 1970s before the impact of the full array of the Swedish experiments becomes apparent, but some have already begun to show results. One of the first to get rolling, as we shall now see, was in a manufacturing plant. If it is typical of the rest, it would seem that the Swedish program is moving along well.

4
A Slow, Small but Sure Start in Department 698

The caution so typical of industrial experimentation is well exhibited in the radical Scandinavian democracy-at-work experiments. Some are kept moving slowly in order to pace, rather than to outrun, changing industrial and trade union values. Others go slowly for the simple reason that launching an experiment requires a lot of give and take between union and management after the original premises and plans have been researched. A good case in point is a small but successful test conducted in Department 698 of the Sickla works of Atlas Copco, a plant which produces mining and construction equipment outside of Stockholm.

At the invitation of the Development Council the management of Atlas Copco agreed to take part in the national program. The guinea pigs were the twelve men on an assembly line in Department 698, where complex drills for boring into rock were put together. The simplest model in 698's line is a drill which takes a total of seven hours of their collective time to assemble. As desired, the group is hardly homogeneous, with its combination of Swedish, Finnish, and Italian workers, who have a spread in age from twenty-three to sixty-three years.

In the eighteen months from the time it was decided to experiment to the actual start, there was a monumental amount of preparation, involving surveys, investigations, conferences, and bargaining sessions. Not only were there management-worker working groups and a major sociological study of the department, but everyone from the foreman's union to the shop union had to be brought into the act. Also, the careful observation and documentation of each step in the process—so that it could serve as an element in the emerging national body of knowledge for other companies and future experiments—added time. According to Bjorn Askert, the chief engineer at the Sickla works and one of the experiment's many architects, "Preparation took us three times as long as we thought it would, but looking back on it, I think that if we had moved faster we might have lost the chance to let the workers create a new environment."

Essentially, the switch made in Department 698 was from a typical assembly line to a team operation in which there are teams of three or four men who are able to change jobs on their team and move from team to team. There is no classification into professional categories of painter, tester, or whatever. From the beginning, the foreman was to fall back to a role of passive observer and senior advisor, and the workers were to be allowed to take on planning and technical responsibilities as they felt they were ready. It was agreed before the experiment began that the workers could cancel the experiment whenever they felt it was not working or when it did not seem to be an improvement over the old system.

The actual experiment got underway in February 1972 for a year's trial run. Not too long after the year was up, chief engineer Askert and shop steward Gerhard Forslund met with me to outline its results. All twelve men in the group agreed that the new system was superior to the old one, and all twelve said that they wanted to continue developing it. On the average, each man in Department 698 was able to perform 80 percent of the jobs—which meant that the swing to complete rotatability was nearly complete. Productivity has shown a measurable increase, and, although it had leveled off, is still well above that of the group when it started. The foreman had become a part-timer in the department, spending an increasing amount of time on higher duties in the plant. During the course of the experiment, management-worker groups were formed to work on improved production techniques and long-range planning. Askert pointed out that the company is willing to give the workers even greater autonomy and responsibility as they ask for it.

With both men agreed that the experiment has been a success, their explanation for that success takes in several major points. Forslund says that allowing the workers to be in on the development of the experiment at every level was important. "We were not used to being asked our opinion, and we now have influence. It was quite important that the decision to continue the experiment past the first year was left up to us."

Another factor in the success of the experiment, according to Forslund and Askert, has been the ability of both sides to show flexibility and good will. An interesting instance of this came when the workers decided that they wanted to junk the assembly line in favor of a system in which they sat at large tables across from one another. The company ungrudgingly agreed, and the large tables were brought in—even though a similar system had been tested and rejected years before. "After a month or two," said Askert, "the workers told us that the line was better and we had the tables taken out one night and replaced with the old line." Askert brought up the incident not to show that workers prefer assembly lines (although they did in this particular case) but to give an example of what constitutes good will in developing new work systems.

Attesting to this point, Forslund said that this mutual willingness to act openly and in good faith has gone a long way toward removing the worker's feelings of uncertainty and anxiety—which he termed the "major problem" which faced the men in Department 698 during the early phases of the experiment. He said, "We could not figure out what was really going to happen, and even our union leaders couldn't tell us what to expect. We kept asking ourselves if there was something hidden in all of this, and we feared that the company would somehow be the only party to gain in the change. There was a definite lack of confidence in the company but this is disappearing."

One facet of this experiment which is interesting in light of the internationally publicized departure at SAAB and Volvo and the publicity problems which bedeviled the Arvika experiment (which will be discussed next) is the low visibility it was given in terms of the press and the other workers in the plant. Rather than put undue pressure on the workers through national publicity or give them the role of an elite within the factory, it was handled with such quietness that most workers in the plant did not know that an experiment was in progress. Askert says that the company was tempted to let the outside world in to see what was going on, to let it be known that it is a progressive outfit, but felt that this should wait until it had actually completed the test operation. The negative aspects of publicizing an experiment among workers, letting TV cameras and reporters come in and make stars of workers, is underscored in the next experiment, which, though flawed, is considered to have been successful by those running it.

5
The Arvika Experiment

Despite strong socialism in the government, Sweden's economy is firmly in the hands of capitalists, with only 6 percent of its total industry owned by the state. The government's position as owner-manager of this small but important slice of the nation's industry, however, puts it in a special position in the development of industrial democracy. Quite simply, the government—as prime advocate of humanized work—is obliged to show that it can act as a model for the rest of Swedish industry by democratizing its own enterprises.

The first experiment to be launched in a state-owned facility began to be planned in 1969 at a tobacco plant located in the small, tourist-poster village of Arvika, close to the Norwegian border in western Sweden. The specialty of the plant is pipe tobacco. One of its hottest items is a blend called Borkum Riff, which it developed for American export; to appeal to American tastes the blend is liberally sprayed with *bona fide* Kentucky bourbon.

In response to a call by the government for industrial democracy to be tested in its own industries, a management-labor working group began here by outlining an experiment for testing and selected a group of twenty-eight male workers in this factory of about one hundred ninety workers. The participating group was the "primary" department, that group whose physically demanding responsibilities are at the center of the factory operation: handling tobacco in large lots, doing bulk processing such as cutting and drying and feeding the tobacco to groups which mix, refine, and package it. These men were picked for the experiment because each had a separate duty which made it ideal for job rotation.

The gist of the experiment has been to give the workers as much freedom and responsibility as possible within the framework of a factory. Although it was considered, its developers stopped short of making the workers autonomous, for the simple reason that it was felt that their jobs were too closely tied to other departments in the plant. The Arvika experiment adopted ideas from earlier trials in Norway and elsewhere, and added touches of its own (such as creating general meetings). Under the new system, these workers were given tremendous latitude not only to move from job to job but to assign themselves to fill in the gaps left by absent co-workers, to put themselves into minor periods of overtime, and to exert a direct role in establishing department policy. Once planned, the experimental program was introduced immediately and in its entirety. As it turned out, it had some bad features, but they were generally overshadowed by its good ones.

The major elements of the experiment were job rotation; the turning over of many of the foreman's duties to the workers (with the foreman given higher managerial responsibilities); and a council for the hiring of new workers, composed of workers, the foreman, and a working "contact" man selected by the workers every six months to act as the information and planning liaison between his peers and management. The contact man works to resolve minor production problems in weekly consultation with the foreman and a management representative.

A unique aspect is the general meeting of all workers with management, which takes place each month outside of company hours (for attending, the workers are paid about five dollars). It features a revolving chairmanship by which both management people and workers get their chance to run the show. During these get-togethers, the workers are given the detailed information on company objectives, operations, and problems which is required for the general discussion period that follows. This discussion is open to any subject, but normally centers on such issues as safety, training, needed repairs, procedure changes, and the need for new equipment. According to Eje Christenson, a young engineer who is the plant manager, major and minor departmental decisions are arrived at in these meetings by consensus—that is, an issue such as the worker's contention that a new machine is needed is hashed out until a general agreement can be made. At the time of our discussion, which was after more than twenty-five general meetings had been held, Christenson said that no issue had yet come to a vote, and that all had been resolved by working to a consensus.

Christenson is convinced that the experiment has been a success although it is hard to pin down in black and white. The productivity of the department has leaped since the experiment started, but although he is sure that the new workstyle has been a contributing factor, during the course of the experiment new machinery was introduced and old equipment modified, so it is hard to tell where the effects of the new work pattern begin and the effects of improved machinery leave off. Since absenteeism has always been low, the fact that absentee rates are unchanged is no barometer of worker satisfaction or dissatisfaction. More to the point, when, in an attitude survey conducted a year after the program was instituted, twenty men who were there for both systems were asked which was better, seven saw no difference, seven indicated that the new system was somewhat better, and six said it was much better. (The same survey showed that four workers felt that the workload and physical strain of the job before and after was about the same, while eight felt it was somewhat greater under the new system, and eight felt that it was much greater.) Christenson predicts from his experience with the workers that a new survey would show greater favor for the new system, which had still not completely shaken down at the time of the first survey.

As a more direct way of getting a feel for the experiment, I asked four workers about it—two who had worked with the old system and two who had been hired recently by their co-workers

—as well as their foreman.* Asked about the advantages, each agreed that it was better than normal work forms in many ways. Both new workers were impressed with their freedom and vastly preferred it to their previous jobs (one in a piano factory, the other as a road grader). A young worker who had taken part in both systems said, "I wouldn't want to go back to the old system because I am now much freer in my work. The rewards are greater and so is the stress, but I accept the new stress for the rewards. For example, I am now under the pressure of helping to hire new workers, but I would rather help pick the people whom I will work with than do it the old way." The other experienced man had this to say: "Before, we worked by the minute and never thought ahead, but now we work and plan ahead and are free to change things around here to the way they should be. I don't think that there is more pressure under the new system; I think there is less because I am happier. Nowadays I can sing when I come to work as well as when I go home." The same man adds that it has even had an impact on his family life, as he is now more likely to go home and tell his wife about what he accomplished rather than to complain about his ineffectuality.

A major advantage with which all four men are impressed is their new-found ability to effect their milieu quickly in the general meetings, rather than having to go through a bureaucracy. These workers point to having a gas tobacco drier—which they judged too hot to work with—replaced, and to getting a new machine to cut the tops off tobacco barrels (to replace the inefficient heavy work of opening them with an ax) as major advances which they orchestrated themselves. Even an instance when the workers had to compromise is seen as a real advance, because they were part of the compromise; the workers wanted improved cutting machines, but the company would only agree to experiment with older machines, which were modified.

* These interviews, as with several others overseas, were not conducted in English. In this case, Plant Manager Christenson and one of the workers translated.

When asked to list the disadvantages of the system, all agreed with the worker who said, "The attention from the press has been too much for us. We're afraid of making even the smallest mistake or bringing up the smallest problem because it feels as if the eyes of the whole country are on us." The same man adds, "If I had to run through the experiment again, I would have strongly pushed for them to wait for at least a year more before announcing that it was a success, because this has put us under too much pressure." Plant Manager Christenson agrees. "The interest of the press has been overwhelming and not good for the experimental group or the rest of the factory. A few newspapers made the experiment sound as if we have come up with the absolute perfect way to work, and never bothered to mention that it was not 100 percent popular with the men who took part in it." A clear lesson from this experiment is that early publicity has drawbacks.

Another worker felt that a further source of stress was created because the experiment was conducted in only one department of the factory, producing jealousy on the part of other workers whose work has not changed at the same pace. The experimental group's foreman felt that still another source of stress was among the older workers, who had to contend with a totally new way of doing things. He told me, "It was less of a problem for the new, young workers who had no earlier work experience to compare it with." The attitude survey conducted when the experiment was a year old records this feeling of psychological stress; only five of the twenty workers polled felt that the psychological stress was the same as in the previous work situation, while six felt that the stress under the new system was somewhat greater and nine felt that it was much greater.

The experiment has also produced its own dropouts. Several men left because they did not like it. One of these men was, according to Christenson, a good and loyal worker who far preferred working on his own without the group, and who was willing to take a wage cut just so that he could get off on his own. He is now driving one of the company trucks.

Looking back over two and a half years of experimental operation, Plant Manager Christenson sees things going better and better all the time, but he does admit that there are certain things—such as the aforementioned business of early publicity—that could have been handled better. He also feels that the introduction of the new ways was too abrupt. "I think we should have done a little more training before it started, as many of the workers were at first confused by the new procedures and were not sure how to handle their new responsibilities."

Christenson still questions the new hiring system, which depends on experienced workers' hiring and accepting new workers after a probation period. He is not sure that it is applicable in all situations, and questions its ultimate potential for discrimination. He says, "We are located in a rather isolated little corner of the country. The only foreign workers who come here looking for work are nearby Norwegians who are so much like us that they are not considered foreign. I'm not sure that this system would work in an area where the labor force is less homogeneous." Indeed, one of the workers points out that the group has decided to steer clear of hiring brothers, cousins, and other relatives to preclude the problems which such nepotism might bring, and that they also hold the line against old people, who might find it hard to keep up with the strenuous work. Christenson himself says that the work in the experimental group is so physically demanding that it precludes hiring women. Ironically, then, the same forces which serve to liberate the men in the department are keeping women out. Although some jobs in the experimental group are not that taxing, under the new system, a woman would be expected to be able to rotate into the most demanding jobs, including such work as hauling around gargantuan tobacco casks. Christenson says that the worst work in the department is being mechanized to permit sexual integration, but one must wonder whether or not management will have

Scandinavian Industrial Democracy

to intervene to get the first woman (or, for that matter, older man) hired to work in the department. In fact, experimenting with an all-male team in a factory whose workforce is two-thirds women taints the experiment, and certainly contributes to the admitted jealousy existing between the special group and the rest of the workers.

Meanwhile, other experiments subsequently underway in other state-owned companies have met with varying degrees of success. Lars Erik Karlsson, a young specialist in industrial organization and the man monitoring these experiments at the Swedish Ministry of Industries, says, "Our results to date have been both positive and negative. What we have learned is that it is possible to engage workers in the lower levels of decision making, but we still don't know how far we can go."

Karlsson's barometer for worker democracy is based on five levels of influence, and he finds this a convenient way of rating projects (for example, an experiment that has reached the fifth level has reached full industrial democracy). The five levels are:

1. The worker has control over his or her job and feels free in it.

2. Control is extended to personnel policy matters like hiring and the division of work.

3. There is control over technical matters such as production planning.

4. The workers have control in resolving product problems—things like quality control and specifications.

5. Managerial control is shared with the workers who now are involved in the long-range planning process, the design and planning of new factories and budgetary matters.

Based on this criteria, Karlsson places the Arvika experiment at a level of about 2.5 and now stretching for three.

His view of the future of Swedish industrial democracy is not altogether optimistic. He thinks that what will on a national scale amount to a gradual change overall has already been accompanied by rhetoric which has led to "fantastic expectations," especially on the part of those in the worst jobs. He notes grimly, "The potential for upheaval is great when a nation is promised that a new working environment is at hand." He sees the Swedish situation as comparable to the rising expectations created by American politicians when they talked about a quick turnabout for blacks and then gave them gradual change. Karlsson is not alone in worrying about the explosive potential of industrial democracy as it passes from academicians and idealistic trade-union and government leaders into the heads of men and women on the factory floor. But according to some, any resulting upheaval will just be a phase on the path to ultimate success. Arne Derenfeldt, a leading Swedish industrial psychologist, has been quoted as saying, "We are going to have turbulence, but by the end of the 1970s, Sweden will be the leading country in the world in the field of industrial democracy."

6

INDUSTRIAL FREEDOM IN DENMARK

Nationally, Denmark has not advanced the idea of industrial democracy anywhere near the degree to which it is being promoted in Sweden or Norway. There are no nationally sanctioned experiments, and the national concern with the topic has not reached the level of discussion and debate it has in the other two nations. Actually, much of the same energy for change going into industrial democracy to the North is being expended on "economic democracy" in Denmark, where ideas like profit sharing and employee stock-ownership plans have become the common aspirations of working people.

However, the story of the democratic workplace in Denmark is no less interesting; diverse developments in that direction are occurring in progressive companies here and there throughout the country. Though undirected by a national plan, some are paralleling developments in Sweden and Norway, while others emerge as unique pieces of Danish modern.

In one remarkable case, the man in charge of a company decided that the most democratic thing he could do for a group of employees was to let them design their own factory. This was, to him, the ultimate expression of trust and personal democracy. (This episode is detailed in Chapter VII.) In another case, the managing director of two small companies grew interested in a totally new way of working when he became involved with students at an experimental education center. He asked them, as an exercise, to create their own model for a company they would like to work for. The resulting model was one of a company with flexible structure, limited hierarchy, and made up of small family type groups of peers with little or no bossing in the traditional sense. From this experience, which indicated to him the kind of working world into which young workers would best fit, and from his readings in behavioral research, he decided to make an abrupt, radical change in the organization of one of the two companies under his command. The company, a small outfit selling cards and forms used in data processing, was broken up into five groups, which were to form themselves based on who wanted to work with whom. The groups were given near-total right to administer themselves. Among other things, they could hire and fire their own members, would set their own sales quotas, and establish their own sales strategies. Since the products of the company are custom-designed for each client, each worker now sets his own price on each job he or she handles. The only real management over the five groups comes through a Friday meeting, when a representative from each group meets with the managing director and the finance manager to resolve certain company-wide issues. When the company responded to this system by posting a sales increase of 40 percent in the year after the change—without adding to its staff—it was instituted in the second company, too.

To give an idea of the various emerging forms the new industrial revolution is taking in Denmark, this chapter will conclude with two examples of a Danish company making itself over in a democratic manner. In the first case, workers are given the right through elected representatives to co-determine their own wages, while the second boasts a novel pay system (which actually started out as paperwork dodge) and autonomous working groups with powers up to and including those of giving each other days off and hiring and firing. The first case takes us to one of those firms which has helped make Danish furniture internationally known and admired.

Having concluded that paying its one hundred eighty workers by the common Scandinavian piece-work system was inefficient because it prevented workers from cooperating with each other, the management of Fritz Hansen's Eftr. Inc. devised an alternative which it felt would be more democratic. In 1970, two groups within the Hansen furniture factory in the Copenhagen suburb of Allerød were selected for the experiment. One was a group of about twenty who produce metal chair frames; the other was a smaller group of seven who develop the new models for the company's line. Each group was told to elect two representatives to sit on a wage council for a two-year term, along with the group's foreman and the company production chief.

In the experimental system, all workers in both groups were to be paid the same base rate per hour; it was the job of the two councils to set and periodically review the sum per hour above the base that each worker was to get. The first job of the councils was to assign each worker to a place in one of four job classes ranging from Class I, in which the worker is paid between 1.25 and 2.25 Danish kroner per hour (about $.16 to .28) above the base, to Class IV in which 4.75 to 5.50 DK (about $.61 to .77) is

Scandinavian Industrial Democracy

added. Management told each council to use common sense rather than any elaborate technical system for placing the workers in and within the four classes. Each council completed its work in one afternoon. Predictably, the frame-production workers were spotted through Classes I, II, and III, while most of the more highly trained model developers ended up somewhere in Class IV. The differences between the two groups were generally based on the traditional difference in pay between skilled laborers and designers.

As was true in setting the original ratings, all four council members must agree on new ratings assigned a worker in quarterly evaluation sessions. Wages are reevaluated by a system in which each member of the council rates each worker on ten weighted variables, which include quality of work, ability to cooperate, knowledge of job, and initiative. The four individual tallies are put on the table and a consensus rating is agreed upon. If the new rating differs significantly from the previous one, the worker's per hour pay either goes up or down. Bech Danielsen, the company's managing director, says that ratings arrived at by each of the four members of each council have tended to be remarkably similar and agreement has not posed a problem. An exception to this is the two worker representatives on each council who have consistently rated themselves lower than have the foreman and production chief. (Although it was not planned this way, Danielsen says that somehow the groups' workers have always been able to find out where each other has ended up on the lists, which suggests that the worker representatives may rank themselves low to prevent their peers from accusing them of taking advantage of the system.)

While pay has been the most important council function, both groups have been offered and have accepted responsibility for their total working milieu by moving into such diverse areas as safety, the purchase of new equipment, and suggestions from the workers. They have also hired and fired.

Danielsen terms the experiment an overwhelming success, and

is quickly moving the whole company to the council form of management. His reasons for this assessment are persuasive. Carefully documented weekly records show significant production increases by both groups; the median extra pay per hour has risen correspondingly. The company's fear had been that the councils would inch the pay scale up without proper cause—even though management sought to guard against this by adjusting the base pay to keep up with industry norms and inflation—has proved groundless. "We told the councils to rate on merit alone and we would keep the base in line with national trends," says Danielsen, "and they did just that." Another barometer of success: After watching the two groups with considerable interest, an overwhelming majority of the other workers indicated that they wanted to work under the wage-council system. In addition, the councils' performance in areas outside of pay has worked out well. For example, the company has found that there is a benefit to letting a council handle the ticklish business of deciding who gets laid off. Due to a slowdown, the company decided that two employees in one of the experimental groups had to be let go. The workers on the council had no trouble naming two men who were about to leave the company—one was about to quit to go back to school and the other had been offered a better job elsewhere which he was planning to take. While company officials knew nothing of the plans of these two men, the workers did, thereby letting them protect the jobs of their peers who wanted to stay. This approach, of course, has its limits, and could only work on small layoffs when the conditions are right.

While he finds no long-term drawbacks to the plan, Danielsen admits that getting it started presented some definite communications problems. He says, "Some workers were initially suspicious and had a hard time understanding it. One man actually quit his job because he felt he could not work in such an environment." Another early problem was that the management could not get the workers on the council involved in departmental planning and economic analysis. At first there was no response to such attempts, but now, says Danielsen, "both groups show great sophistication and are looking at our products along with their co-workers to see how they can be improved. This ability of the councils has developed to the point where we will soon be organizing courses in economic analysis for those workers interested."

A few days before my visit to the Hansen plant, the small company had been named winner of the Danish Furniture Prize, an annual award especially coveted in a nation where, because of the desire to maintain its international reputation and level of exports, furniture design and quality is a matter of singular significance. The award, which normally goes to a company designer or designers, was given to the whole staff of the firm in recognition of the high quality of its work. The award underscores Danielsen's contention that the company's future lies in its ability to make each worker a cooperative craftsman capable of innovation and higher standards. Paradoxically, this successful small company sees its new thrust into self-management a matter of survival. As explained by Danielsen, "In the next few years, it will become impossible to get the best young workers by offering them the stale, established ways of management." Much the same thinking was expressed—to take up our second example—by the management of another Danish firm which has come up with its own ways of dumping the tired and established.

One clear manifestation of the hunger for new approaches to work is the attention that has been given to the firm of R. Bøg Jørgensen, Scandinavia's largest manufacturer of canning and frozen-food equipment, which pays its workers quarterly rather than weekly or monthly. Since the beginning of 1970, on the sixth of February, May, August, and November a quarter of each worker's annual wages (less approximate withholding tax) have been deposited directly into his or her bank account. Each sum deposited represents approximately six weeks' pay for time already worked and what amounts to seven weeks' advance pay.

While the quarterly system has received tremendous attention, the company downplays this notoriety, claiming instead that the reporters who have come there in droves have beaten a path to its door for the wrong reason. Jørgen Eltang, assistant manager of the company and the man who devised the system, says, "The wage thing started out as a practical joke on the tax authorities that worked out rather well. It was not meant to be a social experiment or an advance in industrial relations, but rather a way to save the company money." Eltang created the system when the Danish government announced that all companies had to start withholding the exact amount of taxes from each paycheck. Keeping track of all of this meant either expanding the payroll department or getting a computer to handle the deductions. However, he discovered a loophole; if money was loaned to employees, the exact withholding did not have to be computed until the end of the year. By paying the workers with a quarterly paycheck-loan and withholding the approximate amount, the company did not have to do the exact tax figuring until the year's last payment, thereby keeping the process simple and inexpensive. "This aspect of the story," says Eltang, "is one which you never see mentioned in the articles about us." To prove his point, he pulls out a copy of that week's European edition of *Time*, which heralds the system as the latest in a list of "pioneering" Scandinavian work experiments, and goes on to say that other Danish firms are thinking of copying it. It does not mention that it is, in reality, a paperwork dodge. "Of course, others are thinking about copying it," Eltang replies. "It's a fine way to save money."

Despite the disclaimer that the novel wage system is not an experiment, Eltang concedes that it has, in effect, become one, and that its results have been mostly positive for the one hundred eighty employees. On the plus side, it has given workers some added clout in the marketplace by enabling them to come up with larger sums for down payments on large items, the full amount on lesser things, and has encouraged some bulk buying of household goods such as food. He also claims it has served to give the individual worker a much clearer sense of job permanence and loyalty to the company—a feeling admittedly stemming from the fact that the larger part of each deposit represents an advance payment.

On the other hand, workers have been known to find themselves in budgetary dilemmas as the quarter wears on. Eltang has not yet found an example of a worker who has gotten into really serious difficulty, however, or has gone out and squandered the funds at the beginning of the quarterly pay period. The fact that there have been no major personal problems is all the more remarkable because the company decided that they were dealing with adults and did *not* offer fatherly advice or any special lessons in fiscal matters when the new pay system was introduced.

What bothers the management of the company about the fame of the wage system is that it has served to obscure other developments which it feels are far more innovative and significant. The point is well taken: Its ongoing experimentation in self-managing groups is highly advanced.

The first experiment began informally when it was observed that the workers in the crating and dispatching department seemed to work better when they were not being closely supervised. To see what would happen, the company gradually closed off its supervisory role and replaced it with a contact man from among the workers who would periodically report on the group's progress and problems to management. "The situation was an easy one to follow," says Eltang, "since these men were always working against a tight deadline. They had to have everything ready for shipment in railcars that leave here on Fridays. We found that they would press much harder and work to the very last minute to make that deadline—working harder and more efficiently than they were when we were pressing them."

In October 1970, the company decided to start a much larger experiment involving the whole company. Each worker was told to seek a natural functional group within the factory. To the extent that it was practical, workers were allowed to pick the work they wanted to do within the group so that they could get away from the aspects of their old job that they did not like. With help from management, twenty-six groups emerged, ranging in size from three to thirteen people. Then each group was told to pick from their ranks a contact man or spokesman, who would act as the group leader and who would meet with management once a month in a general meeting in which worker problems would be discussed. In the meetings, the company management would keep the contact men up to date on the company's problems, prospects, and financial conditions, so that they could, in turn, brief their groups on what was happening. From the beginning, the group was allowed to change its contact man whenever and for whatever reason it saw fit.

In addition, each group was given a list of new powers. For example, the group had the right to give its own members single days off without having to check it out with anyone outside the group. Along with this particular right came the warning from the company that it did not want to hear complaints from a group that it could not get its work done, nor from other groups affected, as this kind of problem was to be worked out within or between groups. There was not to be any overtime pay associated with the day-off privilege, which meant that if a group got too liberal with days and half days off, it was the group's responsibility to catch up even if it had to work extra hours without pay. Granting this particular right has worked out well, and with one or two exceptions, individuals have not abused it. Eltang is the rare manager who can take pride in the fact that a worker may blow an afternoon fishing without having to feign sickness or find some other pretext—provided his peers agree he has earned it.

The groups were also given greater powers over hiring and firing within themselves. When a job opens up, the personnel office advertises for applicants and screens out those who are obviously not qualified. Those judged qualified are sent around to the group, which interviews them and decides on which one is best for the job and the group. Once a person is hired, it becomes the group's responsibility to make sure that he works out. The company has made it a policy not to lay off workers—although it admits that in a severe economic crunch it might have to—and has put the firing of individual workers for cause in the hands of the workers themselves. "The company now looks upon wages as a fixed cost, not one that is to be manipulated on a seasonal basis," says Eltang. "This gives management the challenging and invigorating task of rising above seasonal slowdowns."

Has any group yet fired one of its members? Yes and no, said Eltang, who explained to me the one case that has occurred since the company started giving its workers this responsibility. One new worker with personal financial difficulties took advantage of the liberal day-off policy and his coworkers' sympathy to work another job. His absences became so frequent that his workgroup contact man came to management and asked that he be moved elsewhere in the firm. As there were no other positions open at the time, and since his group refused to keep him and management had figured out what was going on, he was fired. "Although management actually gave him his dismissal notice," said Eltang, "he was essentially fired by his peers, who knew full well that by pushing him out of their group he would have to be fired."

One right that has been offered to the group has not been exercised: Eltang insisted that it was important to let the workers know that they were invited to come up with a new system for determining their own wages. "For instance," he said, "if a group decided to get rid of wage differences and pay each other the same median pay, that would be permitted." As it stands, the method for determining wages which the workers have not chosen to overturn is an uncommon one. Each worker is paid a basic yearly rate which is equivalent to that of the median pay of the upper third of the craftsmen of his specialty in the local labor market. Differences come from merit pay, which is decided annually for the year ahead after a session in which the man and his supervisor work out the question of what he is worth. The results of these "speak up" sessions are used by a board of three supervisors who set the amount of the merit pay. The significance of the process, which has been in effect for over five years, is that it allows the worker to advocate his own case in a face-to-face showdown.

Thus far, the company has not regretted its decision to attempt to create its new way of working. Early results from group to group have been diverse, ranging from those which have emerged as paragons of democracy and competence to one which has seen the contact man emerge as a dictator—posing a dilemma for the company because it had set up the ground rule that it would not step into such a situation unless asked to. Supervisors remain on the factory floor, but, as envisioned from the start, their role has shifted significantly from that of boss to that of consultant on particularly tough problems and situations. This has freed the supervisors from the trivial problems—such as granting days off—enabling them to spend more time on product-improvement and long-range planning.

Summing up the change in the company, Eltang says, "When something had to be done, we used to tell the workers 'do it and here is how you do it.' Now we present the contact man with the problem and ask the group to find the best way to do it and we'll help out if they need us." While he points out that this change has cost the company a lot of time in meetings, problem-solving sessions, and the like, the approach to the worker as a craftsman and problem solver has resulted in fewer pieces of canning equipment ending up in the scrap heap, and is therefore more profitable for the company in the long run. Although management tries to keep interference to a minimum, it still has occasions in which it is either asked to or feels it has to step in to straighten out a problem; however, the incidence of this is going down and has been limited mostly to situations of stress such as those in which the company falls behind in filling orders. Eltang says, "If you want to accuse us of manipulating our workers to greater efficiencies, you'd be quite right. We are trying to encourage the kind of worker who is curious, involved, and enjoys problems—perhaps, even to the point of showing up on a Saturday morning without pay to have another look at the problem so that he can think about it for the rest of the weekend. There have been cases in which this has already happened."

As with others who have started to give greater power to their workers, the Jørgensen company knows it can't return to the old way of doing things. It plans to push ahead with logical next steps, which will be attempted in the next few years, including a profit-sharing system and the fostering of greater worker power to determine wages.

While the degree of progress in the industrial democracy movement in Scandinavia varies considerably from workplace to workplace and country to country, there is little question that it is becoming bigger and more powerful. To be sure, the typical workplace in that part of the world is still hierarchical and much like its counterparts in other Western nations, but the number of exceptions is growing rapidly. And while the movement is at its most advanced in Sweden and Norway, it is, thus far, at its weakest in Finland. That country, however, is on the verge of following the course of national experimentation set by Norway and Sweden, and debate is underway there on how it is to be accomplished. Meanwhile, a few Finnish companies have been moving out on their own. Wilhelm Schaumans, a large paper- and wood-products company, has developed a democratic system with a Finnish twist. In a large company plant in the coastal town of Petersari, elected workers meet regularly with management on the subject on the full range of factory issues, including such normally taboo subjects as foremen who are not performing or who are creating problems. In such cases, worker delegates can actually raise—though not resolve—the issue of firing or demoting the erring foreman. The Finnish-ness of the system is that the meetings always take place in a sauna. "There's good reason for this," says Erik Stahlberg, a company officer. "First it makes the meetings more relaxed and, second, when you're sitting in a sauna, you're not reminded who is manager and who is a worker—because nobody has any clothes on."

Ranging from the pioneering Norwegian experiments to the democratic sauna, the Scandinavian nations hold some fascinating cues and lessons for other countries, but the question is: Will they be listened to?

Einar Thorsrud, for one, feels that the impact of his experiments and others like them are still four or five years away outside of Scandinavia. He is quite optimistic about the spread of the democratized workplace in the United States and predicts a major industrial democracy movement here—with American characteristics—by the end of the 1970s if certain basic criteria are met. First and foremost, before experimentation can begin in earnest, top management must come to believe that worker loyalty and skill are important forms of capital. Second, experimentation must take hold on a large scale in leading industries with the latest in technology—at IBM and Xerox rather than in, say, shoe manufacturing. He adds that there are signs that these criteria are beginning to be satisfied, and points to experiments underway at General Foods and Procter & Gamble which he feels are as important as any in Scandinavia. Finally, it will require that managers and union leaders become increasingly more progressive, idealistic, and, for lack of a more formal description, possessed of "an interest in the fun and action of experimentation," a frame of mind which he adds means not being afraid to be called crazy. He says with finality, "America needs this kind of democracy and knows it."

Ironically, Thorsrud feels the term "industrial democracy" may not sit well in America at this point, as it may sound a bit too direct and threatening—the kind of "radical notion" that prompts angry letters from stockholders. As a matter of fact, those in America who have worked with Thorsrud's model, or crated others like them, are given to talking about their work in terms of the "sociotechnical approach" or "autonomous working groups"—perfectly acceptable academic terms which are used commonly in Scandinavia, but which, when used in unrelenting profusion to describe real-life situations, become camouflaging euphemisms for the fact that plain industrial democracy is the issue at hand.

The directness of the term should not be all that alien in the United States. Pro-industrial democracy sentiment goes back a long way in American history. To be sure, the term has been abused, but one of the first sincere expressions of its basic meaning was expressed long ago by Albert Gallatin, Secretary of the Treasury under Jefferson and Madison, who said, "The democratic principle on which this nation was founded should not be restricted to the political process but should be applied to the industrial operation as well." Gallatin was not simply pontificating. He established a glass works in New Geneva, Pennsylvania, in 1787, and with it, introduced the first profit-sharing plan in North America, under which each worker would get his wages plus half the "neat" profits of the enterprise. For its time, Gallatin's idea was a fantastic one. It was not for another thirty years that the first practitioner of profit sharing appeared even in Europe, supposedly far ahead of the New World in organization at the time.

IV
Democratic Designs in America

1
Show and Tell

The flyer read: "Next month's national conference on *The Changing Work Ethic* will be the most important conference on worker satisfaction and productivity ever held in this country." Promotional material for such events commonly overstates their importance, but this didn't. To use an overworked but nonetheless apt description, it was a landmark occasion.

The conference was staged just at the moment when it was becoming apparent that within the United States the seeds of workplace change had indeed been planted and were beginning to sprout. And while there had been similar conferences before and there were others to come, these three days in New York in March of 1973 were especially important because they caught the spirit and substance of that moment.

The format of the conference was not at all out of the ordinary. There were the usual panels at which people with authority addressed themselves to topics like "Labor-Management Cooperation in Improving the Quality of Work," as well as several keynote speakers and a number of workshops in which individual companies reported what they were doing that was special. But there were critical differences. For the first time, there was union participation in such a meeting and, in fact, the United Automobile Workers was listed as a co-sponsor. The keynote speakers were powerful types such as Senators Kennedy and Percy, George Gallup, Jr., and AT&T President Robert D. Lilley, rather than the academicians who normally set the tone at such gatherings. Not only was there an impressive roster of corporations there to tell what they were doing—General Electric, General Motors, and General Foods, just to list the "generals"—but the list of organizations which had sent delegations just to listen read like a who's who of American industry.

While many had come to find out what was going on, it quickly became apparent, as one talked with the listeners, that many were actively involved in work reform and were there also to compare notes on their plans with those discussed at the podium.

A year earlier, at a similar conference, a job-enrichment consultant and a scholar following such matters had made a list of the American organizations they knew about which were "really doing something" in the area of reform; the total they arrived at then was sixty-one. By the third day of this conference, it was apparent that the total had now approximately doubled. Indeed, the March 1973 conference was a coming-out party for the job-reform movement in America; while there was no questioning of the fact that the Scandinavian countries were still years ahead, an American movement with distinctly American characteristics was underway.

Besides signaling a new awareness, the conference also afforded a good vista from which to spot the varied directions of change. Some firms were pursuing job enrichment as their answer; a few were testing the corporate waters with American versions of Norwegian industrial democracy (though true to Thorsrud's prediction, they were not using that term); others were moving into "worker participation" (a term with various meanings); and still others were developing hybrid systems borrowing from more than one philosophy. Several were not announcing anything new, but were smaller companies that had long before deviated from the norm and were now being discovered, or on the verge of it, by an outside world hunting for new solutions.

Following leads gathered for the most part at this conference, I made a series of visits to organizations which typified the character and variety of workplace change in America excluding, of course, job-enrichment cases which have already been discussed. Of these, it is hard to say which is most exciting, but one is hard-pressed to top the American Velvet Company as an elder statesman of reform.

2
AMERICAN VELVET: "THAT CRAZY PLACE IN CONNECTICUT"

From 1892, when the Wimpfheimer family moved its textile manufacturing business into Stonington, Connecticut, until the early 1940s, labor-management relations at the American Velvet Company were bad. Jacques D. Wimpfheimer, the current president of the company and the fourth generation of his family in the business, says that relationship ". . . was one of suspicion, industrial strife, and unrest that now and then led to stoppages and strikes."

A low point was reached in 1938, when the workers, represented by the Textile Workers Union of America, began a sixteen-month strike triggered by management's attempt to get the weavers to increase their work load from two to four looms per person. From the company's position, the situation was a grim one, presenting only three alternatives: to sell out and quit, move South where labor was cheap and unions weak, or stay and somehow work out a solution. Most of the family opted to sell out, but one man, Clarence Wimpfheimer (the father of the present president), chose to stay, and bought out the other interests. After the takeover, a very uneasy truce was negotiated with the union, based on a one-year contract. Jacques Wimpfheimer describes what happened next: "My father was anxious to try some new ideas which I do not believe he could have articulated at the time. They were much more instinct than anything else."

The most immediate change that took place was that management became local and involved—ending absentee ownership. The owner and his top deputies were present in the plant all the time, asking questions, accepting suggestions from the workers, and sharing information with them and their union. A few of the old-time bosses were unable to accept either this proximity or collaboration with the workforce, and had to be let go.

However, the most important new element in the relationship was not instituted until the second contract was negotiated with the union a year later (in 1940). This element was profit sharing. It had been offered in the first contract but was immediately rejected by the membership of the local as a management trick. What got it accepted was an interesting concession the company made to break a deadlock in which the union wanted another one-year contract and the company, for the purpose of business stability, wanted a three-year one. The company told the union, which was still cool to the idea, that if it had accepted the first plan a year earlier each worker would have gotten an extra $.11 on every dollar that they had earned during the year, a revelation which began to warm the union's attitude. Then the company made an unusual offer: If the union would accept a three-year contract with profit sharing, the company would pay each worker the extra $.11 on the dollar for the whole previous year even though it was not in the contract. The union agreed, and the 1940 contract became the basis for a new and lasting relationship.

Today, the results of that 1940 relationship (which has developed considerably over the years) are stunning. Few companies anywhere in the nation can match them. There have been no strikes, work stoppages, or disputes which have had to go to outside arbitration since 1940, and there has been no year in which the company has lost money. The profits shared with the employees have ranged from a low of 5 percent to a high of 39 percent of an individual's wages. Base pay for the workers is the highest in the industry, and the company itself has grown to be the largest in the velvet industry. As for the issue which prompted the 1938 strike, over the years, the union and management have agreed to changes which have changed the weaver's workload from two to eight looms. As for the rates of turnover and absenteeism—key barometers of management effectiveness—the company's are far below the national and area norms, despite the presence nearby of companies in high technology like General Dynamics, which pay more, and despite the fact that working in an eighty-year-old textile mill is anything but glamorous. All of this is especially significant in the face of the experience of the last thirty years, which has seen a large share of the textile mills in New England either gone bankrupt or gone South.

In recent years, these facts about American Velvet have begun to be discussed in the business community, even though the company has not tried to publicize them and has no public-relations program. Wimpfheimer has subsequently spoken before several recent forums on work reform, the United States Government has used the company as a stopping point for tours it has set up for foreign industrial and labor teams studying labor relations, and at least one doctoral thesis has been written on the American Velvet experience.* In spite of this recent attention, the company is generally misunderstood. Some see it as an example of the virtues of profit sharing, but this is only a part of the story. To others, it is seen in the way a Federal expert on employee relations described it: "that crazy company in Connecticut"—an assessment he based on his belief that it was a "pretty" industrial freak with a certain chemistry going for it

---

* Of the man who wrote the thesis, Wimpfheimer has said, ". . . I can barely understand what he says we are. He describes our simple human relationship in the damndest, most complicated technical terms and graphs that I have ever come across. I ordered 500 copies of his work, intending to distribute them to our people, but after I read it, I was afraid to do so. On paper, we had become some sort of mechanical robots—the product of a button pushed on a computer—controllable, predictable, a mathematical equation—the last thing I want to feel I am, the last thing our people think of themselves, and, I truly hope, the last thing we are."

that could not be replicated elsewhere. Based on a visit to American Velvet, the author must disagree, for a number of reasons which will become apparent.

The company is located on a tree-lined side street in the picture-postcard village of Stonington on the Connecticut shore, a few miles from Mystic Seaport. Its main building looks like scores of other aging, red, industrial sites in its part of the country. I arrived there on a September morning in 1973 just in time to observe part of the company's morning routine: the 8:45 meeting. The routine actually starts at 8:00 A.M., when the managers of the business fan out through the plant to talk with some of the four hundred employees on a random basis, mostly to ask questions and get suggestions. At 8:45, the officers, department heads, the union president, and at least one other union member meet in Wimpfheimer's large wood-paneled office. This daily meeting is an informal occasion, where the first order of business is the company but where first names are used and digressions tolerated. (There was some banter about how bad the weather was the day I was there.) Wimpfheimer, who is outwardly relaxed and friendly but firm, is clearly in charge of the meeting.

The meeting began with Wimpfheimer going over the previous day's production figures, making announcements and opening the day's mail and passing it around the circle. The mail reading is a practice that was established to give labor and management immediate insight into what is going right or wrong with the company in the form of customer complaints, purchasing problems, and new sales orders. Next, in clockwise order around the assembled circle, each person in the room had the floor to bring up problems and items of general interest. A few had nothing to say this particular morning, while others dwelt on major and minor concerns. Vice-President Herbert Schell, Jr., mentioned that there might be tough sledding ahead with an expected shortage of rayon, and said that he was looking into solutions. On the other hand, Hank Marquette, who is in charge of maintenance, addressed himself to the problem of "guano on cars" resulting from birds which were congregating on a large tank next to the parking lot. He estimated that it would cost nine hundred dollars to build a barricade. The group consensus, for the moment at least, was to look into less costly alternatives, such as the one Wimpfheimer suggested, which was to get a couple of cats to act as a deterrent force.

Once everyone had been heard from, Wimpfheimer again took the floor and asked why production was down for the week. Harold Main, a vice-president, said that the cause was clearly from absenteeism due to illness. At this point, Wimpfheimer asked union president Frances Ainsworth if she thought anything could be done. "If they're really sick, we can't do anything," she replied. "If not, I'll come down on them." Next a short pep talk: Wimpfheimer pointed out that, at the moment, the company could sell all it could make, and that with profit sharing down everyone had to work to get production up. The final item on the agenda was the daily conference call to the New York sales office to see what was going on there. The only problem that morning was a lost shipment; once it was agreed that the problem would be looked into from both ends, the meeting was over.

By all accounts, the morning meeting is a very important element in the way this company operates. "Some are more important than others," says Vice-President Schell, "because, in many of them, major problems are solved before the day really gets going, but even the less important meetings are important because they show that labor-management collaboration is not just something for crisis situations." Schell and Wimpfheimer both point out that nothing is held back from the union and that the union, in turn, is just as frank. Wimpfheimer says, "We have lots of arguments but few real problems." The meetings also serve the purpose of addressing and correcting minor grievances before they become major ones. Schell sums it up: "By including the union in the business of the company, we have evolved to a point where I can truly say that neither party suspects the other of hiding its true motives."

The morning meeting is not the only collaborative institution at this company whose president brags of "scads of committees." Safety matters are discussed and resolved jointly, as are quality problems, which are ironed out in the Seconds Committee. Workers participate in the selection of new equipment and the design of workspaces. Over the years, an unusual group called "the Pops committee" evolved, which is made up of the present and former presidents of the local union, who are called together on occasion to discuss new ideas and long-range plans with management.

Of this assortment of committees, the most important is the Profit Sharing Council, which meets every few months after work for dinner and drinks. Each department is represented by two workers, a foreman and a member of management. The council serves as an informal session in which suggestions are discussed on improving profits and making the most of the profit-sharing system itself. The system, incidentally, is quite straightforward. Each year, 27 percent of the company's profits before taxes are distributed to the workers. One-third is automatically paid out among the workers in cash—two-thirds cash if requested—with the remainder put into a trust fund payable to individual workers at retirement, disability, or death. This is *in addition* to the company's regular pension plan, which is paid for entirely by the company. A person with more than ten years' service with the company can take his full share out of the trust if he leaves for reasons other than retirement, and a person with less than ten years can take half the amount. Investments made by the trust are tended by another committee, this one composed of two members of management and two union representatives.

The officials of the company are both proud of and enthusiastic about the system. Significantly, this feeling is shared by both the present and the two previous elected presidents of Local 110 with whom I met independently. Former president Joe Sposato feels that the key to the system is communications, and that without it profit sharing would be just another element of the pay system. "If either side stopped communicating, we'd slide back into the Stone Age in a few days," he says, "but I don't think that this will happen because we all like the system we have now, which is that anyone can say what he wants—and has the right to say it." Charlie Gencarella, another former president, feels that another strength of the system is that it can settle 90 percent of all labor-management problems quickly through the morning meetings and other direct contacts. "When we show the bosses that a foreman is wrong, they just go down and work it out with him." Frances Ainsworth adds that the system is a good one for the local because things go so well at American Velvet that Local 110 can handle its own affairs without having continually to call in the parent organization. "The International likes us," she adds, "and I think they'd like to have more locals like ours."

All three of these union leaders are quick to point out that there are things that need improvement in the company. Sposato feels that the company training program is poorly administered and needs upgrading. All three were in agreement that they were going to have to push for a change in the trust fund rules which would allow an employee to have the right to have his or her money taken out of stocks and bonds and put into a savings account at age fifty-five rather than age sixty in order to allow the person to better protect his share from the fluctuations of the stock market. Other problems had been solved. One was the union's displeasure when pension funds were put into the stocks of European companies—a policy which was felt to be bad for American labor. "We screamed like hell," says Gencarella, "and they stopped."

Nonetheless, their overall feelings about profit sharing and the retirement plan were generally very favorable. Sposato points out, "This is not just any profit-sharing plan we have here, but one which we are directly involved in. We are given the kind of information that lets us know as much as management does about the fortunes of the company, and we have the right to examine the books anytime we want." The consensus among these three was that the workers, for their part, understand and work with the system. "We work hard to prevent wasted velvet because that's lost money to us as well as to the company," says one, and another adds, "It's the company's business to warn people about too much absence or goofing off, but we'll talk to them too because they're hurting their co-workers."

The more one talks with the people at American Velvet, the more it is demonstrated just how far it is from the norm in terms of employer-employee relations. Some of the evidence seems downright otherworldly. For instance, the last contract was negotiated in two minutes; both sides were aware of what the company could handle and what was an equitable increase for the workers. Gone was the normally obligatory tug of war in which the union asked for more than it knew it could get and the company offered less than it could afford to give. At American Velvet, both sides agreed right off that a twenty-cent-an-hour increase seemed about right. What is more, management is routinely invited to the union's annual party, and Wimpfheimer recently turned some heads in the textile industry when he got invited to participate in a conference held by the International in New York. "It was a dull meeting, but a significant event," he says.

Although those at American Velvet do not see their experience as an experiment but rather an effective and practical way of working, the company is always testing new ideas. Some work and others don't. One that flopped was a recent attempt to turn over the hiring process to the employees in the department where there was a vacancy. The plan bogged down when two ethnic groups which are heavily represented in the workforce (Italians and Portuguese) began to argue over how many from each group should be hired. At the time of my visit, a more manageable committee of worker representatives was being set up to do the hiring. On the other hand, some years back, the company's salesmen successfully tested the idea of pooling their commissions to protect each other from erratic and seasonal markets. Prior to the pooling, the salesman who had developed customers for velvet in the Christmas novelty market, for instance, had a few good months—and a much tougher time for the rest of the year. The men liked the pooling, and the practice is still in force.

The question raised earlier, and which now begs for an answer, is whether a situation such as that at American Velvet can be established in other operations. Representatives of both labor and management at American Velvet were unanimous in their belief that it could and should. Although Wimpfheimer has done little to push his system—for one thing, he doesn't have the time to do it—he did write twice to Richard Nixon during his first Administration, when the President was grappling with the question of national productivity. Wimpfheimer's idea was that his company's experience would be worth studying for national lessons, but all he got was a form letter saying that his first letter had been received and no answer at all to his second. There seems to be little reason to doubt that other companies should be able to come up with similarly successful systems. In fact, there *are* others already who have come up with highly workable systems that blend the "piece-of-the-action" factor implicit in profit sharing with some other innovative mechanisms for labor-management collaboration. As with American Velvet, it is important that the distinction between a company that has profit sharing as a benefit and one built around it and the principle of participation be kept in mind. A few examples are in order.

Unlike at American Velvet, which has attracted only a small amount of outside attention, the world has beaten a fairly deep path to the door of the aforementioned Donnelly Mirrors of Holland, Michigan. This firm, which produces 70 percent of all mirrors for American automobiles, had turned into an industrial curiosity of major proportions by 1972. So many scholars, industrialists, and reporters were coming to see it for themselves that production was being interfered with and the company had to halt visits. Starting in 1973, the company opted instead for two-day workshops, held in a nearby motel, where managers and workers would tell the story. As befits a shrine to productivity and optimized profits, the charge to companies attending the workshop is four hundred dollars for the first two representatives plus seventy-five dollars for each additional person. The popularity of these workshops is underscored by the fact that seventeen of them were scheduled in 1974 alone. The reason why organizations ranging from GM and GE to the Iowa Beef Processors and the Scripture Press, Inc., pay for this briefing is that Donnelly reduced the price of its mirrors while doubling its productivity and improving the quality of its product.

Donnelly's four hundred fifty workers are all salaried and belong to work teams whose rights include those of setting their own breaks, establishing their own production standards, and, for those involved, setting the speed of the assembly line. In addition, everyone in the company gets monthly production bonuses in those months when profits are increased through higher sales or reduced labor costs. As was true in the similar case discussed in Chapter III, the bonus is not a substitute for wages; Donnelly's base pay puts it among the best-paying companies in its area. Unlike American Velvet, this company is not unionized, but senior Vice-President Richard N. Arthur insists that the company has not tried to prevent unionization. He says that there is no reason to believe that the company's system would not work just as well with a union. Nonetheless, pay scales are negotiated between labor and management through "productivity bargaining."

The basis for the company's way of working is the Scanlon Plan, created in the late 1930s by Joe Scanlon, once research director for the United Steelworkers of America and later a professor at MIT. His idea was that a worker who is totally

Democratic Designs in America

informed about the company's profits and can share in them through periodic bonuses will become an agent for greater productivity and cost cutting. While dozens of companies have adopted Scanlon's premise as their own—often with great success—few have carried it to such creative ends as Donnelly.

Creativity is a big word at Donnelly. Vice-President Arthur is fond of pointing out that the average worker wants to be creative. "One form of creativity is the automobile worker who encloses a marble in the dashboard of a new car," he says, adding that some of the policies and practices which have emerged in the participative atmosphere of his company illustrate more positive forms. Some of the more important examples:

¶ With employee approval, time clocks have been eliminated and all workers are salaried, meaning that they are paid even when they miss work.

¶ As far as is possible, advances are made from within and, ideally, take a person as high as his or her ability will allow. The present treasurer of the company began there as an assembly-line worker. Because of the many good suggestions he made from the ranks, the company sent him to management school.

¶ When a piece of machinery is needed, the work team which will use it elects a representative whom the company sends out to get it even if that means a trip to California.

¶ Such matters as hiring and discipline are largely handled by the work teams. One element of the company's discipline program is described by Arthur as being "very cruel." It consists of sending an erring worker home for a day *with* pay. One need not be a behavioral scientist to realize that this is a far tougher punishment than being sent home without pay in a system where your peers must pick up your slack for that day in order to protect the bonus.

¶ A special system has been established to prevent layoffs due to new technology or increased productivity. When a job is eliminated, the person who held it is guaranteed six months' pay and top priority for the next job that opens, and the company promises to pay those with five years' seniority for two thousand hours of work at the minimum wage per year. Recently, when a work team discovered a way to eliminate a process, eighteen jobs were wiped out, but all eighteen displacees were given new positions equal to or better than their old ones. On the rare occasion when a business downturn dictates a layoff, there are invariably those, often workers close to retirement, who volunteer for a few months off.

The bottom-line results posted as result of these practices are awesome. Between 1967 and 1972, the number of mirrors returned for defects went down from .028 percent to .0011 percent. "We have one customer that we sell three or four 'semi' truckloads of mirrors to a week. I can bring the rejects back in my station wagon when I go up there," says Arthur. By doing away with the time clocks and putting everyone on salary, the reforms have reduced absenteeism from a low 5 percent to a very, very low 1.5 percent; tardiness is down from 6 percent to less than 1 percent. Arthur adds, proudly but sheepishly, that the company has a problem with peer pressure, which is so high that people occasionally come to work when they are ill. Turnover in recent years has hovered at a hard-to-believe one half of 1 percent and when the employees were last polled on their attitudes about work, it was found that 97 percent were satisfied with the company. Meanwhile, company sales have zoomed from $3.6 million in 1965 to over $14 million today, and the monthly bonuses paid out have averaged over 10 percent of pay for the last five years.

No less spectacular is the performance of the Lincoln Electric Company in Cleveland, Ohio—a company whose record has become something of an industrial legend. In 1933, at a point when it was experiencing heavy losses, the late James F. Lincoln created his Incentive Management System, which was based on four major points: no layoffs, large profit-sharing payments when there were profits, price reductions whenever possible, and a continual plowing back of a portion of earnings into the company. This works by 100 percent of all profit remaining after taxes being first used to pay a set stockholder dividend of 6 percent, and a further share being plowed back into the company. What remains is divided up among the workforce. The cash payment has continually amounted to a bonus of *over 100 percent* of an individual's annual pay. In addition to this plan, which commonly yields sums of over $10,000 above a person's normal pay (a combination of base pay plus piece-work incentives), Lincoln has an employee stock-purchase plan, an advisory board of elected workers (which suggests operating changes to management), a strict policy of promotion from within, and a way of working which allows each person to operate as an independent subcontractor responsible for a complete assembly operation. The most remarkable aspect of this is not that production workers can earn $25,000 a year, but that productivity at the company has grown at such a rate that the prices for the company's electric motors and arc-welding equipment have remained fundamentally stable *since* 1934, despite the fact that costs of raw materials and labor have gone up three to six times. Michael Fein, an industrial engineer who reported on Lincoln in his 1971 book, *Motivation for Work*, concluded that the combination of factors at play in the company ". . . is working to produce what I believe is the highest productivity of any plant in this country." Fein also asked himself if the experience of Lincoln was transferable, and answered, "The Lincoln mystique is not a set of profound principles, but a working relationship based on mutual confidence and trust that management and labor will honor the other's interests."

Others which belong on the list of companies involved in workplace change are not restricted to the United States. In France, at the world-famous champagne producer Möet & Chandon, an unusual plan has been in effect since 1947, in which each portion of the production process is broken down into small profit centers which "buy" the produce in process from the group before it and "sell" it to the next. The value added to the product in excess of the norm—a standard negotiated between labor and management—is distributed as a bonus. Moreover, employees get to keep half the profit from all bottles of champagne that would normally get broken. When this incentive was introduced some years back, the breakage rate was a bottle a day per employee; today, it is a bottle a month per employee. The company also features a series of internal mechanisms to promote active participation and good communications, including, among other things, an accountant who is charged with reporting directly to the workers on matters of company business. An incident which reflects the degree to which this has worked out occurred during the broad wave of strikes which hit France in 1968. As reported in *International Management* magazine, the unions at Möet did not want to damage their relations with the company, but, at the same time, were under pressure to strike and show their solidarity with the other workers of France. The company itself, however, was fearful of militant unionists from elsewhere doing damage to the plant, and asked its unions to strike—which they did in order to protect the factory.

While these firms and others like them see the key to their success in the mixture of the principles of participation and profit sharing, a great and growing number of American organizations are employing only one of the two principles and could stand to enhance their success by adding the second. According to the Profit Sharing Research Foundation, there were 122,962 plans in operation in the United States in 1972, involving some 9,000,000 American workers. This compares dramatically to the 3,565 plans in 1949, the 20,117 in 1959, and even the 86,957 in 1969. Today, little companies have them as well as big ones such as Xerox, Sears, Texas Instruments, and Hewlett-Packard. Profit-sharing plans are fairly common in certain other areas of the economy: one of three retail firms, wholesale distributors, and banks, for example, pass on some of their profits to their employees. Individual plans range from those which are excellent, equitable, and invite greater involvement with the organization to those thrown together solely to take advantage of the fact that payments are tax deductible and are therefore better than other forms of special compensation. The tax break aside, many see their plans as a means of morale building, strengthening loyalty, and bringing the employee closer to management's goal of greater profits and productivity through enlightened self-interest. It apparently works, because several major studies have shown that profits and organizational health increase when some of the profits are given away.*

3

GENERAL FOODS:
GAINES IN TOPEKA

The career of Lyman D. Ketchum demonstrates how an individual with a bit of power and freedom has effected change in a large corporation, and has done it so well and in such a way, moreover, that his work has attracted international attention. His is a new variety of the American success story. He is an unassuming, soft-spoken man who, as the cliché goes, would be easily lost in a crowd. Sitting in his office in the General Foods Corporation's headquarters in White Plains, New York, where he is now manager of organization development, he tells the story of how he, with the help of others, created a very unconventional

---

* One of these was a study by the Profit Sharing Research Foundation in which the sixteen largest grocery-store chains in the United States were studied. When the eleven with profit sharing were compared to the five without, it was found that those with sharing outstripped the others in terms of net income to net worth, net income to sales, sales growth, net worth growth, growth of average market price per common share, growth of the invested dollar, and earnings per employee. The same results were obtained in a similar Foundation study in the largest merchandising companies.

workplace for the future—a story he tells with no lack of enthusiasm.

In early 1966, he was given the job of operations manager for the company's Gaines Pet Food plant in Kankakee, Illinois. Before that, he had held a variety of jobs, all relating to the food and grain business. At his new post, one of his first decisions was to employ a behavioral scientist to act as a consultant in developing the plant's human resources. The consultant was Dick Walton, then of Purdue (now of Harvard Business School), who, today, is widely recognized as one of the leading authorities on applying behavioral science to business. Over the next few years, Ketchum and Walton worked to improve the ability and effectiveness of the staff through sensitivity training and other fairly common methods. Improvements were made, but they were not enough. Both men also realized that certain improvements had created other problems. One of these perplexing developments was that as the condition of upper management improved, the jobs of middle managers were being gradually impoverished. Looking back, Ketchum feels that as top management became better and closer knit, they became so adept at problem solving that they began dipping down into the jobs of those below them to get new problems, thereby stripping middle management of much of its challenge.

Sales of pet food boomed in the 1960s, and by the fall of 1968, it became apparent that a new Gaines plant was going to have to be built to meet the demand. This afforded Ketchum the chance for further experimentation. With an okay from corporate headquarters, he set up a special team in Kankakee to draw up plans for the new plant, which was to be located in Topeka, Kansas. Directed by Ketchum and advised by Walton, the team was to create a total system for the new facility, including its organization, work style, architecture, method of staffing, and overall philosophy.

Early in its two-year effort, the team adopted a set of assumptions about people, including recognition of, among other

Democratic Designs in America

things, the ego, social and security needs of the individual. Out of this came the core concept of autonomous work groups, each of which would perform a complete function. Each job on each team was to require near-equal skill and value. Supervisors were to become team members rather than bosses. In addition, teams would be allowed to make their own day-to-day job assignments, would have the right to recruit and hire new members, and would set their own goals. While this setup has been paralleled elsewhere—and is far from rare in Scandinavia—it was accompanied here with a set of new twists. Along with the establishment of such nonhierarchical principles as decentralized decision making, many major symbols of hierarchy were, on the other hand, to be banned. There would be no reserved parking spaces, everyone would come and go through the same door, the carpeting in the locker rooms would be the same as in the offices, and the size of an office would be determined by the work done there rather than by the rank of the person in it. Architecturally, the plant would be configured to make it easier for employees to get together during working hours, because it was felt that such mingling would encourage people to learn about each other's job and provide enjoyable social contact. As far as possible, machines would be used to wipe out all the less meaningful elements of jobs in the plant—dust-collecting equipment would be installed, for example, to minimize sweeping—and the menial tasks remaining would be apportioned equally among team members.

Besides a large daily dose of feedback to let them see their individual and team performance, employees would also be given a great deal of information on how the Gaines line was doing, how other dog foods were faring, and how the plant stood in the overall General Foods scheme of things. And the concept of the employee as a mature adult dictated the banning of time clocks and long lists of rules on behavior. Plant rules, if needed, would come from the people in it—after they had gained experience. While the designers could not prevent layoffs, they worked toward creating the maximum opportunity for stable employment. Workers would be encouraged to learn as many jobs as possible; this, it was felt, would give them a better chance for a job elsewhere for the duration of any layoff. As far as possible, firing and disciplinary layoffs would not be permitted; problem employees would be dealt with through "constructive counseling."

Since the team leaders in the plant would be so important, the planning group next concentrated on drawing up specifications for the kind of person they would need. The list of attributes they developed included analytical ability, a basic optimism about people, creativity, emotional stability, a sense of security (no need to dominate others), sincerity, and skill in dealing with others. The group was obviously not prepared to settle for run-of-the-mill supervisors. To begin the selection process, the following ad was run in the Topeka and Kansas City papers some months before the plant was to open:

GENERAL FOODS NEEDS PRODUCTION SUPERVISORS

To take on a new plant and an exciting new management concept in Topeka, Kansas. General Foods, a leading processor and distributor of nationally advertised grocery products including such household names as Post cereals, Kool-Aid, Maxwell House coffee, and many others, is opening a new Post Division plant. In the General Foods' tradition of progressive, forward-thinking management, a young, new-breed idea in management is being introduced in the new facility.

If you're looking for something different, a flexible management structure, that emphasizes individual abilities, an imaginative program that will set the pace for our multibillion-dollar industry, you may be the young-thinking leader we need.

You must have mechanical skill-potential with a background in production. Previous supervisory experience desirable. You will need an above-average flair for working with people and ideas—with the very minimum of supervision. Excellent salary, benefits, and relocation pay. If you would like to know more about this unique opening, write in confidence or call.

This ad netted thirty applicants, who were first narrowed down to ten through interviews, and then down to the six needed after an intense weekend of problem-solving exercises and structured games designed to reveal the leadership abilities being sought. Of the last four to be rejected, one was hired as a foreman for the parent Kankakee plant, and two requested jobs as team members at the new plant.

The six who made it past the final cut were then specially trained for a full understanding of the technology, business practices, and new value system involved in their new jobs. As the opening drew closer and the rookie team leaders took on more responsibilities, the leadership role of the design group began to diminish. When it became apparent that the team leaders had understood and "bought" the new system, it followed that they would advertise for, screen, and hire the team members. The ad they wrote was similar to the one which had been used to attract them, specifically calling for people with mechanical aptitude who were willing to accept greater responsibility and who wanted to learn multiple jobs and new skills. Of the six hundred twenty-five who applied, more than half were screened out through initial interviews, tests, physical examinations, and self-elimination. More than one hundred more were eliminated after in-depth interviews with the six team leaders, and a final thirty-five did not make it past a "selecting" weekend of gaming and role playing. Those left, sixty-three in all, were hired and put into training for the new plant. (During the elimination process, all those taken out of contention were offered the chance to discuss their rejection with a team leader. This was seen to be fair to the applicant and a good way to give team leaders an early opportunity to deal honestly and openly with people.)

In February 1971, the Topeka plant went into operation. The workforce of about eighty was divided into six teams of seven to fourteen members each, with a single processing and packaging team operating during each shift. Before the year was over, General Foods had put out a rough interim report on Topeka which indicated initial success. It told of uniformly high product quality, an absence rate of less than half a percent, negligible turnover (four left, two to go to better jobs elsewhere), virtually no theft and "property misuse" (significant problems at Kankakee), and a boost in productivity over similar operations elsewhere of 10 to 40 percent a person—despite the fact that about 30 percent of each person's day was being spent in training, meetings, and breaks! From the outset, it had been the plan to keep the management and workforce as "lean" as possible, not just for the obvious economic reasons, but also because of the belief that overcrewing and overmanaging naturally reduce accomplishment, autonomy, and self-esteem. Based on the usual standard engineering and production standards of American industry, the plant should have had one hundred ten production workers to accomplish its mission, but it was, in fact, functioning quite well with about forty less than that.

By the time eighteen months had elapsed, the degree of success had become even more apparent. The safety record was one of the best in the company, and there were 92 percent fewer rejected batches of dog food than was the norm in food processing; the combined value of all the improvements was computed by the company to be worth $600,000 a year.

A number of incidents typify the particular spirit and mood of the place. When the leader of the morning processing team left for several weeks to take on a special engineering job, his team not only worked well without him but devised a plan by which breaks were rescheduled to improve product flow. Another leader reported that the fourteen members of his packaging team were consistently showing up for their jobs twenty minutes before they were supposed to. When a business writer for the *Topeka Capital-Journal* came in after eighteen months of operation, she interviewed employees at random but was unable to find anyone cool to the system. Typical of the comments that ran in her article was this one from Richard Young: "I doubt if anyone has a bad word for the system. Oh, occasionally everyone is going to gripe, but there's nothing major. It's one hell of a fine place to work."

This is not to say there were no problems. Walton carefully watched for them and reported them in a 1972 article in the *Harvard Business Review*. A few team members had a hard time accepting the demands of the new system—one refused to work in the product-testing lab because the responsibility was too great—and a few team leaders had a hard time not acting like traditional bosses. When team members took on roles normally reserved for management (such as running the plant safety committee, hiring, leaving for a few days to see how a particular problem had been solved at another plant, or dealing directly with outside vendors), this usually worked out well for the worker but occasioned mixed reactions elsewhere. Walton cites cases such as that of the vendor who was disappointed to find himself dealing with a worker rather than a manager, and the plant worker who was sent to a corporationwide meeting of safety officials all the rest of whom were managers and who could be presumed to be "potentially threatened" by this man in a blue collar. Walton concluded, however, that the workers' "seriousness, competence and self-confidence" have usually earned them respect in such situations.

The most serious problem he noted was the unresolved—and perhaps unresolvable—one of pay. This "source of tension" is inevitable in a system like this one which is trying to promote equality at the same time that it rewards performance. At Topeka there are four basic rates for team members: a starting rate for everyone, a rate for mastering a single job, one for learning all the jobs on the team, and a plant rate for mastery of all jobs on both types of teams. A person can also qualify for a special "add-on" by showing particular ability in a certain area, such as machinery repair. Certain workers moved rather quickly to the team rate, and others became unhappy.

In addition to collecting problems, Walton also took note of certain indicators of success beyond the measurable ones watched by General Foods. In line with a theory suggested by several social scientists to the effect that participatory democracy on the job spills over into other institutions, he found that plant employees have become more active in local civic affairs than employees from other plants in the area. He also observed that distrust and cynicism were shorter-lived and less frequent here than in other workplaces with which he was familiar. And while he acknowledged that the workforce in Topeka was not without some evidence of prejudice toward racial minorities and women, he believes that such social ills have a much better chance of being cured in this kind of innovative environment.

Reasons for the initial and continuing success of the Topeka experiment are many, and range from the technical and economic feasibility of eliminating boring tasks to the freedom Ketchum and the plant manager were given by the company to experiment. (Walton feels that the physical isolation of the plant from the other parts of the company made it easier to be unique.) One factor that stands out is the highly selective process for employing team leaders and members for the plant. Recalling that only about one in ten of those who responded to the ad for workers was finally hired, one must assume that a certain degree of success was due to the fact that these were superworkers whose abilities had nothing to with the system into which they came.

Ketchum himself sums up why he thinks it worked:

> The key is that we created a total system with values, behavior, ideas and technology consistently aimed at mak-

ing sure the individual is not separated from the whole, giving him a sense of self-worth and offering him a chance to identify with the success of the organization. If you take part of the system and treat it with job enrichment, or sensitivity training or whatever, things may improve and look good for a while; but eventually they return to normal because the old system still controls.

This might seem to suggest that the Ketchum approach demands starting from scratch with a new plant and a hand-picked workforce to create a new system. Ketchum says no, explaining that, if that were so, he would not now be working to diffuse the Topeka system into other plants in the General Foods operation. In fact, as the Topeka plant was going into operation, changes were also being engineered at the Kankakee plant, changes which Ketchum has said have ". . . resulted in continued substantial improvements in productivity as well as other indicators of organizational health, such as attendance, grievance load, turnover, quality." At the time of our meeting in 1973, he was in the early stages of some other renovations, representing a real mix of situations: a plant in a rural area of New York State, an inner-city plant in Chicago with a heavily black workforce, a Northeastern plant with what he terms "a militant union situation," and another in Quebec.

Ketchum is emphatic in stressing the point that Topeka is *an* answer—not *the* answer—and that he uses it these days as a means of explaining principles rather than as a model. He admits frankly that Topeka is so far ahead, so successful, and so well known both inside and outside the company that it tends to inhibit others, so he tries to downplay it.

In lieu of trying to turn the approximately fifty General-Foods plants in the United States and Canada into carbon copies of Topeka, he now concentrates on helping other organizations in the company change from traditional to innovative ways by changing the climate of thinking. To do this, he has come up with a basic methodology. It is set in motion with a request from the management of the local plant, which prompts a three-day meeting of Ketchum with the plant manager and his immediate staff. The first day opens with an examination of such traditional assumptions of management as "Man is an extension of the machine, useful only for doing things the machine cannot," "Men are unreliable and require control," and "Job fractionization is a way to reduce costs by reducing the skill contribution of the man." As each assumption is discussed, the group begins to spot exceptions, problems, and flaws in it, and, in some cases, see how those above them in the larger organization must be making the same kind of assumptions about it. Once they begin to see that these are the assumptions of most organizations—including their own—Ketchum leads them into an examination of the kind of jobs these assumptions dictate. The picture that emerges is of a job as a point in a hierarchy in which people are interchangeable cogs, make a minimum skill contribution, are machine-paced, have little dependence on one another, and communicate at a minimum level—in other words, a coercive system composed of simple jobs and many rules. He also points out that these assumptions lead to traditions with a special meaning for the worker. For example, he says that there is a "distinct message" for workers in the fact that, in most corporate accounting systems, the salaries of managers are treated as a fixed expense, while workers' pay is a variable expense. The second of the three days is spent looking at the Topeka system as an example of what was done in one instance; the third dwells on what can be done with the particular system managed by those in the room.

This initial intervention by Ketchum produces individual reactions which are not always positive. Some participants are overwhelmed by the attack on the managerial assumptions of the last seventy years. The important thing, though, is that in most cases the process of rethinking has begun. Four to six weeks later, he returns for a second three-day session, this time with those from the next lowest level in the plant hierarchy, who are

Democratic Designs in America

subjected to the system overhaul philosophy, but with more emphasis on the "how-to" side of implementing it.

The two three-day sessions plant the seed for change and will germinate if certain conditions are present—the most vital being the support of key managers. Ketchum is quick to point out that there will be problems, tensions, and dislocations, especially within an existing operation. Certain members of the staff will feel threatened, managers will fear that their careers can be hurt if it doesn't work, rivalries will result, people who pride themselves on their abilities as problem solvers may have trouble transferring these abilities to others, and so forth. While it will be some time before the full impact of this form of systems changing can be assayed, Ketchum feels that it is beginning to take hold and will work in most cases.

As the Topeka plant is not a union operation, an important question is, What happens when there is the added factor of a local union? In a recent conference address, Ketchum answered: "As yet, we haven't enough experience with unions to generalize with the exception that union members and union officers are no more monolithic than managers and are equally human. . . . We will be expanding job redesign experiments in our unionized plants. The strategy [thus far] has been to get union involvement, build trust, give information and training in methods." If this policy is followed, it should serve the company well; much of the general union skepticism and lack of enthusiasm for job redesign has been prompted by exclusion of the unions from the process.

The systematic design of the Topeka plant system initiated by Ketchum and the seeding he is doing elsewhere are not unique (although they do have unique characteristics). Universally acknowledged as the first application anywhere of this type of reform are the experiments conducted by Eric Trist (formerly of the Tavistock Institute and now at the Wharton School at the University of Pennsylvania) in the British coal-mining industry which began in the 1950s. Such organizations as TRW Systems and Procter & Gamble have created similar systems since then.

All have reported success. More recently, still others have begun to experiment with what is becoming commonly known as the sociotechnical approach. At the time this was written, the consensus of several authorities in the field was that at least a dozen American companies had gone past the stage of studying what others had done and were deeply involved in experiments of their own. One such experimenter is Alcoa, where a young assistant professor of organizational behavior named Thomas Cummings has been helping with trials in white- as well as blue-collar areas of the company. He feels reform in the former are just as essential, but often tougher because of the ability of office bureaucracies to resist change. Meanwhile, because of the pioneering Trist and others, like Walton at Harvard and Lou Davis at UCLA, an increasing number of new business-school graduates are going into industry already armed with an appreciation of the potential of the sociotechnical approach.

4

MORE DESIGNS ON PEOPLE

The task force which put out *Work in America* estimated that as of the end of 1972, when its report went to press, the number of Americans who had been or were involved in extensive redesign efforts numbered about three thousand—a small fraction of 1 percent of the total workforce. The three thousand was, however, too conservative for the time at which it was made and has fallen even further from the mark since then. Nonetheless, the number involved is even now very small; even the most liberal but still reasonable estimate would not go much over 1 percent of the nation's working population. Clearly, ideas such as those in force at General Foods, American Velvet, and AT&T are ideas whose

Democratic Designs in America

time has only come to very selected firms. But if the number participating so far is low, the relative number of success stories is not. To further illustrate what can be gained by the variety of approaches available to those shedding the old one, let us consider the following from the potpourri of recent developments on the job-redesign front:

¶ While SAAB and Volvo have gotten a great deal of attention for their assaults on the conventional assembly line, several American companies have gone even further by eliminating them entirely in selected locations. One of them is the Communications Division of Motorola, Inc., where a single person is now responsible for the assembling, testing, and packaging of each Pageboy II (a pocket radio-paging device). As many as one hundred people had taken part in the production of the earlier model Pageboy! Thus, each "assembly technician" now has 100 percent responsibility for the new models, as opposed to less than 5 percent on the first model. To further enhance the sense of individual craftsmanship, each operator has been charged with repairing any unit that does not test out correctly and, just before it goes in the box, gets to put his or her name on the finished pager.

The company concedes that the new system has imposed certain penalties, such as the need for far more training for each individual and the need to increase the size of the assembly force by a quarter, but feels that, on balance, the advantages for the company and the individual far outweigh any disadvantages. Motorola says that it has been able, among other things, to cut handling time, rid itself of the many problems which cropped up when the line was changed or people were absent, make better use of plant space, cut its parts inventory, shorten the length of the delivery cycle, lower repair costs, increase quality, and cut turnover and absenteeism. Through demonstrations like this, Motorola and others are showing that new and highly workable job designs can be built around autonomous individuals as well as autonomous work groups.

Motorola, incidently, has been active in other areas of reform as well. The company has a program for getting its people to participate in decision making and problem solving on a volunteer basis. The program, called TEAM (for Total Effort at Motorola), dates back to a situation in which a group of women on an assembly line in the communications division were having such problems that the company was on the verge of shutting the line down. The women asked for and got permission to meet on company time to work out the problems among themselves—which they did. Now over one hundred TEAMs have been created by workers in the company.

¶ Driving home the point that job redesign is appropriate for any kind of job no matter at what level of employment, psychologist Harold M. F. Rush was able to tell of two existing extremes for his report for the National Industrial Conference Board called *Job Design for Motivation*. On one hand, Texas Instruments, Inc., had applied the principles of participative management and group goal setting and decision making to cleaning and janitorial jobs with remarkable results, such as a large and measurable improvement in cleanliness, cost savings on the order of $100,000 a year, and a *quarterly* turnover drop from 100 percent to 9.8 percent. After a week of special training, cleaning attendants were given the opportunity—which they took—to change anything from their cleaning materials to their relationships with other employees. The changes they actually made ranged from working with a supplier to develop a special disinfectant that did not cause chrome to corrode and dermatitis to appear on their hands to taking it upon themselves to approach factory, office, and lab workers to get them to help keep the company clean.

On the other hand, at Arapahoe Chemicals in Boulder, Colorado, redesign efforts have not only changed production jobs but also those of managers and scientists. For example, before redesign, the company's Ph.D. chemists were assigned pieces of projects, and were told just what to do, how, and when. This was

Democratic Designs in America 169

changed so that each chemist was responsible for an entire research-and-development effort—becoming a combination project manager and working scientist whose duties now include ordering materials and setting schedules. The results were improved morale, higher productivity, and fewer missed deadlines.

¶ Although the Federal Government has been slow to experiment with job reconfiguration, local governments have not been as reluctant, according to a 1973 report from the Urban Institute. The police in Kansas City, Missouri, have been experimenting with several alternative schemes for bringing patrolmen into the department's decision-making process; Parks Department employees in Scottsdale, Arizona, are now routinely involved in the process of designing and planning new facilities; and the city of Simi Valley, California, has been experimenting with various participative management schemes, as well as a "total approach" to law enforcement in which an officer has complete responsibility for all police matters on his beat, including investigations and follow-up. It is too early to report on the overall success or failure of such governmental departures from the norm—most are so new—but some have already proven themselves. Several years ago, seventeen experimental teams of sanitationmen in Kansas City, Missouri, were given the responsibility for creating their own operating procedures and safety programs to replace the old system of rules and regulations administered from above. Teams having the best safety records were given small cash bonuses and extra days off as rewards. The system was quickly made citywide when the experimental teams posted remarkable gains in the critical area of safety. Vehicle accidents were cut by one half, bodily injuries by 41 percent and lost man-hours by 72 percent.

¶ Short of full redesign, some companies have taken limited but commendable steps to involve workers in problems and decisions normally reserved for management alone. It generally goes by the name of "employee participation." As most are finding out, it is a move that both gives workers an increased sense of responsibility and satisfaction and often serves to post substantial gains for the company in the bargain. The Minnesota Mining and Manufacturing Company took a simple approach when it decided that something had to be done after its manufacturing costs had gone too high. It went out and asked its employees to set up their own programs for cost cutting. Within a year, costs had been cut by $10 million, with the added benefit of people getting more deeply involved in the business and problems of the company.

At Lockheed several years ago, when morale was low because of the company's specific financial problems and the general bad shape of the whole aerospace industry, it junked its old system of morale and production building (which amounted to the awarding of prizes) and replaced it with a program which is based on the assumption that "the individual performing a job knows more about that job than anyone else, including the changes that are necessary for improving the conditions or techniques of his job and the products of his effort." Under the new system, even the lowest-level employee was now considered to be a problem solver and an individual whose suggestions and thoughts meant something to the company. A system was set up so the workers at all levels would not only be heard when they uncovered problems, but would also be assigned to solving them. Based on the premise that being able to solve one's own problems is reward enough, the prizes, plaques, and platitudes of the old system were abolished. Similarly, the Ralston Purina Company has developed its "Operations Improvement Plan" which, like the Lockheed plan, is based on the idea that the company's own employees are its best consultants. Both companies see their plan as one which provides personal motivation and individual growth as well as techniques to save the company money and improve the way it operates. These programs have been so successful that both companies are now offering to show others

Democratic Designs in America

how it is done (for a fee). John Schmid, the man in charge of Ralston Purina's program, has helped install the Operations Improvement Plan at a variety of sites, including a bank and a university.

Although the techniques for employee participation which have been adopted by these companies involve fairly complex mechanisms (workshops, program coordinators, training sessions, and the like), the idea is remarkably simple and rational. Lockheed, Ralston Purina, and 3M have all made news in the business press with these programs, and have attracted wide corporate attention. This not only shows that these companies are on to something new and important, but demonstrates that they are rare exceptions in a world where most organizations feel that a suggestion box on the wall is enough to absorb any participative desires from its workforce. (Incidently, the suggestion-box form of employee participation first appeared in the 1890s, when it was embraced by the progressive businessmen of that era and was a daring departure for its time.)

As such developments show, job redesign has produced some excellent results. But there have been failures as well. One stunning flop occurred at Non-Linear Systems, a small electronics firm near San Diego. In the 1960s, with the aid of a team of behavioral scientists, it proceeded to tear down its assembly line, form autonomous work groups which kept their own financial records, and put workers on a salary far above the norm for the area. The innovations (as well as half the workforce, which had to be laid off) did not make it through the aerospace industry slump which began in 1970, and the company drifted back to traditional management practices. A detailed postmortem which appeared in *Business Week* revealed a number of possible reasons for the failure, but the major overall reason seemed to be that the slump merely accentuated the management's weakness in having gotten too deeply involved in experimentation and having forgotten that it had certain responsibilities for day-to-day operations (such as making sure that parts inventories were in balance) and keeping tabs on the outside world (seeing the signs of the impending slump). Andrew F. Kay, the president of the company, told *Business Week,* "I must have lost sight of the purpose of business. . . ."

Failures, of course, must be expected in job redesign as well as in any other new and still mostly experimental venture. But unless a number of failures have been very well hidden, they have been few and far between, which is all the more reason for others to enter this area which offers so much in terms of individual satisfaction, organizational improvement, and profits.

Finally, it should be mentioned that the Scandinavian and American examples used so far are part of a larger international picture, in which many countries and organizations are moving toward more democratic work. Such companies as Alcan Aluminium and Northern Electric in Canada, Phillips in The Netherlands, and the Shell Refining Co., Ltd., of England have been at the leading edge of experimentation in the sociotechnical approach. Worker consultation (and sometimes participation) in company decision making—through work councils—have emerged in the post-World War II era across Western Europe and in Turkey, India, and Canada. Some function well while others are of little value, but recent initiatives in many of these countries have begun to help the council idea realize its full potential.

Then there are those national political and social systems which have moved in the direction of greater self-management. Passing up both the traditional Soviet and capitalistic industrial models, both of which are authoritarian and hierarchical, Yugoslavia has made worker self-management an organizing principle. At its best, it works as it does at Energoinvest, a dynamic Yugoslav mining and manufacturing conglomerate with 24,000 employees. Workers there not only elect the company's directors but ratify major decisions in votes taken right on the factory floor. Despite—or, perhaps, because of—this, it is a highly profitable operation, doing over $200 million in sales a year. Because Energoinvest has acquired thirty-three companies since being founded in 1951, *International Management* magazine has called it ". . . one of the world's fastest-growing conglomerates."

V

Support Systems

1
The Customizers

While many organizations trying to develop a new working environment tend to adhere each to a single prescription (job enrichment, job enlargement, profit sharing with participation, or whatever), others have chosen to develop under no single unifying principle other than the very broad one of trying to improve the way people work, therefore improving the overall health of the organization. Sometimes, these custom-tailored approaches borrow some elements from, say, job enrichment, and other elements from other categories, but are still a breed unto themselves. About all they have in common is the desire to create a climate in which people are given support and responsibility, and little fear of the trial-and-error process—a generalization which covers a lot of ground.

Although there is little direct borrowing, such American systems often bear resemblance to some of the supportive environments which have been created in Japan. One of the most noticeable of these is at Sony's Atsugi plant, which has become known worldwide for, among other features, trust-building devices such as an honor system for paying for meals in the company cafeteria, new formulas for internal communications (for example, an interviewer who moves through the plant to question and listen to those not commonly heard from), and small production teams that set their own goals.

Giving support can take many forms, from a single, simple act of trust and respect to a whole raft of changes. A few examples of such acts will show the many forms they can take:

¶ Appointing an ombudsman to serve as every worker's representative—outside the formal hierarchy—with broad powers to receive, investigate, and resolve employee complaints, as the Xerox Corporation has done.

¶ Taking a major step to eradicate the second-class-citizen

role conferred by an hourly wage rate by abolishing the time clock and putting people on straight salary with sick pay as Motorola did for its 22,000 line workers in 1969.

¶ Giving production workers instruction in the underlying theories of the technology they are working with, as several major electronics companies are doing.

¶ Setting up a special office within the organization to help people deal with personal problems ranging from bankruptcy to drug addiction, as the Kennecott Copper Corporation and several others have done.

¶ Letting automobile workers test-drive the cars they worked on and giving them an advance peek at the new models they will be assembling—which are two ideas that the Chrysler Corporation has been experimenting with.

¶ Establishing new scheduling patterns, and redesigning workspaces to fit human needs better—two areas of reform which will be dealt with in forthcoming chapters.

The most interesting innovators, however, are those which have come up with larger, multifaceted systems to fit their needs. To better understand the infinite variety of approaches that can be taken, we will now examine three different corporate plans, which have little in common save for the fact that they have gone beyond the old but seldom-acted-upon cliché about supporting the worker and, in actual practice, found new ways to do it.

2

GENERAL ELECTRIC'S
COLUMBIA EXPERIMENTS

One obvious approach to improving jobs is to treat them as another item to be worked on as part of the company's overall research and development program. Today, however, with even small companies investing great amounts of talent and money in R&D on new products, it is astonishing how little effort goes into systematic inquiry on the working lives of those who will make the new products and use the new techniques. Some organizations have begun to adopt "personnel research" as an approach, but they are a very small minority. The number of firms with large-scale programs are rare indeed.

One of these rare ones is the General Electric Company, where, under the direction of Herbert H. Meyer, director of personnel research, a group of "practical consultants," mostly psychologists, have been assigned to selected GE plants to spend time framing experimental solutions to real problems, and developing new approaches. Once one of these consultants develops something which he and Meyer feel is worthwhile, it is sent to other plants for implementation.

The newest of the selected sites with an active practical consulting program is the new General Electric Appliance Park, a sprawling complex making electric ranges and air conditioners, situated adjacent to the "New Town" of Columbia, Maryland, midway between Washington and Baltimore. The consultant at Columbia is Dr. Wilton Murphy, a psychologist with previous experience in the space program, who feels that the Columbia situation is an especially good one for introducing change: "For one thing, this is a new plant which gives us a relatively fresh place to start, without some of the built-in preconceptions and customs of an old factory, and, second, we share in the aura of experiment in being part of a New Town." He adds, "Of course, this new plant in a 'New Town' situation sometimes works against us, as it tends to heighten expectations, but generally the impact has been favorable."

The term which Murphy uses to describe what is going on at Columbia is a "nondogmatic approach," meaning that it follows varied approaches. The best way to describe it is to portray some of the individual and often unrelated items which it encompasses.

One item in the collection is a program in product identification established for the benefit of production workers. Its point is simply to give the individual a sense of how he or she fits into a process and so identify with what is being made. Workers are introduced to their jobs by being shown and told about all elements of the production line, and are encouraged to take an interest in others on the line so that, for instance, one worker will be able to show a second the problem he has when the second man does not do the job right.

Another element of the program has been to introduce the workers to what happens to their products in the outside world. When big GE customers come to the plant, workers give them tours of the plant and get to talk to them about the product. In one pilot effort, workers making air conditioners have also been taken on field trips to see their products being installed in motels and housing developments, and to talk with the installers. And at the time of my visit to the Columbia plant in 1973, a trip was being planned to take the workers out to talk to customers in their homes about their new GE air conditioners. Murphy feels this program has been highly successful, and it is going to be continued and expanded. "Quite simply," he says, "it seems to work, in that it allows a person to see that his work has more meaning than just bending a tube or whatever." For all of the ease and obvious rationality of this program—akin to letting a chef taste the food he prepares—such efforts are still quite rare. Murphy knows of no other company which has gone so far as to take workers on field trips to see their products in operation!

This practice of working to give employees a bigger picture of their jobs first started with feasibility tests at other GE locations in the late 1960s. Termed "stewardship" training (as in the idea of feeling stewardship toward one's job), these experiments with workers in various operations proved that such treatment brought greater happiness at work, more productivity, and a new willingness to take on responsibility. The premise was starkly simple; as explained in a 1967 GE report, if a woman is wiring a circuit board that is going into a television camera which will be

Support Systems 181

used to televise the Rose Bowl (or whatever), she might have a greater sense of accomplishment and responsibility if she were aware of that fact.

To cite another manifestation of the same principle: A group of one hundred twenty people working on an assembly line producing electronic equipment were treated to a rich set of orienting activities, including a plant tour, the showing of a film about the product they made, and plantwide meetings in which each unit's work was related to the total operation and its goals. The group picked for the experiment was one which had been performing quite satisfactorily by company standards, so the before-and-after comparisons are especially interesting. When production records for the ten-week period before the training and the ten weeks that followed it were compared, they showed that the number of broken welds in the welding operation was down from 6.5 to 2.8 percent, the number of products which required reworking was down from 22 to 17 percent, the number of overall defects detected was almost halved, and the incidence of tardiness was quartered. By GE's accounting, the experiment had cost the company about one thousand dollars in wages paid during training, but the improved quality of work was computed to have saved fifty thousand dollars the first year. What is more, before-and-after attitude surveys revealed a significant increase in job satisfaction. Other trials measured by other yardsticks netted similarly impressive results. One not only produced a 20 percent gain in productivity, but the give-and-take group sessions in which the group's operation was discussed generated what the engineer in charge described as seventy-two good, directly applicable suggestions for improvements. Predictably, the technique produces the best results in places like assembly lines, where work tends to be repetitive and tied to a single location, but GE found that it also had some definite positive impact in areas where there was greater freedom and autonomy.

Besides showing the ease with which a good, simple idea works out in practice, GE's development of this particular idea in a variety of installations shows its consultancy concept off to good advantage. By the time the Columbia plant opened, the idea was already well developed and ready for added refinement.

A second group of new customs at Columbia relate to giving employees a voice in company affairs and simultaneously making management more visible. One such custom is the "round table," in which top management periodically picks ten to twelve workers at random and meets with them for several hours to discuss plant affairs. Management opens these sessions with a general business review, and then the meeting is thrown open to a discussion of items of major and minor concern to the workers. Questions and answers from these meetings are written up and distributed throughout the factory. At one round table, employees said they were not sure that they fully understood all benefits available to them from GE and were, therefore, afraid that they were losing out on some of them. Consequently, the company assigned people from the personnel office to hold court in the cafeterias at lunchtime for several weeks to make sure that all questions were answered. Of course, some gripes do not lead to positive action, but the fact remains that they are addressed and handled publicly. Round-table meetings are also held at a lower level; each month each foreman gathers those under him for a like give-and-take session to resolve smaller, localized problems.

The Columbia plant has also come to rely on temporary-employee task forces as a means of addressing specific problems, many of which are first identified in round-table meetings. These temporary task forces are a mixed lot. Some, like the one formed to look at employment practices, are made up only of salaried employees, while others, such as those addressing floor-level issues, are a mixture of salaried and hourly employees. Since the factory opened, some fifteen task forces have been formed, on issues as far apart as minority affairs, recreation, and soldering practices. "Together they have brought about a great deal of positive action," says Murphy.

For example, when it became apparent that people were not happy with the way we were filling jobs as they opened up, the task force which looked into it was able to recommend and get approval for a system of job posting so that people in the plant could get a crack at better jobs as they came available. A very different kind of example would be that of the task force which was formed when we found that there was an unacceptable rate of damage occurring in our warehouse. A task force of supervisors and workers was formed, and they put together a new set of operating procedures which has drastically reduced the damage rate.

Another group of new practices deals with the selection and grooming of foremen. When the plant opened in 1971, some foremen were brought in from other parts of the company to get things started. Since then, however, all prospective foremen have come through the plant's foreman-assessment center. Rather than selecting foremen on the traditional basis of an application and an interview, the personnel office picks them through a series of structured events which sample their abilities in simulated work situations. Included in the assessment are: situations in which they must relate to a group; "in-basket" exercises; and role playing.

In the in-basket test, for example, the man is set up in a mock-up situation in which he has come in to replace a foreman who has died; his first duty is to handle the business in the other man's in basket. Among the other items found in the basket are:

¶ A note from several employees complaining about "the long hair and silly clothes" of one of their co-workers.

¶ A request for time off from a worker who has used up all of his vacation time but needs the special consideration because of the death of a distant relative.

¶ A complaint from a worker about a screwed-up paycheck which is short of the amount due him.

¶ A reminder from the maintenance department that it is time for a major overhaul of equipment in the foreman's shop.

¶ A note about a production problem which will require the new foreman to put his workers on overtime for two weeks.

Although the prospective foreman has been briefed on company policies before the test is given, the test offers borderline cases and conflicting demands. The requests for equipment overhaul and overtime, for example, conflict. Exact answers to the situations which conflict are not expected; the test is looking instead for a series of responses which indicate an ability to handle the conflicts. Some answers are clear-cut, however; the man with the long hair and the silly clothes should be let alone unless his hair or clothes present a danger to his working around machines.

In the role-playing exercises, the applicants are put into one-to-one situations in which they show how they will react in a given situation. In such a test, a foreman-to-be might be asked to act out how he would react to a man who is not producing (played by an actor). Says Murphy, "This shows us a lot about a person and how he will operate and treat others. We have found that some people do quite well in group exercises, but when they're in a one-on-one situation they come on like gangbusters and try to crucify the man who is not producing. Things like that don't show in normal job interviews."

Although Murphy is quick to concede that the process is subjective, he feels it is the best way he has found to select people for jobs. The process is being introduced in other parts of the company and being tested as a way for picking people for other jobs, such as salesmen. How well does it work? Murphy says, "Our indication is that the replacement rate among new foremen is much, much lower than the norm."

Once selected, foremen at Columbia can look forward to ten four-hour sessions of special training which Murphy sums up as ". . . practical lessons in protecting the self-esteem of others in dealing with them on the job." It is geared to getting away from the father-son relationship traditional to the foreman and worker, and moving closer to job partnership. The sessions employ such techniques as role playing and the use of videotaped situations acted out on the shop floor, to teach such things as introducing a new employee to the job, introducing changes in the job, and telling someone he or she is doing a good job. "What it amounts to," says Murphy, "is behavior modeling for those in supervisory positions. Our next step will be to introduce it to middle management."

In addition to these techniques, the plant is witnessing experimentation aimed at answering the question of how to best nominate a man or woman for a foreman's job. A series of experiments are using both existing foremen and nonsupervisory workers as talent scouts. In one test, all the workers who had been on the job in the warehouse for six months or more were asked to nominate candidates from their peers. "Because two of the men nominated by the sixty-seven workers in the warehouse are now working as foremen, this technique has already proven to be successful," says Murphy.

A good deal of Murphy's time these days is being spent in such experiments. There are now nine groups in place which are trying out the team approach to assembly work to see if it is feasible to start phasing out some of the more fragmented jobs. Thus far, the results have been encouraging. Another series of tests has been set up to find the best ways to give workers the most immediate feedback on how they are performing. Still another trial will see if the plant, being shifted to the much more informal and personal practice of a discussion between the worker and supervisor, can effectively get away from formal, structured grade cards as a means of evaluating individual performance.

Looking at the overall list of plans which have been introduced or are being tested, Murphy says, "There is probably not one thing that is going on here that is truly unique and not being done somewhere else, but I think that the total list taken together adds up to something significant, a real attempt to give the people who work here the ability to feel self-esteem and to feel that they are working in a supportive environment." Harking back to his work as a psychologist working on the space program, he says, "What we're trying to do here through a variety of plans and programs is to try to get the same sense of coherence that existed on the Apollo program."

One question that is brought up by the thrust of the work at Columbia is its relationship to the specter of unionization. Many of GE's plants are unionized, but some, like Columbia, are not. In its first two years in operation, there were two attempts to organize the Columbia workers; both failed by a margin of approximately two to one. Coming directly to the point of whether or not the menu of new ideas is as much an attempt to stave off union organization as it is to make people happy and productive, Murphy answers, "No," adding, "I'd have to be frank in saying that it is probably easier to do some things in a nonunion plant, but if we were organized here there is little doubt in my mind that we would be doing things in much the same way—and we are doing similar things in unionized plants."

Unlike many other big companies, GE has acknowledged that it is faced with a problem. Recently, its senior vice-president, Walter Dance, told stockholders that the company saw a vast potential threat to all industrial companies: the rising feelings of "frustration, irritation, and alienation" among employees. Speaking of blue-collar workers, he said, "It involves a gut feeling on their part that industrial society has left them with the dull, hard, dirty jobs—and doesn't care." What is going on at Columbia and other GE plants indicates that this company is showing signs of caring. While much of what is most exciting, such as work teams and peer nomination, is still in the experimental stage or in the early phase of implementation, GE's varied approach appears highly promising.

Attesting to the fact that the company is willing to look at and develop ideas which would be considered too radical for much of

American industry is the fact that it has experimented with situations in which workers are literally unbossed. While GE had already learned that morale and output were improved by giving minor decision-making options to workers, it decided to test the results of giving the *full* range of decisions to the workers. A group of a dozen union men who staffed a welding shop in GE's Heavy Military Electronics Systems Department in Syracuse, New York, were picked and offered the opportunity to take complete charge of their operation. They would be given drawings and specifications of jobs to be done and would then be on their own until the jobs were completed. All of the bosses and specialists who normally surrounded them—ranging from their foreman to the production-control specialist—would step back and only enter the picture when the men in the shop needed their help. Management clearly outlined why this option was offered: ". . . to reduce operating costs while maintaining a quality product and to meet scheduled commitments by removing any constraints that might prevent the shop from performing jobs at a competitive price."

The first reaction to the proposal was one of skepticism and disbelief. A series of meetings were held, some with the workers and some with management, in which the proposal was discussed and eventually warmed up to. Shortly after the experiment was finally agreed to, there was a plantwide strike—and the experiment was off for the duration. However, two interesting things happened. Before the strike was called, the men had asked for and gotten the company to pay for their tuition for a seminar on advanced welding techniques; during the course of the strike, only one man missed a single session of the seminar. And after the strike, the union asked that the men hold off for six months before picking up the experiment, but the men refused.

The results of the experiment were such that the company termed it "remarkably successful." Among the components of that success were these: There was an improvement in output, quality improved substantially, and, due to the new self-sufficiency of the workers, there was a 50 percent savings in shop overhead. The experiment's overseers not only noted a new enthusiasm and cooperative attitude toward management on the part of the men in the shop, but saw new management trust and respect for the workers. One of the most interesting results of the experiment was the way in which the men valued their own work. This was a job shop in which the men were paid on an incentive basis for the amount of work done. Before the experiment, the value of individual jobs was set by time-study specialists, but as part of the experiment, the men were allowed to set their own prices. As it turned out, the men set values which were no higher and often lower than those set by the time-study men who were computing the value of the jobs independently on the side as a control. After seven months, the men had actually cut their average earnings by 3 percent—perhaps one of the best examples current in the world of industrial experimentation that working people do not abuse new freedoms and responsibilities provided they are given to them freely and ungrudgingly.

3

Edwin H. Land and His Polarized Family

Commonly referred to by his employees as "He" (in such a manner that the word sounds at once upper case and vaguely suggestive of immortality), Edwin H. Land, the shy, photogenic, college dropout who has built the thriving Polaroid Corporation on an ever-growing pile of patents issued in his name, is the founder, chief inventor, board chairman, president, and director of research for what, until a sharp 1974 earnings decline, has been one of the most glamorous of the glamor companies.

Support Systems

Land is a private person given only to an occasional public speech and very infrequent press interviews, but one who has nonetheless captured the popular imagination as the perfect embodiment of the tinkerer who was able to build an industrial empire out of the ideas which came from his own head. His life presents us with the kind of story which, when looked at in isolation, tells us that the American Dream is in fine shape. All of the components of the classic dream story are there, including that of the bold young man pursuing hunches at all costs (in this case, we have a teen-ager secretly slipping through an unlocked window into a physics lab at Columbia University to further his experiments in light polarization).

While Land is best known for his cameras, his genius, and his ability to realize a dream, there is another facet to him: He is an idealist with very specific ideas on creating the ideal working environment. His ideas are not a warmed-over version of the Protestant ethic and the inherent dignity of work, but rather are built around a vision of a workplace which recognizes the inherent dignity of the people who come there to work.

Back in the early 1940s, when the small company's major products included sunglasses and sheets of polarized plastic—and the first instant camera was just beginning to take shape in his mind—Land talked about a new kind of company which would carry the world into "the next and best phase of the industrial revolution." He predicted this new day would dawn first in the small scientific manufacturing company, which promised to emerge as a democratic social unit where all involved would regard themselves as "labor" in the sense that their common purpose would be ". . . learning new things and applying that knowledge for public welfare." Land envisioned a "vigorously creative" company whose scientific accomplishments would rival those of the university. At intervals over the years, Land has amplified on this heady theme. During the 1958 annual meeting, he compared the contemporary corporation to a feudal aristocracy and went on to assert, "What we would like to build at

Polaroid is a nonfeudal system." Later that same year, he called his managers together to make sure that his goal did not get lost in the shuffle as the company really began to take off. The crux of that message, reported in *Fortune*, was this:

> I think we are going to be magnificently successful and in a very short time . . . [but] if after we succeed in *just* doing that, we are just another large company, we will have contributed further to the hazard of the degradation of American culture. . . . A country without a mission cannot survive as a country. There may be many ways of creating that mission, and many groups will play their role, but I want to talk about the proper role of industry. Its proper role, I believe, is to make a new kind of product—something that people have not thought of as a product at all. When you've reached a standard of living high enough for most people, where do you turn next? It seems to me there is only one place to turn. Industry should address itself now to the production of a worthwhile, highly rewarding, inspiring daily job for every one of a hundred million Americans.

Making sure that everybody got the word, Land then went to the employees' Christmas party to talk about creating jobs where a person can maintain the same dignity possible at home. He added, "Now I don't mean anything silly—I don't mean you're all going to be happy. You'll be unhappy—but in new, exciting, and important ways. You'll fix that by doing something worthwhile, and then you'll be happy for a few hours. Alternatively happy and unhappy, you will build something new, just as you do at home in the family."

Land's tantalizing vision of a new industrial world leads to the obvious question: What kind of place is Polaroid today?

As a company, Polaroid is nearly as shy and unpublic as Land himself, and tends to keep its internal activities as much under wraps as it does its next generation of cameras. To be sure, it pushes its cameras with big, zesty advertising campaigns, but otherwise, it has no public-relations department as such. It issues no press releases and turns down droves of press requests for a glimpse inside the company. Robert Palmer, Polaroid's director of community relations and the closest thing that Land and the company have to an official spokesman, estimates that Polaroid commonly turns down as many as two hundred requests a week from the press. The reasons for this reluctance to let the outside world look in are not as irrational as they may seem at first. For one, the company's perception of self is that of a local Boston company (it has all of its plants in the Boston area) which just happens to have an international product.

Another reason is that the company has gone a long way in employing the hard to employ. At the time of my visit, for instance, it had one hundred eighty-three former convicts on its payroll; according to Palmer, there are many writers and TV people who would love to cover them, but it is Polaroid's position that they should be kept from being exploited as "industrial freaks." Still another factor in Polaroid's fear of the outside is the paranoia born of an enterprise built on proprietary ideas; the company looks upon all intruders as potential industrial spies. Furthermore, Polaroid doesn't need publicity to attract new employees; the word is out that this is a good place to work. During early 1973, as many as twelve hundred job applications and résumés were coming in a week. Despite the fact that the New England economy was depressed and had a high rate of unemployment, this is a spectacular number of applications for a company which only has nine thousand employees.

I was one of the fortunate reporters who, for reasons unclear, was able to gain limited access to the company, in the form of a two-hour audience with Palmer. Normally, a meeting with the person who represents an institution to the local community might be expected·to yield no more than public-relations puffery and tales of employee unity as expressed by thriving in-house bowling leagues; yet, the disarming frankness of Palmer in painting a portrait of life at Polaroid leaves one with no doubt that he is giving it straight. For instance, in talking about the company as a liberal institution, he was direct in approaching its dark side, which he termed "typical liberal stupidity." Example: When the company first hired former convicts, it made a big deal of it internally, with the result that theft of the company's highly fence-able product immediately jumped by 50 to 60 percent. "We were done in by our regular employees, who were given the ex-convicts as an excuse to rob us blind."

Palmer himself is worth dwelling upon because he is the prime outside representative of an important American corporation and underscores the singular nature of his company. He seems to delight in not avoiding the controversial, and is the kind of person who would drive the management of a garden-variety American corporation to distraction with his candor. His personal involvement in community affairs goes far beyond the normal pattern of the corporate man who works with the local community chest—in fact, Palmer is an outspoken critic of the local United Fund and has gone so far as to air his controversial views on the subject before a TV camera. Palmer (in his role as a member of the company's foundation, an employee-run operation which grants money to high risk, often volatile, causes), is a key man in the distribution of Polaroid money to the community. As Palmer describes it, "We currently support one hundred forty-three projects, many of which are the kind of thing which keeps our marketing department nervous. At any given time, the kind of thing I'm talking about might include a Black Panther breakfast program or an abortion clinic."

Freedom of personal expression is looked upon as an employee right rather than a benefit at Polaroid, and Palmer's own actions back up the fact. He had recently taken time off from his job to act as a mediator working to settle a prison revolt, has been a vocal opponent of a plan to use photo identification cards for Massachusetts welfare recipients (a system which might well have meant business for Polaroid), and has worked internally to develop sales guidelines to keep the Polaroid camera from being sold for purposes which hasten the day of "an oppressive I.D. card society."

Nor does Palmer have any trouble talking about the turbulence which rocked the company and his office during 1970, a year that brought Polaroid enough ferment to give it an aura closer to that of a college campus than that of a glamor company. Two 1970 events, and the way they were handled, show that free expression is more than a slogan at Polaroid. In May of that year, employee concern over the American invasion of Cambodia and the subsequent tragedy at Kent State had fostered an intense frustration within the company. A number of employees began to openly push to get the company to make a statement of concern. The demands were laid at Land's feet. He decided not to make a statement on behalf of the company because he felt that this would not be a fair expression of all opinions. The issue was not avoided, however, as a memo went out to all employees which read (in part):

> Believing as we do that this is a time for vigorous political participation by individuals in the democratic process, the company has undertaken to cover the cost of a telegram to be sent to the President, your Senator or Representative, or any other member of the Congress with whatever argument, point of view, or comment you want to have heard.

Within a week of the May 8 memo, over twenty-two hundred telegrams were sent out at company expense.

The second event took place in October, when several militant black employees attacked the company (and Land personally) for racist activities: specifically, for support of South African *apartheid*. What was charged was that the company was supplying cameras and film being used in the country's oppressive internal passport system, and supporting the South African dual racial system by allowing blacks working for Polaroid's distributor there to be paid less than whites.

Reaction was quick. The first response in the company was

generally the typically hollow and defensive reaction of a liberal reacting to a devastating indictment, taking the form of comments like, "After all that we've done for them, how can they do this to us?" But this quickly gave way to a more sincere response, which was to question what was really happening in South Africa. Land himself was shaken, and looked for a way to resolve the embarrassing situation, which was attracting much press interest and subverting morale in the company. The first attempt at a solution was to appoint a committee of eight blacks and seven whites who were to examine the issue and come up with policy recommendations. This failed when blacks on the committee balked at the idea of making policy in Boston for blacks thousands of miles away—a situation smacking of classic colonialism.

The next decision was to send four employees (two of whom were black and two white) to South Africa. Says Palmer, "At that point, Land told them to come up with a solution and he would abide by that decision no matter what it was. The company would have been quite happy to cut out South African distribution entirely and have the whole thing over with, but when the group came back, we had four votes to stay there and act as a positive force."

As it turned out, there was substance to the original charges. Polaroid's distributor in the country was paying its black workers the typical below-the-poverty-level wages paid to blacks in that country. Corporate policy on equality of opportunity was unheard of there, let alone practiced. Polaroid's initial argument that the South African operation was that of a distributor and not part of the company per se might have been technically true, but the distributor was distributing Polaroid products and was, therefore, part of the system. The only original charge that fell somewhat flat was the allegation that Polaroid products were bolstering the insidious South African system of internal passports for blacks. About 8 percent of the photo shops making photos for the passbooks were using Polaroid film, which hardly made Polaroid the mainstay of the system.

The unanimous decision on the part of the four-person committee to stay in and attempt to have a positive impact yielded these actions: One hundred thousand dollars was pumped into the country for the benefit of blacks there in the form of education and training grants; the wages and benefits of the blacks working for Polaroid's distributor were brought up to those of the whites; and Polaroid would strive to prevent any further use of its products in the passbook system (for example, no Polaroid I.D.-system equipment would be let into the country for any reason).

Looking back on the South African affair, Palmer, who was in the middle of the action, says that its net effect on Polaroid was jolting but good. It tested the company's liberalism. Two of those who had led the attack on the company were fired early the next year, but not for the attack; they refused to stop attempting to launch a boycott of Polaroid cameras while on the Polaroid payroll. What is more, the South African affair made the company look closer at all aspects of its operations to see if there were traces of racism or discrimination elsewhere. "If nothing else," says Palmer, "it made us as determined as ever to retain the practice of free speech within the company, even with the kind of problems the incident brought." But if the event showed Polaroid that it could handle such freedom, it had a bad side effect in the Boston area, which bothers Palmer: "Other companies were saying, and some still are, that if such a thing could happen at Polaroid, imagine what could happen here. Pure and simple: It didn't make it easier to get a job in this area if you were black." (For its part, Polaroid has achieved the goal of making sure that it hires blacks at the same ratio that they exist in the general population. Today one of ten jobs at the company is held by a black.)

On a more mundane level, free expression is part of the

Polaroid routine. One example is the company's "Interact" system, whereby employees can sound off on company policy and practices on a confidential basis and are guaranteed a reply. Representative issues raised through Interact appear in *The Polaroid Newsletter*. Everything from the price of coffee in company cafeterias to excessive dealer profits is fodder for the Interact columns in the *Newsletter*. It was an Interact complaint (about Polaroid's role in fostering an oppressive I.D.-card society) that got the company to set policy guidelines on the use of its products.

Freedom of expression, however, is just one element in the Polaroid experience. The term which Palmer uses to sum up the entire situation is "total support system," a catchall reference to a rich bag of benefits, career opportunities, and freedoms. The net effect of these offerings—from profit sharing to the availability of five full-time psychologists (who don't report back to anyone)—indicates that Land's dream of a democratic, industrial society has come a long way from words to actions, at least under his roof.

An important facet of life at Polaroid is its determination to make promotion, internal movement, and career development realities. These may sound like the very same principles which most companies pay lip service to, but at Polaroid, they become believable. Its training department offers the substance of mobility, with offerings up through, and including, the ability to get in-house courses applicable to a B.S. degree and free courses in such subjects as scientific Russian. It has a long-established program in "career exposure," which amounts to the right to ask for, and probably get, a chance to work in a new field within the company. There is no guarantee that one will be given a permanent spot in the new area, but one is given a chance. Polaroid has progressed in career exposure as far as its Pathfinder program, which has allowed blue-collar workers to split their days between work on the line and apprenticeship as a researcher.

Any open position up to, and often including, that of division manager is posted around the company, so that anyone who feels that he is qualified can call in and be interviewed. When a person is finally selected for the job, the unsuccessful applicants are formally notified, and reasons why the successful applicant was picked are made public. It is not uncommon to have one hundred apply when a good job opens, making the process extremely time consuming, but, according to the Polaroid litany, it elevates the notion of promotion from within from a tarnished and only sometimes-observed industrial cliché to a reality. Polaroid claims to have the most advanced "job posting" system in the country.

Although there is no question that Land and his top managers make the major corporate decisions, there is a distinctly democratic consciousness at work which is expressed in many ways. All employees vote each year for holidays on which the law permits flexibility. Companywide surveys are commonly employed to shape policy in the area of personnel practices and benefits. Both the life- and medical-insurance plans were created by majority opinion. An elected Employees' Committee takes an active role in suggesting new policies for company operation, and localized plans and progress meetings are held to keep everyone abreast of the company's direction. The stress is on "being your own boss"; official policy decrees that the supervisor's role should be that of helping the supervised on the job and helping them advance, rather than that of an overseer. In the same vein, the company has developed Land's idea that the person working at Polaroid should "own" and control the machinery with which he or she works rather than have the machinery own them. To this end, production workers are routinely involved in equipment redesign and the purchase of new equipment.

Another internal institution of note is the ad hoc committees which come and ·go with regularity. Some of these are formal company-sanctioned panels appointed into being to address a particular issue or grievance, and which disappear when they have brought the issue to rest with new policy. These groups have emerged to address such specifics as the opportunities for women in the company and the advancement of blacks. Other committees pop up on their own, without the formal approval or disapproval of the company (although lack of disapproval implies approval). One such group was created as the result of a cafeteria conversation in which some employees were bothered by the fact that the overall performance of the stocks in the company's retirement fund portfolio was not as good as that of the overall market. They formed a group, investigated the situation, and made recommendations to management, many of which were acted upon. For instance, the ad hoc panel told the company that the fund should be managed by a better-performing brokerage house, and the company agreed.

In addition, there are the benefits: Polaroid pensions are transferable and built on company profits invested in the name of the employees. Pay is good and generally in line with that of the Boston area's other leading manufacturers. Also, the company has a policy of doing everything it can to avoid layoffs. Finally, it is a firm believer in profit sharing, and for many years, has given out an average of 15 percent of annual salary in cash bonuses to everyone in the company with three years' seniority (with a smaller percentage for those with less time with the company). While the bonus has hit 18 percent in a few boom years, there was no bonus at the beginning of 1973 because the company needed every cent it could lay its hands on to bring out the SX-70, the new pocket-sized magic box with such touches as film that advances automatically and instant pictures which pop out without messy negative papers. Although there were long faces aplenty when the news came out that bonuses were off, there was clear evidence that the decision was understood. There was no rise in the company's low turnover rate, and complaints—in this company which encourages complaints—were few. Land was betting $250 million of the company's money on a product that could eventually be the most successful in a long line of camera successes dating back to 1948, when the first Polaroid camera hit the market. Palmer claims that the company has built up a loyal body of employees who understand the risk being taken and realize that risk, especially a Land risk, can beget long-term profits to be shared by all.

If there is a convenient symbol for work life at this company, it is *Polaroid Newsletter*, which bears only passing resemblance to other American corporate periodicals. To be sure, it contains its share of stories of employee good deeds, promotion and retirement acknowledgments, jogging club news, and the other pap and fodder common to its breed. But what makes it different is that the uncommon institutions and freedoms of this company pop up in some form on almost every page. Aside from the aforementioned Interact column, the things that strike you as you browse through a few copies are varied expressions of the unfolding week-by-week development of the company. Examples:

¶ A report from the company's Equal Opportunity Office, outlining its new overall Affirmative Action Plan, a redoubled equality effort incorporating such existing plans as the "10–75 program," a plan to achieve 10 percent black representation at *all* levels of the company by 1975, and "the Woman's Action Plan," which calls for "equitable representation" of women at *all* levels by 1978.

¶ Bad news is presented with the good: One typical issue contains news of new sales records along with a story telling that Polaroid has been named co-conspirator (with Kodak and Sylvania) in an antitrust suit.

¶ An article on the company's "Intercultural Workshops," which are weekend-long affairs at which employees of different groups (black and white, male and female, and management and nonmanagement) meet for the purpose of ". . . supporting personal growth and assisting corporate equal opportunity programs."

¶ Reports from the employee-elected nonmanagement Employees' Committee (EC), in which its grievances, demands, and opinions are given full treatment.

It is here that the news appears when the quasi-union questions management overtime practices or starts its push for fuller hospitalization insurance. Minutes of the meetings between the EC and its management equivalent, the Personnel Practices Committee, are approved by each and published so that the interplay may be open. For instance, one agenda item reported in a March 1973 issue of the *Newsletter* is an EC report of a survey it conducted, comparing employee benefits at Polaroid with those offered by Kodak, DuPont, IBM, Xerox, General Motors, and TRW. The report showed that Polaroid came in number two overall. The EC then listed the steps that should be taken so that Polaroid would become equal to or better than the leader in each of eight benefit areas (retirement, short-term disability, group life insurance, long-term disability, medical insurance, vacation, holiday, and profit sharing). In response, the Chairman of the Personnel Practices Committee said that the company could not possibly match the best feature of all of the other plans, but recognized the need for improvement and asked the EC to determine the changes it felt had top priority.

What the *Newsletter* does is to confirm Land's vision of a workplace with dignity for the people who work there. That vision shows up elsewhere. *The Polaroid Handbook*, the manual of benefits and company rules given to all new employees, contains on the first page a short message from Land entitled "The Purpose of Our Company." It outlines the basic aims of Polaroid, the first of which predictably is to make high-quality, useful products which will keep the company prospering. "The other," says Land, "is to give everyone working for Polaroid personal opportunity within the Company for full exercise of his talents, to express his opinions, to share in progress of the Company as far as his capacities permit, to earn enough money so that the need for earning more will not always be the first thing on his mind—opportunity, in short, to make his work here a fully rewarding, important part of his life." In the jargon of the company, when you have personally accepted these two goals and can relate them to your day-to-day work, then you have been "Polarized," and are referred to as a "Polarized member."

This company has been built on the model of a politically liberal family headed by a respected, humanitarian father who, after all, is in charge of the family but has let his children have a lot of support and freedom to develop themselves and so improve the family itself. It attracts the adjective "familial" rather than "paternalistic." (For this reason, the term "Polarized member" is wryly descriptive of this liberal family if you look at "polarized" in the sense of being a pole apart from political conservatism.) By adhering to this model, rather than a unifying programmatic approach like job enrichment or some other recognized school of management thinking, the place exhibits a collection of refreshing trend-bucking abnormalities. Job boredom is not viewed as evil incarnate but rather as a reason for the individual to move his or her career in a new direction. Curiously, Palmer boasts that the company could not come up with an organization chart, and that, instead, it remains a loose operation with what he calls ". . . a lot of healthy confusion"—a pattern which is a lot closer to that of a family than to the dicta of nearby Harvard Business School. Similarly, the company has rejected the urge to consolidate itself into one campuslike central facility; rather, it has spread its operations in a hodgepodge of buildings scattered around Cambridge, Waltham, Needham, Norwood, and New Bedford, again harking to small familial operations rather than a monolithic central operation.

As all of this works for Polaroid, one wonders what spillover lessons are in it for others without Polaroid's history of profitability and success. For that matter, one wonders what the future of innovation is at Polaroid itself if it is in for a long period of decline. It is a hard question to answer. Nonetheless, it is obvious that this place is full of ideas worthy of much wider test and application.

Meanwhile, it is worthwhile to look at another kind of operation to see what kind of support a very different type of company can give its employees. Unlike Polaroid, the next company is not effecting new technology, but is being affected by it. While Polaroid has its eyes on bigger things, this one is going through a period of consolidation—a nice word for plant closings.

4

The Deal
at the Dairy

On March 30, 1973, I met with Whitfield Browne, Jr., who is the manager for Personnel Administration Services for H. P. Hood, Inc., the large 125-year-old dairy combine headquartered in Boston. The date of the meeting is significant because, by the end of the day two unprofitable company plants, one in Manchester, New Hampshire, and the other in Providence, Rhode Island, would close. Given this situation, one might logically suspect that any personnel man with an ounce of sensitivity would be depressed. Not so. Browne was pleased with himself and his company because almost all of the employees involved had been taken care of either by being moved elsewhere in the company (some as far away as the company's citrus operation in Florida— a move paid for by the company), by being helped to get new jobs with other companies, or, in the case of those nearing retirement, by being given early retirement. Browne bragged, "In the New Hampshire case, we were able to find new jobs for everyone who wanted one, and in Providence, we did pretty well but couldn't hit 100 percent because the area is one of the most depressed in New England."

The attitude of Hood in matters of job security and layoffs is, if not unique, at least uncommon. For over twenty years, the company has had a running deal going with its employees, geared to keeping them working, even though the dairy industry has gone through a series of mostly technical changes aimed at reducing the workforce. During that period, industry processes have been automated, the use of the home delivery milkman has been cut drastically or eliminated in many firms, and even the national shift from glass milk bottles to cardboard cartons has enabled dairies to get along with fewer workers (for one thing, the shift eliminated cleaning rooms where the bottles were cleaned).

The deal with the employees is simply this: Nobody with two or more years seniority with the company will be laid off because his job has been eliminated for reasons of technological change. Moreover, it is agreed that a worker cannot place himself in that not-too-uncommon situation where he suggests workplace improvements and then finds that his good ideas have effectively served to suggest himself or a co-worker out of a job. While Hood will make no such guarantees on plant closings or operations cutback for purely economic reasons, it will do all that it can to find the displaced worker a new job in the company or at another.

Besides this overall layoff policy, Hood has worked to further foster worker confidence by adopting supplementary practices. For instance, if an employee is fired for cause, the person has the right to ask for an investigative panel of peers to review the case. If a deliveryman is told that he is going to be fired for taking milk from a truck for his own use, he can appeal; five deliverymen will then be picked at random and given company time to make a full review of the case. "Reviews are seldom asked for," says Browne, "but the right to have your case reviewed serves its purpose, which is to make sure that the facts support the firing."

Another Hood practice is to announce a plant closing or a cutback as far in advance as possible. Some closings have been announced as far ahead as a year before the event. The aforementioned March closings in Manchester and Providence were announced before Labor Day the year before. Conventional industrial wisdom is to wait until the last possible moment, for fear of antagonistic acts and attitudes, people walking off the job immediately, and the like. Because the employees know that Hood will go to work in their behalf, the company has had few problems with its practice of giving advance word. According to Browne, the doomed plants normally work at near-peak efficiency until the final whistle. Once the decision has been made to close or cut back an installation, the company takes a variety of actions. It holds one-to-one counseling sessions with workers to find out how it can help them, helps train them for new jobs, puts in hiring freezes at other plants so that it can make room for those in the closing plant, and beats the bushes to locate new jobs elsewhere. Says Browne, "Other companies are always amazed when one of our managers arrives with a carload of workers and says that there are good people whom we have to lay off and we'd like to help them find jobs. That kind of thing just isn't done too often."

The deal that Hood has with its employees has its roots in the firmest common sense. It has apparently worked. Not having issued a pink slip for reasons of technological change for over twenty years has made employees willing partners in that change. When better trucks, better refrigeration, and procedures which give milk a longer shelf life made it attractive to cut home milk delivery from an average of three deliveries a week per family to two, the routemen worked with the company to help create consolidated routes. Also because of the deal, as we have seen, Hood boasts of a very active employee suggestion system (with awards of up to $5,000).

Besides being able to claim "very low" turnover and absenteeism rates as well as high productivity, Browne adds that there is a genuine trust in the motives of the company. "A month after we made the announcements that the plants were closing [in Manchester and Providence], we took a survey of the employees affected, and the majority of them supported the closing in the sense that they agreed that Hood would not have decided to close them down unless they were totally unprofitable."

Hood may be a large, paternalistic, nonunion operation, but it has a definite inclination toward the experimental. At the time of my visit, it had just put its office staff on a flexible workday, and was on the threshold of introducing job enrichment. With twenty years behind it, however, the company's policy of job security and employee participation in change has long ago passed out of the experimental realm and has become a totally ingrained part of the way the firm operates. The company has, in Browne's words, ". . . chosen to balance economic and human needs." While claims like that tend to sound a bit too self-serving, an incident occurred while I met with him which supported the point. A personnel officer came into Browne's office to report a corporate foul-up that had been caught in time. It seems that one of the men leaving the company in that week of cutbacks had only a few months to go to qualify for pension and retirement benefits. The man was going to be kept on so that he could qualify. In an era when people are often canned *because* they are about to qualify for such benefits, the personnel man's decision to protect the man in question is significant.

VI
Breaking the Time Barriers

1
Dogmatic Days

There are few facets to the Western way of work which are more depressing and unimaginative than the way in which worktime is arranged for us. Our jobs generally demand forty hours of service in five consecutive eight-hour clips, during which we obediently come and go at rush hours appointed by others. Except for layoffs or prolonged periods of illness, a worklife is laid out in front of a person: Five-day, forty-hour pieces stretch out like a seemingly endless passing train, terminating abruptly at age sixty-five at a chicken à la king banquet where a gold watch is presented and the boss picks up the tab for the drinks. Unless we dearly love our work or are blessed with a rare professional flexibility, we tend to work toward 5:00 o'clock, the weekend, vacations, and retirement itself. The worktime system encompasses some profound absurdities: for instance, that a person's workday should have the same 9:00 A.M. to 5:00 P.M. boundaries on a dreary February day as it does during the best days of late spring, or that big industrial employers have only recently begun to seriously question the rush-hour problems which they themselves are responsible for, or that a person can work for forty-five years with no single workbreak longer than a piddling three-week vacation.

While it is the lot of many to ride this train, others are slighted by derailments. The woman who has chosen to bear children but is prepared for another work role as well finds herself unable to reenter the kind of work that she is qualified for when the kids reach the age when they are all off at school. Women who would like to work less than a full forty hours or work in blocks of a few years between children are commonly relegated to sitting around going nuts in an empty house, doing volunteer work, or filling in at clerical work which often falls far below their ability and training. Similarly, others derail in this era of high-paced technological change when it is found that their skills have become outmoded and they cannot keep up with the changes in their field. Then there is the jolt which commonly occurs when the train comes to the end of the track, an event that is not necessarily as promising in reality as it seemed in the abstract.

While few aspects of work seem as deadening as the way time is handled, few are so easy to challenge, experiment with, and change. And few offer such easy potential for quick employee and employer rewards.

In recent years, the concept of a standard worktime has begun showing definite signs of erosion. Even though only a relative few have been able to participate in these timely departures, their number is increasing. The high-visibility groundbreaker for all of this has been the four-day, forty-hour workweek. Its importance has been to focus attention on the idea that worktime need not adhere to a strict formula and that there is plenty of room for experimentation. The four-day workweek made us realize that at least one major alternative existed in an area which had seemed to be locked into an immutable format.

What is happening is that challenges are beginning to be hurled at our institutions of time. Increasingly, what were yesterday's utopias are starting to be looked upon as today's time traps. The five-day workweek was a late-nineteenth-century radical dream, as was the eight-hour day. At the turn of the century, the average working American was expected to put in six ten-hour days. The old-guard trade unionists successfully led the fight to prune this back to five eight-hour days; but now, younger workers tend to look upon this once-radical arrangement as the essence of the commonplace, ripe for toying with. Although it attracted little national attention at the time, there is significance in the fact that a Fargo, North Dakota, local of the International Typographical Union chose to withdraw from the parent organization because it did not allow the local membership to go to a four-day workweek. The International held that four ten-hour days was a violation of overtime rules and a step in the wrong direction from the eight-hour day. Another example of an element of worktime under fire is the long-held assumption concerning overtime. Since World War II, the institution of compulsory overtime has been generally regarded as the right of the employer *and* a boon to the employee, giving him extra wages at the preferred rate of time and a half or better. Led by the United Automobile Workers, the effort had begun to change compulsory overtime to voluntary overtime when the reverses of the 1975-model-year hit the auto industry and the issue became temporarily muted by massive layoffs. However, the first major blow against forced overtime had already been scored in late 1973, when the UAW got Chrysler to agree to a contract provision whereby a worker could not be made to work more than nine hours a day, on Sundays, and not more than two out of every three Saturdays. Virtually the same pact was then made with GM and Ford.

On a more fundamental level, the very nature of the way one's worklife is laid out is coming into question. A new consciousness is being tested. For example, the great dream of going to a four-year college and subsequently following a single career was formulated at a time early in the last century when the average American was not destined to live much beyond forty; so, it was natural then to want to be educated in one short four-year burst to make the best of what was, by today's standards, a miserably short life. That dream still made a lot of sense in 1900, when our average life expectancy was 49.2 years. But today, with life expectancy at over seventy years, and with more and more people attaining the dream of a four-year college education, there is new interest in seeking alternatives to it. The notion of having two careers or stopping more than once for an education is not uncommon today; while only a limited number are actually doing it, many more are at least talking about it. It may well be that the lifetime with two full careers may emerge as a major aspiration in the years ahead.

Meanwhile, new patterns are being advocated in which the

lines between work, study, leisure, and retirement tend to shift and fade. Sabbaticals for people other than professors, voluntary midlife career switching, long leaves of absence from major companies to do socially useful work, and other novel breaks from the standard pattern are beginning to show here and there.

This trend to a time-varied worklife is not a movement without its thinkers and strategists. For instance, it was growing international interest in new time arrangements that prompted delegates from twenty-three nations to meet in Paris in late 1972, under the sponsorship of the Organization for Economic Cooperation and Development (OECD), to explore new patterns in working time. The intention of the meeting was ". . . to promote diversification and variability in the regulation and allocation of time for work, study, and leisure under the highest freedom of individual choice." Challenges are coming from other quarters as well. The Department of Health, Education and Welfare's report, *Work in America*, took broad swipes at the normal patterns of worktime and presented a gaggle of new ideas which could serve to radically change the life of the average American. One plan it put up for consideration was that of a "Universal Worker Self-Renewal Program," which would provide *all* workers with the opportunity to take a ". . . six-month paid sabbatical every seven years or a one-year sabbatical every fourteen years." This idea and others like it will be examined in more detail shortly, but the point here is that an idea of the scope of the paid sabbatical for working Americans of all strata is no longer in the far-out realm of utopian thinking and futurist projection, but has been put forward by an official agency of the United States Government.

All of this strongly suggests that a new dream is in the wind and ready to unfold. The old dream, born of the abuses of the past, was to create humane standards based on shorter worktime. Now that those standards are the norm for most, many are discovering that the dark side of that dream is its inflexibility. Therefore, the new dream will stress flexibility and individuality in an area where there is presently little of either. Commenting on the timeliness of the aforementioned OECD meeting on flexible work patterns, Janice Hedges, an economist for the Bureau of Labor Statistics, wrote in the *Monthly Labor Review*, "The growing tendency of workers in many countries to achieve flexibility through absenteeism lent urgency to their discussions." She is not alone among those who observe labor trends in asserting that in many work situations the main path to flexibility and individualism at the moment is to be absent, tardy, or quit.

It is not hard to see the stuff from which this dream will emerge. The sons and daughters of office and factory workers whose parents dreamed of coffee breaks wonder why they have to take their break at 10:10 A.M. or some other exact moment determined by others. Men who grew up dreaming of situations in life which would allow their wives to be free from work, now find that their wives want meaningful part- or full-time work. Some find retirement at sixty-five just fine, while others want and are meant to work beyond that age, or, perhaps, to retire earlier. Still others would prefer to phase out gradually, avoiding the jolt of stopping cold on a given day. Dreams can go sour at the top as well; in recent years, many top executives have seen the far-off dream of retirement turn into the unexpected reality of "early retirement"—a nice way to say that you are being forced out of a job while still in your prime.

Complementing such thinking, there appears to be a new awareness that patterns and schedules can be rearranged. Examples of time rearranging are on the rise, and contribute to a tradition-breaking mood. In 1971, for instance, a Congressional bill went into effect which made Washington's Birthday, Memorial Day, Columbus Day, and Veteran's Day all fall on Mondays. In terms of our thinking about time, the importance of the move was that Congress guaranteed Americans four three-day weekends (five if you count Labor Day, which was long ago decreed for Monday) with relative lack of antagonistic debate.

Time-related alternative-seeking is also beginning to show up in the public speeches of American business leaders. Addressing himself to the subject of the corporation in 1990, James P. McFarland, chairman of the board of General Mills, said, in 1972:

> [By 1990] we may, for example, be providing "second career" opportunities through a substantive reduction in the retirement age but with full benefits. We may well see the rapid development of corporately sponsored day-care centers for employee children, and a great increase in programs that give employees lengthy leaves of absence to pursue interests in nonbusiness-related fields.

In short, worktime and its arrangement has become a matter for concern. Starting with the four-day week and other versions of the compressed week and moving one at a time through a group of lesser-known time changes, here are some of the major new time options.

2

THE COMPRESSED WORKWEEK

While the four-day workweek existed before Mrs. Riva Poor came along, it was she who spread the word and parlayed it into a national phenomenon of some proportions. A restless mother with two children, two masters degrees, and a varied work experience, she was admittedly looking around for a new idea to develop for national consumption and, thereby, create a calling for herself. It was an unusual quest; she really did not know what form the idea would take, only that she would know what it was when it appeared. The spark came in the form of a *Boston Globe* article on a local company which was experimenting with the idea of having its workforce come in for four ten-hour days rather than the traditional five eight-hour days. "When I saw that piece in the paper," she says, "the little hairs on my arms stood on end. I knew that this was the idea I had been looking for."

Her first action was to begin tracking down leads to companies which had converted from five to four days and from this came *4 Days 40 Hours: Reporting a Revolution in Work and Leisure*, a book built around case studies of twenty-seven firms which had adopted the 4/40 format. Beginning with the appearance of that book in 1970, Riva Poor became the unchallenged spokeswoman for the four-day week, and her office became the central clearing house for information on employers which had converted to it. Out of this grew innumerable speaking engagements and media interviews, several Congressional appearances, *Poor's Workweek Letter* (a newsletter that keeps tabs on the movement), and a 1973 expansion of the original book to include more than one hundred new pages of information on the phenomenon. Riva Poor has succeeded in her goal of hitting on a big idea for national consumption and has indeed been, in large part, responsible for the major flurry of interest which attended the four-day workweek during 1971 and 1972, years when it was hard to pick up a newspaper or magazine without finding something about the compressed workweek complete with a few quotes from Riva Poor.

Today, with that flurry of media interest over, the four-day workweek itself is anything but over. Close to two thousand working places—which taken together employ about a million workers, a small but significant percentage of the population—had converted to it by the summer of 1974. The energy pinch of the previous winter had spurred renewed interest in it in some quarters, where it was viewed as a means of cutting gasoline consumption for workers' commutation and cutting heat and electricity bills at the plant. At one point during that winter, the *Washington Star-News* reported that the United States Government was going to put most of its workforce on a four-day schedule if other energy-saving measures did not work. At least a half-dozen organizations are currently converting each week. There also continues to be broad experimentation with various forms of the compressed workweek. During the summer of 1973, for instance, the Motorola Corporation announced that it was experimenting with a three-day, thirty-six-hour week for some of its production workers. The idea there was to offer people long leisure breaks, but also to give the company maximum utilization of its plants and equipment (with three twelve-hour shifts a day).

In short, from all available indications, the compressed workweek is here to stay, although it is as yet unclear as to how fast it will continue to move and whether or not it will ever become, as some have predicted, the dominant work schedule for the majority of Americans.

Now that a variety of organizations which have adopted the idea over the last several years have had experience in its practice, it is clear that those conversions have included some failures, but the overwhelming number have been happy with their decision and plan to stay with it. A good case in point is the company which was featured in the item in the *Boston Globe* which first attracted Riva Poor's attention: Kyanize Paints, Inc., of Everett, Massachusetts, which started experimenting with the idea in 1969. As one of the elder statesmen of the four-day movement, it is a good example of a company where the memories of the five-day week are getting hazy and the advantages of the four-day schedule are accepted as givens. At the time of my visit to Kyanize five years after the initial experimental period, enthusiasm for the "new" system was still strong, even though its novelty had worn off.

Kyanize's main plant and headquarters are located in a plain, three-story brick building surrounded by particularly grubby surroundings—the number of scrap and junk yards dotting this treeless industrial outback render it a true wasteland, just the kind of area which one might not especially relish coming into five mornings a week. The company employs two hundred in its main Everett plant, who are represented by a local independent union, the Kyanize Shop Association. The company has an established reputation for flexibility and good employee relations. Its benefit package is among the best in the paint industry, and it has long let workers routinely shift jobs, not because it fit in with any theory of job enlargement but because it seemed like a natural way to fight boredom.

Inspiration for the four-day week at Kyanize came more from the way paint is processed than it did from any desire to pioneer a new and pleasant work schedule—although this became a contributing factor. Quite simply, it was found that the company, which could produce only fifteen batches of paint during the shorter days of the five-day week (three batches a day), could produce sixteen batches in a four-day week of nine hours (four batches a day). In short, it fared better by having its employees cut out a few coffee breaks and get the same pay for thirty-six hours spread over four days than it was for a forty-hour, five-day week.

From the beginning of the experiment, all production office and management people have been on the four-day week, although the sales force still works five days because of the nature of its work. Even the president stays out on Friday; he felt that if he started coming in, except in real emergencies, other executives would drift in to make sure that they were not missing out on the action—and that would sabotage the whole plan.

Approval has been near-universal in the company. Although the union took a week or two to warm up to it, 78 percent of the members approved trying the idea for the test period in March 1969. A month later, 90 percent of the union members approved its permanent adoption. Only one man was so opposed that he requested (and was granted) arrangements that allowed him to work five days—he has since changed his mind and now works four days.

An executive who has been in on the Kyanize four-day week

since its inception, and who has become the company's unofficial spokesman for it, is Grant Doherty, the sales promotion manager. Speaking for the company, Doherty says that the major benefit of the switch has been what he terms ". . . a nice production increase, which amounts to at least 7 percent." He attributes this, in part, to the extra batch of paint which can be processed in a four-day thirty-six-hour week and, in part, to the sustained morale boost afforded by extra leisure time. Like other four-day converts, Kyanize harbors a host of examples of how people use the fifth day to their advantage. A man in the shipping department is an avid theater buff, and he and his wife find the long weekends ideally suited to occasional theater trips to New York; another man finds time to go three hundred miles to see his son play college football; and Doherty himself finds the extra day invaluable for household errands and chores which he has assumed since his wife became seriously ill. The number of employees with vacation cottages has gone up, and others talk enthusiastically of near-empty fairways and uncongested stores. Doherty says that employees are using the time for themselves, and that he knows of no instance of moonlighting, even though there is ample opportunity. (Critics have assumed that four-day workers would use their three days of free time to tire themselves out with other work.)

With special relish, Doherty—as a sales promotion man—emphasizes the good publicity value inherent in having been a pioneer. He says that the company's advertising agency figures that the four-day week has been worth about $1.5 million in free advertising for Kyanize. *The Wall Street Journal, Newsweek, The New York Times* and AP, among others, have carried articles featuring the Kyanize conversion, and there have been enough TV crews on location at the plant to have led to the development of a repertoire of standing jokes about the local union affiliating with Actor's Equity. His files now contain an estimated seven thousand inquiries from companies, unions, and scholars who have requested information on the company's experiences, to which it has responded with a mimeographed report (which asserts at the end, however, that Kyanize is as forward-looking in paint research as it is in employee relations). Sales have gone up since the conversion, and Doherty is convinced that the publicity has "helped a great deal" in that. Citing one specific aid, he reports that Kyanize dealers say that people remember the paint's name more easily because of the four-day week.

Another lasting benefit has been the ease with which the company has been able to attract new workers. "Twice as many respond to our ads," he says, "and in the case of millwrights and experienced maintenance men who are usually especially difficult to find, this has been a fantastic boon. Absenteeism rates have continued to drop, and are now at about one-tenth of the level before the conversion. And those who call in sick these days are really sick." The Kyanize list of advantages also includes the elimination of certain fixed costs—heat and electricity are the most important—associated with the eliminated fifth day, and improved service to customers because the "shipping day" is now longer. Summing it up, Doherty terms the system "better than ever," and one which improves with age. He is unable to come up with a single negative side effect of the conversion for the company, its employees, or its customers.

Kyanize is certainly among the most enthusiastic of converts. However, its very positive results have been experienced by others. A 1972 survey by the American Management Association of one hundred forty-three converts revealed that four-fifths agreed that the four-day week "improves business results." To be more specific, the four-day week was credited with increasing production at 62 percent of the companies, increasing efficiency at 66 percent, and boosting profits for 51 percent. Similarly, a Bureau of Labor Statistics study revealed that companies which had installed the plan had generally achieved their objectives in doing so, whether they were to reduce costs, improve efficiency, cut absenteeism, or give employees a more satisfying work schedule.

Of course, not all results have been good. The A.M.A. study pointed out that some companies had some scheduling problems, especially when they were beginning the system. Of the one hundred forty-three converts, eight reported that worker fatigue was the principle problem in their experience—but since only eight reported this as a disadvantage, the problem may not be as serious as some critics have maintained. The issue of fatigue is not to be written off too easily or quickly however. The Labor Department's Janice Hedges reports, "Worker fatigue and its effects on output and work injuries over the long term are still an unknown factor."

Other disadvantages which were uncovered in the A.M.A. study and other reports include complaints from working mothers (who find the longer day harder to fit in with their family schedules), shipping problems, customer confusion about new hours, and cost increases. While it must be emphasized that these are points which have been made by a small minority of converts, they are all problems which must be considered by a company before it adopts the plan. Another problem, which would seem to be a major one, would occur in places where there is a lot of overtime, which could push ten-hour days into twelve-hour nightmares and most decidedly produce fatigue and lowered morale.

Estimates on the percentage of firms that have adopted and then dropped the four-day week vary only slightly. Riva Poor's files on fifteen hundred four-day conversions contain seventy which converted back to five days, yielding a 4-percent rate. Allowing for the possibility that her file of case histories may not be a scientific sampling, she says, "At the most, I would guess it to be 7 to 8 percent." Some estimates have ranged as high as 10–15 percent, but these now seem out of line since the American Management Association survey revealed an 8 percent failure rate. The A.M.A. study also said, "Most observers don't consider this rate of failure any more significant than the record of similar incidents which accompanied the advent of the five-day week some thirty-five years ago."

The reasons why the few have failed are many, and hardly indicate any basic major flaw. "In many cases," says Poor, "the reason they have failed is that management botched it, such as by starting it suddenly and without consensus and explanation, which generates resentment. I also know of some cases where the company has run into circumstances, like a major fall-off in business, which put them out of an experimental frame of mind and back to the old way." As culled from the expanded edition of *4 Days, 40 Hours*, other reasons include: several attempts were stopped at unionized plants when the international refused to let their members continue in light of national policy; a few firms used to getting "casual overtime" from salaried workers without paying for it lost this in a ten-hour day and reverted; and a few experienced lower productivity on the four-day system. *Forbes* magazine adopted the four-day system, but later dropped it when it announced that many of its women employees did not like going home from work at late hours in New York City. Although this was the announced reason for the cancellation of the four-day week, a reporter for that magazine points out that there was more to the problem. He says that the idea was an ill-conceived one for a news-gathering operation, and that the system fell apart as people found they had to come in on the fifth day to get their work done. A New York architectural firm, Haines, Lundberg and Waehler, liked the plan but dropped it when some of its major clients complained that they were unable to reach people on the new day off. Several retail operations, such as the Jules Gillette men's clothing stores of Miami, tried a four-day operation but stopped when they felt they were chasing customers away by being closed an extra day. Such failures clearly illustrate the fact that the four-day week is not intended for everybody, and becomes cumbersome in certain applications.

In some vocational areas, the results show a greater degree of disparity than in others. Police operations are a good case: a number of departments have seen it work to great satisfaction, while others have dropped it. On the positive side are the departments like that of Huntington Beach, California, which has attributed increased morale, more arrests, and a cut in the need for overtime to the four-day week. On the other hand, the Memphis Police tried it for half a year and dropped it when squad car accidents went up—many of them taking place during the last two hours of the longer day. An experiment in the District of Columbia ended all interest in four-day police work in that city when those in the experimental precinct were unable to perform as well as those in the rest of the city. During the course of the sixteen-month experiment, the District was in the process of pulling out all the stops in an attempt to push back its nationally known high crime rates. The rate only went down 3.3 percent in the test group while it dropped an average of 20 percent in the rest of the city. Days after the D.C. experiment ended at the end of 1972, Arlington County, Virginia, across the Potomac from Washington, put its whole force on a four-day week with the avowed intention of reducing crime. Arlington adopted the new schedule to put more patrolmen on the streets during the hours when crime rates were highest. Instead of putting on a whole new shift each ten hours, as in the D.C. experiment, ten-hour shifts in Arlington overlapped during the high-crime hours. Eight months into its conversion, the Arlington Police were reporting success with the new plan. A conversation I had with a patrolman got this response to the system: "I don't know of anyone who doesn't like it." I asked him about fatigue. "No. I never get tired and I've never heard anyone else complain." Interestingly, he apparently did not know that the District of Columbia had tested it and dropped it when he added, "I don't think it would work in a place like the District, in a high-crime area, because there is lot more going on and a lot more tension to make you tired in a situation like that."

The distinction between big and small has also shown up in

research by the Urban Institute, which concluded, on the basis of looking at seventy-five departments which have tried it, that it works best in small and medium-sized cities and not as well in large cities.

The strongest negative reaction to the idea has come from the national leadership of organized labor. This opposition is understandable since the idea touches two sensitive nerves. First, most unions have been on a long campaign to shorten the workday, not lengthen it. In the early 1960s, an effort began to make the five-day, thirty-five-hour week the norm, and despite effective opposition, that desire is still very much alive. Second, the idea of the four-day week, with its ten-hour days, violates the five-day, eight-hour configuration which only took root after decades of struggle. AFL–CIO opponents were quick to point out that the eight-hour day had been their major goal since 1886, when it was adopted at the first AFL convention. Typical of the reaction of national union leadership was that of Steelworkers' president I. W. Abel who, reflecting the fear of hidden motives and the return to the hours of the sweatshop, told a convention of his members in 1971, "The way some of these 'benefactors' maneuver, we have to be careful they don't offer us a two-day week—with two twenty-four-hour days, of course." Nor was this reaction confined to the United States. When the Canadian Parliament began studying the issue in 1972, the Canadian Labor Congress supplied a seventeen-page brief opposing it, with reasons ranging from threats to safety to the encouragement of moonlighting in the midst of high unemployment. Generally, unions in the United States and Canada are against it, and only find it minimally acceptable if it provides workers with time-and-a-half pay for the hours worked over eight. Some have gone beyond this. The Oil, Chemical and Atomic Workers (OCAW) has adopted the policy that all work done over eight hours should be paid for at double the normal rate.

Strong union objection—especially that of the AFL–CIO—to letting people work in excess of eight hours a day without overtime has played a strong role in thwarting a series of bills introduced in Congress in 1971 through 1973 which would have opened up many new four-day opportunities. The bills sought to amend two laws, the Walsh-Healey Public Contracts Act and the Contract Work Hours and Safety Standards Act, that prevent companies on Federal contract from keeping anyone on the job for more than eight hours without paying time and a half. The bills have all died from inaction, with the main reason being vociferous objections which were first aired by union witnesses at Labor Department hearings on amending Walsh-Healey in 1971. The Department found no reason to change the act and, from then on, Congressional interest waned. One of those still plumping for changing Walsh-Healey is Rep. William A. Steiger (R.-Wisc.), who has been re-introducing his own bill each year. His legislative assistant says, "Our hopes are dim, as it is hard to get cosponsors or a legislative hearing on an issue which is so firmly opposed by the AFL-CIO." Expert witness Janice Hedges feels that some of the momentum behind the four-day week was lost when attempts to change the act failed. "I'm not saying that this hurt it badly, as there are still many conversions, but it did take some of the zip out of the movement because it effectively prevented some 4 million workers covered by Walsh-Healey from participating."

Besides having to face the tough hurdles of Congressional and trade union coolness, the four-day workweek has encountered another problem: the impression now current that the idea has faltered. This has resulted, ironically, from its initial success in gaining the attention of the media. The idea had a brief and interesting time in the media spotlight from the beginning of 1971 until mid-1972, when it was big news, with literally hundreds of newspaper and magazine articles appearing on the subject. Especially at the beginning, the largest chunk of these articles were of a simplistic, noncritical nature, glorifying the idea without pointing out its drawbacks or side effects.

Then there was a second reaction. In case after case, periodicals which had given the idea rave reviews the first time around came back for second looks—which tended to go in the other direction. *US News and World Report* opened with a gee-whizzy article called "How the 4-Day Workweek Is Catching On" and caught up with some of its critics in a later article entitled, "As 4-Day Week Spreads, It Meets Some Doubters." *The New York Times* opened up with the enthusiastic duo "Coming Soon? The 4-Day Week" and "4-Day Week: One Less Day to Drag Yourself out of Bed," and later came back to earth with "4-Day Work Week Getting Mixed Reception." *Parade* magazine, the nationally distributed Sunday supplement, provides what is probably the most dramatic turnaround. The first *Parade* article, "The 4-Day Work Week Is Spreading," began by proclaiming, "A new revolution is spreading in the United States. . . . It's a revolution in work and leisure. . . ." and went on to cite a long list of the most positive quotes and examples—a perfect case of home-on-the-range journalism (". . . where never is heard a discouraging word"). Six months later, *Parade* came back with "Second Thoughts on the 4-Day Work Week," which listed a group of organizations which had "junked" the plan, and moved on to a list of "unexpected problems." The later articles gave the impression that the idea was faltering and had pretty much run its course.

By 1973, the four-day week was not generating much interest in the popular media. Ironically, many of the critical articles had pointed out correctly that no really large company had adopted the four-day week except in small experiments. In May 1973, when the John Hancock Mutual Insurance Company announced that it was going to implement the plan for its massive clerical staff, there was hardly any coverage of the decision, save in Boston, where the company is based.

The John Hancock decision is interesting because it shows that the idea still has substantial momentum, and that even after a long, hard look at its potential disadvantages, the idea still appeals to a major corporation. The company had begun dabbling with the idea when it was new, and only moved on to large-scale application after it had been running experiments on the four-day week for four years.

Peter Janetos, a John Hancock vice-president in personnel operations and head of the committee evaluating the experiments, talks about the four-day week in light of his experiences: "It hasn't lived up to its publicity and the claims which were being made for it at the beginning. For instance, we haven't found any of the great economic gain claimed for it. In fact, we can find neither significant economic advantage nor disadvantage. But it is a very acceptable way of working for both the company and its employees and it does have its advantages." Results from the test groups yielded these conclusions, which were enough to put it over the top: There was a high degree of employee acceptance (89 percent of those in the tests indicated that they liked it); the majority of the managers involved favored it and recommended its continuation and expansion; the experimental groups maintained productivity levels with lower overtime requirements during the experiments; and, finally, the four-day week represents an employee benefit having a minimal cost and a high degree of acceptability. The major disadvantage the company found was that tardiness and absenteeism had a much more noticeable effect on operations in the four-day test groups.

The rise of the four-day week shows that a new working idea can be moved far and fast by one dedicated individual prepared to exploit it. As the prime scholar-oracle-advocate of the four-day week, Riva Poor may come to parallel the influence of another Bostonian who emerged over one hundred years ago to advocate a change in the workweek. He was Ira Steward, a union machinist, who went down in labor history as "the high priest of the eight-hour movement." Although it was not until the 1940s that his idea became the norm, it was he who first fired the imagination of the American worker. Among other things, Steward organized across the country a string of "Grand Eight

Hour Leagues," which pressed for the new day and debated its impact on the nation. Steward assumed that the worker would be paid the same for eight hours of work as he was for ten or twelve, and he foresaw this as a great boon to the nation, as it would give the workingman more free time for leisure and the consumption of products. Steward thus foreshadowed the rise of the twentieth-century consumer economy. His point was first acknowledged on a broad scale by Henry Ford, who, by 1926, had all of his workers on an eight-hour day and a five-day week—without cutting wages. Ford reasoned at the time that the forty-hour week was essential in order for the nation to absorb its own production and remain prosperous. There was significant self-interest in this because, as he later pointed out in arguing for the universality of the eight-hour day and the free Saturday in his book, *Moving Forward*, ". . . a workman would have little use for an automobile if he had to be in the shops from dawn to dusk."

While the four-day week per se may not work out as having the impact and final universality of Steward's idea, in a wider sense, the drift away from conventional hours begun by Riva Poor may. She has long made the point that the four-day workweek is merely the flagship idea for a host of ideas for rearranging time, and that when she refers to the four-day week she is really talking about a variety of new schedules.

In the meantime, as the four-day workweek develops, it is moving with one major social trend, in which people are acquiring more usable leisure time. But it will also come up against another major trend toward greater self-determination and freedom for the individual. The most serious limitation of the four-day week in this regard is that, in most applications, it amounts to replacing one rigid, inflexible system with another. Even in the cases in which workers have successfully petitioned management for the adoption of the four-day week, the system is still one in which the bosses tell the workers when to work. As far as can be determined, nobody has yet tried a four-day week in which the worker can pick his or her extra day off; invariably, these days are assigned by others. What is more, only a small minority of firms will, like Kyanize, accommodate those who wish to stay with the five-day week when the majority goes over to four. If there is liberation in the four-day week, it is only through the extra day of leisure, not in any basic change on the job. However, at about the same time the four-day workweek began to spread in America, another intriguing but completely different time-related option became just as popular in Western Europe. Today, just as the four-day week has begun to move across the Atlantic to Europe (and across the Pacific to Japan and Australia)—a movement which will no doubt be spurred by the recent appearance of *4 Days, 40 Hours* in several foreign editions—this European idea has arrived in America. And this idea does fit directly into the urge for greater day-to-day freedom at the workplace itself.

3

The Flexible Day

The freedom to come and go at personally convenient times carries an obvious appeal for almost any working person whose life is tied to rigid hours. Within limits, that freedom has been extended to tens of thousands of European workers, mostly in West Germany and Switzerland, and has recently begun to show up in the United States in a handful of companies.

The flexible day's rather prosaic origin dates back to 1968, when several firms in Munich created the system in desperation as a means of coming to grips with severe rush-hour traffic jams in the city's industrial areas. The largest of these pioneers was the Bölkow aircraft factory which put more than a quarter of its twenty thousand employees on the "gliding workday" as an experiment. Bölkow slipped into the system after having tried two more conventional solutions—an ordinary staggered system and a variable-hours plan under which workers set their schedules in advance. Both of these compromise systems were abandoned because of the added paperwork and administrative costs required to run them. Early newspaper reports that Bölkow had not only achieved the desired goal of lessened congestion—at no extra cost—but had estimated that it was saving some forty thousand dollars a month through increased productivity and lowered absenteeism brought an avalanche of inquiries from other German companies.

Floating work hours spread quickly in Germany with one estimate that over two thousand firms there have now adopted it. Recently, the government put its Transportation Ministry on the system as an experiment to see if it could be applied throughout all government offices. By 1972, 5 percent of the German workforce was participating. The rate of conversion has been even greater in Switzerland, where in the same year, 30 percent of the industrial workers were picking their own hours. Meanwhile, extensive experimentation has begun in Holland, Japan, England, France, and the Scandinavian countries.

A prime instance of *gleitende arbeitzeit* (gliding worktime) in operation is at the headquarters of Lufthansa Airlines in Cologne, where it was introduced in 1970. For all but a few employees, the official workday is twelve hours long, from 7:00 A.M. to 7:00 P.M. One can arrive anytime between 7:00 and 9:30 in the morning and leave anytime after 2:30. The catch is that a full forty-two-hour workweek, the German norm, must be completed, but this, too, is flexible, as workers have a 10 percent leeway each month. Minus hours can be made up the next month, and extra hours can be "banked" as credit for a day off the next month. Time cards are still in use, but their main function is to aid employees in figuring out how many hours ahead or behind they are. Occasionally, the time cards are spot-checked by the company, but for the most part, the system depends on the workers' own calculations.

Since introducing the system at its new headquarters, Lufthansa has brought gliding worktime to as much of its domain as possible, and it now embraces six thousand of its workers in Germany alone. As with the four-day week, there are limitations. Lufthansa had to draw the line in some areas—most notably for its flight crews—but the company is looking into modified versions of the plan for possible use among its maintenance and reservations staff (presumably some sort of flexible system under which the employees guarantee that the public will not be kept waiting).

The Lufthansa experience has been overwhelmingly positive. Flex-time has cut traffic jams coming in and out of the building, which is primarily what it was intended to do. Absenteeism is down and a Lufthansa personnel officer told a reporter from *The New York Times* recently, "We've virtually done away with one-day sickness." The problem of the chronically tardy worker has almost disappeared, of course, as it is now downright difficult to be tardy. Lufthansa, along with others who have adopted the system, reports that the plan has also made recruiting much easier. In particular, it has served to entice mothers with school-age children back into the labor market because, under it, they can juggle their schedules to handle the duties of motherhood, such as getting junior off to his 3:30 dentist appointment. These additional job applicants are particularly significant for a company in West Germany, where there has been a severe labor shortage.

Of all Lufthansa's results, the most impressive is the near-universal nod of approval the gliding workday has gotten from the workers involved. In April 1971—about a year after it was introduced—the four thousand workers then working under the system in Germany were polled. Not one registered a serious protest of any kind against it, 98 percent said they liked it and 95 percent said it had been helpful in regulating the rhythm of their lives. The poll also revealed that it was eliminating a half hour or more of commuting time for 23 percent of the workers and that 65 percent had used it to accrue time for free days off.

Also significant is the poll taken among Lufthansa's managers at the same time which showed that 39 percent of them felt it had increased efficiency in their departments, 55 percent felt efficiency was unchanged, and only 6 percent felt it had decreased.

Unlike in Cologne, where the system was first introduced as an experiment, its incarnation at the company's North American headquarters in East Meadow, Long Island, took place in 1970 as a permanent operating procedure. Because of New York State labor laws which require overtime payment for any hours worked over forty in the same week, there is no leeway here for coming up short one week and long another, but in other respects, the system is like the one in Germany. David Buisch, personnel manager for Lufthansa's North and Central American Divisions, says that, in all probability, an attempt will be made in the near future to work out some sort of an accommodation with the state so that even the week-to-week flexibility of the system can be introduced.

While the American version is not yet as liberal as its European prototype, it shows all indications of being just as successful. Says the very enthusiastic Buisch, "The results have been outstanding. To name the most obvious thing, it has given our people the ability to figure out and deal with automobile traffic, and this has relieved frustration so people don't come in all tied up in knots." He also feels that it has heightened the individual responsibility of workers, fostered greater teamwork, and contributed to higher morale. Like his counterparts in Germany, he reports that word of the system has gotten around and that he is getting job applications from people who would prefer to work a gliding workday. Although he has no statistics to prove it, he believes that it has contributed to lowered absenteeism and that it may have been a factor in increased productivity. Buisch also feels that it has been a positive force in public relations, by adding to Lufthansa's reputation as an innovative outfit.

Since granting his employees the option of coming in anytime between 8–10:00 and checking out between 4–6:00, Buisch has seen some definite work patterns emerge. In the summer months, for example, more people tend to come in early and leave early so they can get off in time for golf, tennis, or a few hours at the beach. Housewives also tend to come in earlier to get home earlier. About half the workers tend to switch their hours from day to day, while the other half are relatively steady in their habits, whether it be 10–6:00 or 8–4:00. (Buisch adds that the "steadys" seem to be the type of suburbanite who never goes to Manhattan while the "swingers" go often.) The overall impact of these patterns has been favorable; Buisch says that because the various patterns tend to average out, there is never any problem with coverage in various departments.

One accommodation which was made for the system was the creation of departmental secretarial pools so that there would never be a problem in providing a secretary when one was needed. Buisch feels that this move in itself has been advantageous, and that if for any reason the gliding workday was ever dropped, the pools would be kept. "We believe that this has had an enriching effect on the secretaries, who now have a much wider world in which to work and a better idea of what is going on. It has also proven to be more efficient, as they have a steady flow of work." *

Another American subsidiary of a European company which has successfully transplanted the idea is Sandoz-Wander of East Hanover, New Jersey. Its parent firm, Sandoz Ltd. of Basel, Switzerland, made a daring innovation when introducing the system by taking away the time clock and putting its workers on an honor system in which employees keep their own records.

* Others would debate this conclusion; many observers feel that pooling people is a sure-fire way to give them a feeling of rootlessness.

The Swiss version—honor system and all—was introduced as an experiment involving one hundred seventy-five workers of the American Colors and Chemicals Division in July 1972. After six months, the system was made permanent for those employees, and since then, thirteen hundred other workers have been put on flex-time, with the remaining 30 percent of the workforce now experimenting with variant time systems. One such variation was put into operation in the company's research and development department: Workers may come and go at anytime they wish, so that if a person works best from 6:00 P.M. to midnight, he or she can probably work then. I say "probably" because this system works under the proviso that the worker must get an ok for such erratic hours from his or her supervisor. It is unlike the new system in force for most of the rest of the company, in that the rest must work during certain block times during the day (9:30–Noon and 2:00–4:00 P.M.), but within those blocks can begin and end their days at times which do not have to be checked out with supervisors.

Sandoz-Wander's basic system is slightly more flexible than others in force in most other American sites because it allows workers to bank up to ten hours in advance, or to go into debt for up to ten hours. Here is the company's listing of time periods allowed:

Earliest starting time:	7:30 A.M.
Latest starting time:	9:30 A.M.
Earliest leaving time:	4:00 P.M.
Latest leaving time:	6:00 P.M.
Lunch period:	12:00–2:00 P.M.
Maximum lunch period:	2 hours
Minimum lunch period:	1 hour
Block time (or time each employee is required to be present):	9:30–12:00 Noon 2:00–4:00 P.M.
Average workweek:	37.5 hours

Maximum workweek:	40 hours (unless overtime is authorized)
Minimum workweek:	22.5 hours (if at least +5 hours have been accumulated)
Average workday:	7.5 hours
Maximum workday:	9.5 hours
Minimum workday:	4.5 hours

Just as at Lufthansa, reaction to the system at Sandoz-Wander has been overwhelmingly positive. During the experimental phase, a poll of workers revealed that 92 percent of them wanted it to be made permanent. Although the company acknowledges initial reluctance over the system among supervisors—many of whom felt it was a threat to their authority—a poll among supervisors administered two months into the experimental period revealed that 91 percent felt they had not lost control over their subordinates, 82 percent found their role as supervisor the same or improved, 79 percent felt that production scheduling was as easy or easier than before, and 38 percent felt that production had increased. None felt that production had suffered.

As a corporate matter, Sandoz-Wander has given the idea its fullest sanction and has even prepared a report on its experiences which it is distributing to potential flex-time companies in the United States. The report stresses improved attitude and morale and increased productivity as rewards of the system. The report describes how individuals become better workers under flex-time: ". . . a secretary may work a shorter day when her boss is out of town and make up the time later when the workload is heavier. Similarly, a laboratory worker who cannot start a new experiment an hour before quitting time because the chemicals will not keep overnight, can leave work an hour early instead of using the time unproductively."

Summing up his assessment of the system, personnel boss Donald Kuhn says, "I think that the most important thing to

Breaking the Time Barriers

come out of this is that the people who work here now have an added feeling that they are trusted adults. In a sense, I think it has affected management more than the workers because the people who work here have responded so well to flex-time that management is now looking at added freedoms it can start giving."

Kuhn believes that an important part of the success of flex-time at Sandoz-Wander is the honor system that goes with it. "In the year and a half since starting, we have found no reason to worry about the system. In fact, the closest thing we've had to a problem in all that time among over one thousand employees was a complaint from a supervisor that a person had come in early and had not done much work, but this was not really a problem of the honor system, but a simple matter of not working—which the supervisor should have taken care of." He goes on to say:

> No matter what system you have, if a person wants to cheat he will find a way. Also, under an honor system you have the added check of peer pressure. It's not that workers are consciously checking on one another, but rather because the flexible system requires people to coordinate more with one another, and a co-worker is going to know when you come and go. I know that people here like the system and want it to continue—they have told me this often—so therefore I believe that there is pressure not to cheat.

Of the companies to adopt flex-time in America, the largest of the early converts is the Hewlett-Packard Company, the large electronics combine headquartered in Palo Alto, California. It had first tried the idea in a German plant in 1967, tried it again in a facility in Scotland, and tested it on American soil at its medical electronics division in Waltham, Massachusetts. Convinced of its worth, in early 1973, it decided to give all divisions the green light. Larry Motzkus, Hewlett-Packard Corporate Benefits and Compensation manager, estimates that fifteen thousand of the company's twenty-five thousand employees were on flexible hours by July 1973, and that the number has since increased steadily.

The Hewlett-Packard system requires one to work an eight-hour day (there is no banking ahead or going into debt), with a person in a typical situation being able to come in between 6–8:30 A.M. and leaving between 3–5:30 P.M. It also features an honor system, with hourly workers keeping track of their own hours. Larry Motzkus says, "There have been no problems so far, and we are very pleased with it. We have no firm information on how it has affected productivity in the company, but we know it hasn't dropped and think it has gone up. Frankly, we feel that the primary reason to have flexible hours is to improve morale. We know that this has happened."

Other early experimenters in the United States have had similar results, and are just as sold on the system as Lufthansa, Sandoz-Wander and Hewlett-Packard. The Nestlé Company of White Plains, New York, introduced flex-time in the summer of 1972 as an experiment and because of its initial success has extended it to year-round operations. According to S. T. Forbath, assistant to the president, "Our experience has been that both supervisors and employees seem to like the system which, in many cases, has solved employees' problems which previously proved troublesome, such as getting children to school or being home when they come from school, car pools, coping with rush-hour traffic, and so on." Another convert is the General Radio Company of Concord, Massachusetts, which introduced the gliding system as an experiment in May 1972 and liked it so much that it lost its experimental status after a few weeks. Personnel administrator John R. Herbert tells why: "It didn't take long to see that absenteeism was down, productivity up, recruiting easier, and the general state of mind in the company was improved."

Despite early successes in America, and broad European

experimentation, the number of American companies to implement flex-time has been small. It is still an idea primarily tied to Europe, and thus far, many of those companies which have introduced the idea in the United States have been European-based companies with American operations or else American companies which began working with it in their overseas plants.

The American total is growing, however. Janice Hedges, who has been monitoring flex-time at the Department of Labor, estimated the total number of American applications to have been less than a dozen in May 1973. A year later, she estimated a new total of over one hundred organizations, with a collective employment of around twenty thousand people. That estimate might be conservative; Donald Kuhn says that he is convinced that others are implementing it quietly without announcing what they are doing. "I know of several companies keeping it under wraps for the time being for two basic reasons. First, there is an awful lot of curiosity about this and they don't want to be bothered with a lot of inquiries at this point and, second, after all the prematurely glowing reports on the four-day workweek, people involved in experimental schedules have become more conservative and careful before making such announcements."

Even though there are not yet that many Americans working a flexible day, American interest is very strong. A briefing on flex-time conducted by the American Management Association in April 1973 attracted representatives from over sixty interested companies. Lufthansa's Buisch says that news of his airline's way of working has prompted ". . . a never-ending stream of inquiries from other companies"—a point that he makes graphic by fanning through a pile of letters from a broad sampling of American industry. And Sandoz-Wander has handled hundreds of requests for a copy of the report on its system.

The idea has its drawbacks and unanswered questions, one of which is suggested by Janice Hedges when she points out that a plant or office that stays open extra hours to accommodate flex-time will use more energy. However, she is quick to add that certain shortages can *help* flex-time. The gasoline shortage that hit its peak in early 1974, she says, actually led to more conversions, because employers felt that a flexible day would give their workers a better opportunity to find an open gas station. Many who converted for this reason stayed with it when it was easier to get gas because they had discovered that their employees wanted to keep it. "My concern is for the long run," she says. "If utility rates go too high in some areas, I think there will be an impact." Others, however, debate the point. Kuhn says the energy consideration is ". . . minimal at best," explaining, "Most plants and offices don't shut off their heat or air conditioning at five because of clean-up people and people working late and always have these things on in the morning well before people come in. Also, if a person comes in an hour early and turns on his light, he will also turn it off an hour early when he goes home." He points out that, in deference to the crisis, his company has been prodding its workforce to save energy, with the net result that (he is convinced) its operations use less electricity than before flexible hours. Motzkus of Hewlett-Packard basically agrees that it has had not much, if any, impact on his company, but adds, "Of course, we don't rely on heavy equipment, and this might make a difference if we were a heavy industry."

There is little question that the point Dr. Hedges raises will be debated and studied as flex-time gains in popularity. If, as time passes, the energy issue is one merely of more expensive energy rather than a serious shortage entailing energy rationing, the cost of extra hours may be relatively small in comparison to labor costs and so flexible worktime may prove worthwhile in terms of morale, productivity, and other advantages claimed for it. For the time being, at least, the external influence of the energy shortage poses an important and unresolved question.

One of the major inherent drawbacks to flex-time thus far has been its apparent inapplicability to certain work situations.

Breaking the Time Barriers 239

While it will take considerable imagination to find a way for it to work for flight crews and others with strict schedules, flex-time is, however, finding its way into some seemingly impossible areas. Until recently, conventional wisdom said that the assembly line could not employ the system, for the simple reason that the work of one person was dependent upon the work of others. Recently, though, Omega Watches of Switzerland solved the problem by placing ample buffer stock at each point along the line. Its productivity dropped a bit but quality jumped enough under the new system to produce a gain. In an attempt at a different solution, an experiment is now underway at Tandberg, the Norwegian electronics firm, in which the gliding workday is being extended to workers in a television assembly area. The key to this plan—and the reason why it took a long time to start—is that each worker has to know a whole set of jobs on his or her section of the line, thereby permitting workers to fill in for each other. This flexibility demands a long period of training but, if it works, will give workers two new freedoms at once: flex-time and job rotation.

Imagination goes a long way in extending flex-time to new areas, as the Omega and Tandberg solutions show. Another such application of the gliding workday to an area where superficially it would not seem feasible is at a foundry where large industrial furnaces are operated by teams. For this situation, the Swiss firm of Sulzer Frères has created the "floating team," by which a team of foundrymen agree on the group's starting time for the next morning before leaving at night.

As for flex-time's other disadvantages, most of them seem to be minor and of a temporal nature. First, there is the fear that it will have an adverse impact on internal communications. But this rarely becomes an actual problem, and some who have introduced flex-time claim that it works to enhance, rather than detract from such communication. Another factor is the initial resistance that the idea can find among supervisors and managers—perhaps stemming, in part, from resentment that this new system tends to give others the kind of freedom from rigidity which has been exclusively theirs. Administrative costs are also a factor, as new methods of record-keeping are called for and people normally have to be made available to answer questions about the system.

One possible solution to supervisor resistance, at least, is a product being marketed by the Flextime Corporation, a New York-based subsidiary of Hengstler AB, a large German manufacturer of counting machines. Hengstler builds a special time clock for flex-time application, and has worked in Europe to market the idea and the product. Its hardware, called an "automatic personal time totalizer," is basically a clock connected to a panel of individual slots—one for each employee. Each worker is given a coded plastic card which he pushes into the slot to activate the counter when he arrives at work. The card is then taken out at the end of the day or when he leaves for lunch. What makes this clock different is that it does not record starting and stopping times; rather, it displays a running total which began at the beginning of an accounting period. For example, a person coming in on Friday and sees 35.4 hours displayed for his card knows that he has only 4.6 hours to go to complete forty hours. Besides giving an employee the amount of time spent and time owed, this system lets supervisors see if anyone is abusing the system. Before announcing its presence in the United States, the Flextime Corporation worked on two pilot projects: one with the Industrial National Bank of Providence, Rhode Island, and another with a small New York publisher, the Alexander Hamilton Institute, Inc. Both reported a series of improvements—from increased productivity to better morale.*

---

* Hopefully, Flextime will be able to restrain itself as it gets rolling so as not to oversell the idea. Unfortunately, it came on the scene hyping itself with embarrassing vigor. A flashy, expensive brochure it gives out, called "A New Work Style for a New Life Style," carries a bird motif all the way through (à la *Jonathan Livingston Seagull*) as a symbol of the

No doubt the Flextime Corporation hardware will spark debate as the idea gains and philosophies clash. The company is promoting its new time clock as a necessity, but to Donald Kuhn, who is sold on the honor system as part of the flex-time liberation, the use of such a device amounts to ". . . replacing one set of childlike rules with another."

One aspect of flex-time which will increasingly stand it in good stead is its favorable reception by trade unionists—unlike the compressed workweek, which attracted much union animosity in the United States because of its reversion to the rigors of ten-hour days. In Germany, for example, some of the unions have adopted an attitude of wait and see, neither hindering or promoting its implementation, while others have embraced it. One union has introduced it into its own offices. Great Britain, with its highly volatile labor situation, provides another interesting example. When, in 1972, a few companies had begun to experiment with it there, it was predicted that it would be held to a handful of maverick firms where there were no unions, or weak ones. After checking around, the *Sunday Telegraph* reported, in early 1972, that ". . . opposition from British unions is liable to be strong." A year and a few months later, another British paper, the *Evening Mail*, was able to report that the number of British firms which had adopted the idea had gone from no known example, in early 1971, to over one hundred fifty organizations representing twenty thousand workers by the spring of 1973, and that ". . . their popularity has been stimulated by the white-collar unions." Similarly, a report from a Scottish newspaper in the same month said that the idea was catching on fast in the Edinburgh

---

freedom it is selling. The text uses just about every buzzword now in vogue to push the idea—e.g., "quality of life," "job enrichment," "human resources," and "social responsibility" (one wonders how it missed "environmental quality"). Its initial press release claims that the company had, by way of the announcement, "introduced formally" the concept of flex-time to the United States. This is a convoluted and misleading claim resting on the vagueness of the word "formally."

insurance industry, in large part due to the push it was getting from ASTMS (the Association of Scientific, Technical, and Managerial Staffs), the biggest union in the industry.

It would be a bit premature to predict how American organized labor will react to flex-time as it gets going. With so many unions plumping for fewer, rather than looser, hours, it may become a secondary issue. If Europe can be used for clues, along with a few initial reactions from American labor, it should come in for a lot of hard questioning. It is difficult, however, to see where any serious labor-management snags will occur. One early positive signal occurred in Baltimore in 1973, when it was proposed by a councilman that the city government enter into a series of flex-time experiments. The resolution was passed by the council with the enthusiastic endorsement of both the concept and the proposal by the Classified Municipal Employees Association of Baltimore City.

From all available reports, the advantages of this system far outweigh any of its disadvantages. This seems to be borne out by the fact that the author was unable to find anyone among the people he talked to about flex-time who could cite an example of a company in the United States or Europe which had tried it and dropped it. Although one should assume that there must be a few who have quit, there has evidently been no significant number of them. Willi Haller, the man directing activities for Hengstler Flextime, has said, "Virtually no enterprise that has seriously tried flex-time is willing to return to the old rigid schedule." He adds melodramatically, "Flextime may have been revolutionary when it was introduced, but workers now would probably stage a revolution if they were taken off flexible hours once they have experienced them." Donald Kuhn's position is, "If you introduce flex-time, you can never go back to the old system."

The importance of flex-time is that it is becoming the number-two punch in a one-two punch assault on worktime rigidity which was led off with the sudden flurry of interest in the four-day workweek. Only time will tell, but from its initial and widespread success in Europe and the enthusiasm it has begun to create among its American converts, the second blow may be more damaging than the first—assuming, of course, that it is not seriously hampered by the energy pinch.

But these are just the beginnings of what can become a more devastating assault on standard worktimes. If the workweek can be compressed and flexed, so, too, can it be sliced in half and carved up to meet the needs of those who see the full forty-hour week as an anachronistic barrier to a fulfilling life—as we shall now see.

4

PAIRING, SHARING, AND SPLITTING— BRINGING ON THE PERMANENT PART-TIMER

Catalyst is a nonprofit organization dedicated to the idea that today's college-educated woman should not have to make that old and tired choice between family and career. Its reason for being is to open the doors that will permit women to be active in both spheres at once. It was founded in 1962 by five college presidents and an energetic woman named Felice Schwartz, who serves today as its president.

For more than a decade now, it has served as the combined information clearing house, think tank, pressure group and source of inspiration for untapping what iconoclastic executive Robert Townsend has termed "the largest untapped labor source in America today." It has sponsored research into the availability of women for part-time careers, launched projects to show the advantage of the permanent part-timer, and supplied thousands of women with the needed "how to's" of getting back into the job market (its master blueprint is a guidebook entitled *How to Go to Work When Your Husband Is Against It, Your Children Aren't Old Enough, and There's Nothing You Can Do Anyhow*).

The key to the Catalyst program is the fervent belief that traditional work patterns are outdated and need to be subverted; its stock in trade is uncovering new options in life. The impact of the ideas which it is pioneering bid not only to have a major effect on its client group of fourteen million college-educated women, but could go a long way in changing the lot of others, such as, to cite one possibility, freeing many men from the sole responsibility for breadwinning.

At the heart of today's Catalyst program is the need for new forms of work to support the permanent part-timer. To this end, Catalyst has identified five new categories of work. While each of these variations on the standard work situation exists today on a very minor and informal scale, it is Catalyst's hope to make them commonplace. These targeted work formats are:

Paired or Partnership Work. Two people fill one full-time, full-day job with equally shared responsibility for time on the job and the subject matter at hand. A good example of an easily paired job is that of an elementary school teacher. In such situations, two part-time workers cover one job in two sessions. Such pairing has its advantages; for example, one teacher can easily cover for the other in case of illness and each can bring complementary skills to the job.

Shared Work. Two people divide a job with each taking responsibility for half the total work. Unlike paired work, the two do not necessarily have to split the day; rather, they split the total workload of a single job, making this method ideally suited to work parceled out in individual assignments or cases. It is clearly not suited to schoolteaching, but easily fits welfare casework.

Split-location Work. Simply, a job in which work is done both at the office and at home. One's work schedule is defined in advance, so that appointments can be held at the office. Such jobs can either be part- or full-time. The advantage of this method is that a woman can hold a job and yet be at home when family responsibilities so demand.

Split-level Work. One full-time job is analyzed into its functional components. It is seen that the skills involved require distinctly different levels of training and ability and can be split along these lines. A case in point would be a full-time job in which a person is required to compose letters as well as type them in their final form; this job could be naturally split into two jobs: for a part-time writer and a part-time secretary.

Specialist. The person takes on a single aspect of a job which requires less than full-time employment, such as a teacher of a specialized subject not in heavy demand or the editor of a house organ for a small company.

Catalyst's contention is that these now-rare formats are destined to become more and more common in the future, and it is doing all that it can to push, publicize, and demonstrate them. According to Felice Schwartz, two factors are presently working against Catalyst. "First, there is the general state of the economy which does not encourage new hiring. What is more, our intention is not to go out and kill full-time jobs. Second, there is the inertia of employers." She explains that most of the hundreds of employers which Catalyst has contacted generally find what Catalyst is proposing to be feasible and fascinating—yet pull up short of actually hiring.

Nonetheless, Felice Schwartz is optimistic about seeing a breakthrough in the near future. Just as corporate inertia and the economy work against Catalyst, there are positive trends working for it. One is the increasing pressure to hire women for increasingly meaningful and responsible jobs. Another is the changing attitude toward working mothers. Most important, however, is the logic which lies behind pairing, sharing, and the other variant schemes. "The appeal of what we advocate is not philanthropic but economic," says Mrs. Schwartz. "Our message is that we are presenting ideas which will enable companies and public agencies to get more for their money."

What Catalyst has determined—which is the punch line to its message—is that the permanent part-timer can easily become proportionally more productive and less liable to leave her job than her full-time counterpart. The mathematics of a shared job is that two half-timers add up to more than one full-timer. This assertion is not a glibly tossed off bit of overenthusiasm, but is backed by solid documentation.

One major Catalyst work-sharing demonstration project has been conducted in conjunction with the Massachusetts Department of Public Welfare. Working with the United States Department of Health, Education and Welfare, Catalyst began hunting for a proving ground for work sharing in 1963. The welfare departments in all fifty states were contacted and four years of discussions were held with nine of them—interested but reluctant—when at last Massachusetts agreed to let Catalyst recruit and train fifty half-timers to fill twenty-five full-time positions. It was decided that the experiment would last for two years and be evaluated by an outside consultant.

Starting in May 1968, Catalyst began recruiting for part-time caseworkers. Some fifteen hundred inquiries were received before Catalyst stopped counting. Applications and inquiries continued to come in during the two years of the project—graphically demonstrating the vast pool of qualified women ready for meaningful part-time employment. That was the end of the presumption on the part of many observers that comfortably situated housewives would not leave their suburban nests for welfare work in the inner city. Of the final fifty who were qualified and selected, the statistically "typical" woman was a forty-five-year-old college-graduate mother with three children in their early teens. On the average, it had been fourteen years since she had held her last job. All those selected were assigned to offices in Boston, and nearly all were assigned to Aid to Families

Breaking the Time Barriers

with Dependent Children (AFDC) cases. Each was offered the choice of two schedules: either five hours a day for four days a week, or two full days plus one half day a week. Because of family obligations, most chose the four-day schedule. After the women had been trained, the project ran for two years, from September 1968 to September 1970.

The results were dramatic. The turnover rate among the women was 13 percent as opposed to the usual 40 percent; the half-timers were carrying an average of forty-two cases as compared to an average of seventy-eight for full-timers. The Catalyst group, on the average, had 89 percent (not the expected 50 percent) as many face-to-face contacts with clients as the full-timers, and averaged 20 percent *more* (rather than 50 percent less) telephone contacts with their clients.

The high level of performance of the part-timers did not just show up on paper and in the statistics. Some two dozen evaluation sessions held with supervisors and administrators—many of whom had opposed the part-time program at first—yielded some interesting observations. Almost all praised the work of the Catalyst workers, and it was generally felt that these forty-five-year-old (on the average) part-timers had added stability to the pool of generally younger caseworkers, whose mean age was 29.4 years. As one supervisor put it, "They spend less time than their full-time counterparts in expressing anger about the system . . . and are therefore free to devote their energies to work with clients." Another supervisor gave this testimonial to stability in a paper she delivered at a meeting of the American Public Welfare Association:

> The young social workers come to the Agency from all over the country. In most instances, this is their first job, although not their first time away from home. These workers did find a "mother image" in the Catalyst. For example, one young worker probably never could have survived the emotional trauma resulting from an office

demonstration without the understanding patience and support from one of the Catalysts.

It was generally agreed that welfare clients related extremely well to these women who had children of their own, and who talked frequently with their clients about their children's education. It was also observed that the half-time group was able to maintain a level of effort hard for others to keep up for eight hours a day, five days a week—strongly suggesting that the shortened day has real advantage in a job requiring great emotional and intellectual energy.

Standing alone on the negative side of the ledger are a few problems which cropped up when the new workers first came into their new offices. There was some general resistance and misunderstanding—especially strong at one office where the existing staff had not been briefed in advance (because it had not been originally scheduled to receive part-timers). At this office, the supervisors feared extra duties and uncovered cases, while full-time caseworkers there were so rattled that one even feared the part-timers were spies, and some of the others were convinced that they were getting a full week's salary for a half week's work. However, even at this problem office, the problems of misunderstanding disappeared with time and explanation, giving way to cooperation and mutual trust.

The lesson from the Massachusetts project is a compelling one: An eager, easily trained and untapped resource is available and ready for quick productivity. Despite this lesson and the intrinsic success of the project itself, though, the spin-off from the project has been local and less than overwhelming. Almost all of the Boston caseworkers have stayed on—some converting to full-time billets as family responsibilities have diminished—and the Connecticut Department of Public Welfare has begun to offer part-time casework positions, but there has been no other breakthrough in job sharing in welfare offices or in other fields that operate on a casework basis.

Breaking the Time Barriers

Another Catalyst effort, undertaken in the late 1960s, reveals the value of part-timers as teachers. Instead of sponsoring demonstrations, Catalyst examined existing examples of school systems that used part-time teachers (a part-time teacher being defined as one who works regularly on a part-time schedule, and who is not to be confused with the substitute teacher who fills in when needed). The study, made in 1967, concentrated on five diverse communities which had adopted the practice of hiring part-time teachers.*

Of the five school systems investigated, the most unusual was in Framingham, Massachusetts, where a paired, or partnership, plan was in effect. Started in 1965 by the Woman's Education and Industrial Union of Boston and Framingham and seven other cooperating Massachusetts communities, it had gotten off to an impressive start. Within the first two years, more than eight hundred women had applied for pairing, and the Union had placed some one hundred twenty teaching partnerships. The idea, tested and proven here, was that two teachers could easily split the day into two equal sessions—with equal responsibility for planning, curriculum innovation, dealing with parents, and extracurricular activities.

As administrator of the program, the Women's Union recruited teachers, sorted them by preferences for morning or afternoon sessions, and paired them so as to complement skills and keep them fairly close to each other by home location. (The Union felt that since the pair would need to phone each other frequently, they should live close enough to avoid toll calls.) Pairings were made in the spring, so the partnership could

---

* Earlier, in 1965, Catalyst conducted a poll of seven hundred-odd school systems in order to sample the attitude toward part-timers. The poll yielded one striking result: The superintendents of the schools which employed no part-time teachers were cold to the idea and expressed a wide range of objections, but the reaction of the superintendents in the nearly three hundred school systems which did use part-timers was overwhelmingly favorable.

develop its plans and curriculum during the summer. An all-day orientation session was held just before the start of school.

The Catalyst study of pairings in Framingham yielded a host of pluses. Parents and PTA officials stressed such points as the benefit for children in having two teachers, that each teacher concentrates on her specialty, and that a fresh teacher comes in at noon. One principal phoned six parents of first-graders being taught by a partnership and found them all positively impressed even though three of them admitted they did not like the idea when they first heard about it. Administrators, too, were impressed with the total impact of two teachers. "They're part-time on payday only. We get about two-thirds of a teacher for half-time pay," said one principal. Another expressed the belief that each partner tended to put in as much preparation time as if each were working full time. Other virtues of the arrangement mentioned by administrators included the benefit of parents getting two points of view on their child, the ability of the two to cover for each other in the case of illness, and the tendency of partnership teachers to put more time than expected into extracurricular activities. The full-time teachers contacted showed no resentment toward the partnerships—in fact, one of them hoped that the partnership option would be open to her when she herself got older. The paired teachers spoke almost exclusively of the positive values of the arrangement, both in terms of personal satisfaction and practical advantages. One teacher made an interesting point by quoting one of her students as saying, "If the morning teacher is down on you, you always have a change in the afternoon." By this and other accounts, the children took well to the system. In one class, some of the children adapted by addressing each teacher by both names, as if they were hyphenated.

Since Catalyst investigated Framingham in 1967, pairing has started in other Massachusetts schools and in several other systems across the nation.

Breaking the Time Barriers 251

The other four communities in the original Catalyst study, taken together, serve to show other ways in which the part-time teacher can play an important role in the schools. Cedar Falls, Iowa, had been using part-timers for over a decade as teachers for high-school subjects which did not require a full-time teacher, as specialists to work with small groups that had fallen behind, and as part-time administrators. The community had one novel partnership arrangement: A teacher of retirement age was forestalling her retirement to share a sixth grade with a woman with one year's experience—the older teacher called it a "wonderful transition to full retirement." In one of several applications in Miami, Florida a high-school principal was bringing in part-timers to enrich the curriculum. One woman was brought in to teach Chinese and Asian studies; another was teaching Arabic. In the case of the Chinese teacher, the principal was using a nonaccredited specialist, but was able to bypass the rules and hire her because she was brought in for a noncredit course. The Detroit school system, suffering an acute shortage of teachers, employed over four hundred part-timers to meet the emergency. Retired teachers were being brought back two days a week to teach remedial reading, and others, who could not work full-time, were splitting classes on a three- and two-day basis. Niskayuna, New York, a suburban Schenectady community, had been using part-timers to reduce class sizes and to teach special subjects where a full-timer was not needed.

Lumping together the five experiences, Catalyst was able also to conclude that part-timers are more apt to stay put than teachers in general, that they are not more prone to absenteeism than full-timers—and frequently are less so—and that their contributions have been widely applauded by administrators who felt they were getting their money's worth—or more. It was generally determined that the use of part-timers eases school scheduling rather than complicating it. A typical comment on this came from a principal in Niskayuna, who said, "We have pieces of jobs that don't really fit together and that's where the part-time teachers come in handy. It allows me to schedule better."

Catalyst also felt that there was an even broader variety of part-time applications and scheduling arrangements than showed up in the five diverse situations studied. For example, at the time of the study, Cedar Falls was planning to introduce the use of part-time librarians in its schools. It was concluded that of the different reasons for hiring part-time teachers—from Framingham's urge to innovate to Detroit's need to keep a system *in extremis* from going under—the reasons most likely to lead ultimately to success have to do with improving the quality of education, rather than emergency needs or expediency. Finally, Catalyst concluded that the obstacles to greater use of part-time teachers were extrinsic to the proven ability and actual performance of the women in question. Mistaken preconceptions on the part of administrators, inflexible rules on the use of retired teachers, and rigid certification requirements are the commonest hurdles. For instance, one of the problems faced by Niskayuna in trying to hire more part-time teachers was New York State certification rules. In a classic case of bureaucratic inflexibility, the Catalyst study revealed the plight of a teacher who could not be hired part-time because she had not *taken* one course needed for certification. She had, however, taught the course as a college teacher.

In addition to these major demonstrations in welfare casework and education, Catalyst has launched other experiments to show the soundness of its ideas. One of the most recent was the "Westchester Project," which sought to show that, with proper counseling for the applicants and a little pressure on employers, it could place a number of part-timers in diverse fields. While it accomplished its limited goal of placing a fairly small number of women, its major result was unexpected: the vast number of women uncovered who were ready for part-time employment. Despite the fact that it was not that well publicized and that it was limited to women in Westchester County, over fifteen thousand women contacted the organization during the eight months of the project to make it known that they were interested in reentering the job market on a less than full-time basis.

Increasingly, Catalyst is moving beyond projects which merely demonstrate its ideas to actions which will enable those ideas to be implemented on a national basis. One step toward this is a computer-based registry of women available for part-time work which has currently begun to function. A periodical lists women in many fields on a line-by-line basis, with a typical entry giving the person's job title, years of experience, salary range, preferred location, and highest academic degree. There are several reasons behind this national roster. "For one thing, it will serve as a tool for representing the number of women available," says Felice Schwartz. "As we come up with many women chemists, we are no longer going to hear that there are too few women looking for part-time jobs as chemists to bother with." It will work as an actual talent guide, enabling a personnel officer to find a pharmacologist in Des Moines, for example. It will also serve as a place where potential pairers and sharers can find each other.

Catalyst is also working through an ever-expanding network of local "resource" units, which are either existing groups such as women's centers, YWCA's, and counseling centers, or new groups which have come into being to work for new worktime arrangements on local levels. Such groups as New Ways to Work of Palo Alto, the Boston Project for Careers, Project Eve of Cleveland, Options for Women in Philadelphia, and close to fifty others are now part of the Catalyst network.

One of the local groups pushing to create new positions is Washington Opportunities for Women (WOW), which has been working to open part-time employment in the government. One of WOW's clients is Mrs. Marie Malero, an attorney with two small children, who came to them to help her get a part-time job. She and another woman attorney were encouraged to apply for a job at the Smithsonian Institution as Assistant General Counsel, and were subsequently hired as a pair to fill the job. For these two, sharing turned out to be a way to get into other jobs; today they hold two *separate* part-time positions. "This is the kind of job that really can't be shared in the sense that one picks up where the other left off," Mrs. Malero says of her later position. As to how it has worked out: "I really think that the Smithsonian is getting a great deal, because I consistently get more than a half-day's work done. I do much of my work at home in free hours in addition to office time."

As a permanent part-timer, Marie Malero is a rarity in the government, which has hardly moved in this area. However, there is a move afoot to change the situation. Legislation called the "Flexible Hours Employment Act" has been introduced in the Senate by John Tunney (D.–Cal.) and in the House by Bella Abzug (D.–N.Y.), which would require that 10 percent of all Civil Service jobs be opened in the next five years to people who want to work on a less than full-time schedule, whether it be for a half-day five days a week, two full days a week, or whatever. The intent of the bill is not only to open government service jobs to mothers, students, and the handicapped who can only work part time but, in Tunney's words, ". . . hopefully would serve as a model to be emulated by private and other public employees."

Meanwhile, as such major proposals as this bill begin to circulate, Catalyst is working on some of the logistics problems which could arise as new time arrangements become more common. One such question is, How does an employer handle fringe benefits when two are holding down one job? Catalyst knows that employers are not going to be willing to give away two full collections of benefits for two part-timers, and so is now working on a set of alternative options which could be presented by the applicants when a job is being approached. These packages will amount to carefully worked out details of several approaches. Catalyst is now cooperating with labor leaders, personnel experts and professional arbitrators to refine these packages. One of the most promising alternatives being worked on is that of the "shopping basket," or á la carte, approach, in which each benefit is prorated to a certain cash value and the two part-timers are given equal credits to shop for a tailored half-package of benefits. Under this system, both, one, or neither of the two persons sharing a job may use their credits to buy hospitalization insurance or whatever.

Of course, many of the social and economic forces which could bring on the day when the permanent part-timer is common lie beyond Catalyst's powers to manipulate. For instance, a period in which there was a shortage of skilled workers and professionals would send employers scurrying for able bodies no matter what schedule they wanted to work. Nonetheless, until that occurs, Catalyst is doing all it can to advance its ideas and to demonstrate their feasibility. This includes the way its own offices operate. Although not billed as such, Catalyst's Manhattan office may serve as its most convincing demonstration project. Eight of the ten women who work there are part-timers, and the two full-timers are "split-location" workers. Then there is chief Catalyst agent, Schwartz, who, between graduation from college, when she helped found the National Scholarship Service Fund for Negro Students, and the founding of Catalyst, raised three children—underscoring the essence of the productive premise behind Catalyst.

While Catalyst has chosen to serve a particular clientele of married, college-educated women, the lessons it is trying to teach bid to have an impact on a far greater number of people. Women not at the professional level of those served by Catalyst may be the first to benefit; in fact, in The Netherlands, a large grocery chain which was faced with a labor shortage, has had success with its paired-mothers program. The company advertised for, and got, pairs of mothers who would share jobs in the stores and would alternate with each other as baby-sitters. Being a wife and mother seems to be just one reason for a woman to fit into permanent part-time employment. A person, regardless of sex, might want to go back to school as a part-time student and still hold half a job. Two older people, working at the same level, might want to become partners, one quitting one job and both holding the other job between them, thereby allowing them to work half-time as they approach retirement—and making space for someone else to enter the workforce. Similarly, two retired people, who have become restless with too much free time but do not want to go back to working full time, fit into this plan. Nor is there anything which says that a man in his prime should not opt to work part time while he pursues some other interest or job. Such an arrangement might be perfect for a person wanting to transfer himself or herself into a second career or into a self-employed situation. In such cases, a working mother and a man might wish to pair up for a job. Or the situation might present itself where a husband and wife would prefer to share a job and child-care duties. In light of the Catalyst study of shared teaching positions, one can see how easily this might work with a husband and wife who are both qualified to teach at the same level.

The impact of this group of predominant part-timers is not to be underestimated. By individual contact or through speeches at meetings, over one thousand companies have been given the message, and Catalyst has been able to pry loose from foundations the money which it needs to get its information out to its clientele. To say that it has not overturned the basic employment pattern in America is not to hint that it has failed. It has, in fact, taken a giant stride in softening things up so that such an overhaul can occur. Giving what is almost a dictionary definition of the word catalyst, Felice Schwartz sums it up, "It's going to happen. We think we're going to make it happen faster."

5
The Sabbatical (Not for Professors Only)

While the academic world long ago made the occasional year off a matter of course, the practice of granting sabbatical leaves has never made deep inroads elsewhere. Exceptions have been relatively minor. Each year, a few top journalists have been granted their Niemans and other fellowships treating them to a year back at school; the military has regularly platooned promising young officers to civilian graduate study; and several alert companies operating in the realm of high technology have let their key engineering and scientific hands take a year off with pay to go back to the classroom and catch up on the latest in their fields.

Lately, however, a lot more thought has been given to sabbatical leaves for others, and there are even a handful of companies experimenting with it. One such company is Eastern Gas and Fuel Associates, a Boston-based combine with interests in coal, gas, and barges. It has a solid reputation as a progressive company whose management has earned the description "freewheeling" from *Business Week*. Among other Eastern Gas proclivities which are not typical of firms in the prosaic gas and oil industries is its interest in the arts. Its executive offices in Boston's Prudential Tower are a veritable art gallery. A few years ago, it commissioned artist Corita Kent to transform the outside of a gas storage tank in nearby Dorchester Heights into a gigantic work of art. Much of the company's progressiveness came from Eli Goldston, its chairman and chief executive officer, who died suddenly in January 1974. He was a leading proponent of corporate involvement in the welfare of the community, a cause which he espoused in his book *The Quantification of Concern*.

The sabbatical idea got its start here when Goldston petitioned for, and got, permission from the company's board of directors to take off for six months to lecture and study. As a result of Goldston's green light, another officer, William Helm, the comptroller, got permission for a sabbatical of his own. Because of the success of these two sabbaticals, the idea has gained acceptance in the company, and it is now planning to encourage others to take time off at half pay.

As he fast approached fifty, William Helm's position in life was not unlike that of many of his age and ability. He had come out of the Second World War, headed straight for college, and from there, straight to work. His working life wound its way through a number of jobs and promotions, serving to move him further and further from his original field—engineering. Now, as a comptroller, he had spread himself into such areas as marketing, corporate recruiting and computer systems management. "I had ceased to feel comfortable doing the things I was doing, and was more and more responsible for things I knew less and less about," he says, adding, "*Future Shock* and *The Peter Principle* were more than just book titles to me."

With a wife, four children, a nice income, a nest egg of appreciating company stock, and community responsibilities (he served on the community finance committee and school board in his suburb), Helm was cemented into a way of life—so much so that, he admits, "I had become so locked into the company that I had become reluctant to take a vacation or a day off because I wanted to stay close to the action. I had come close to believing that I was indispensable." Despite this and, perhaps, because of it, he made up his mind that he had to do something to break out of his plush rut and take advantage of the world outside before it was too late. A friend at the Harvard Business School got him interested in going back to school, and he applied and was admitted to the Stanford Graduate School of Business, specifically to the Stanford Sloan Program, a prestigious course in the humanities and advanced management for young executives. He

Breaking the Time Barriers

then came to his boss to ask for the better part of a year off. Luckily, his boss was Eli Goldston, who was then about to take his own six-month sabbatical at the London Graduate School of Business Studies to study and lecture. The deal was this: Goldston liked the idea, offered him half salary for the school year (just as he was to be on half salary in London), and told him that the company would try, but could not guarantee, to keep his job open for him. Simply, the company had to keep moving, and if his absence jeopardized it, someone else would have to be appointed comptroller. Accepting the risk, Helm decided to go off to Stanford with his family.

Today, Helm is back in Boston at his old job. His feelings about what he did are varied but overwhelmingly positive. He recalls some of the more obvious joys of getting into a new environment: the kid-in-the-candy-store feeling of being able to pick courses from among the rich course listings at a major university (predictably, he stuffed himself during the first two academic quarters); taking his family West to see and live in a new part of the country; the distinct feeling of his family's coming closer together during the time away from home; and the fact of being totally removed from the company and its problems (he had eliminated Harvard Business School in making his decision to go back to the classroom because it was too close to work and he feared being sucked back into his normal routine). At one point in our conversation, he said, "It was a real opportunity to pick myself up, vacate the life I was leading, and see if it was meaningless or not. As it turned out, it did have meaning, but the important thing was that I had the luxury of being able to find that out now, rather than having to wait until retirement to see where I had been."

Finally, Helm believes that his experience has made him better able to function in business since it served to take off some of the pressure he was feeling about his own ability to be current and competent. Or, as he puts it, "By getting myself into an excellent academic environment, I was able to move myself from a level where I felt I had to do all I could to keep up with things to a new one in which I now feel that I am at the front of the wave."

Another advantage, according to Helm, is that the enrichment of an academic sabbatical serves to make one's skills broader and, therefore, less dependent on one job or one company. "Unlike, say, a welder whose skills are basic and quite portable, the skills of a person like myself get more and more tailored to the needs of a single company and become less and less transferable." In this regard, Helm talks about "The 128 Syndrome," his way of summarizing the intensive build-up of electronics and high-technology companies along suburban Boston's Route 128 during the early to mid-1960s—followed by a similarly dramatic winding-down, starting about 1970 when funds for defense and space electronics were cut. He says, "Many people around here became so tailored to the needs of Route 128 that they have had an extremely tough time converting to another field, or are now driving cabs waiting for 1965 to roll around again. It is just this kind of dependence that a carefully planned sabbatical can prevent."

Speaking as a corporation executive rather than as an individual who has benefited from a sabbatical, Helm sees major advantages accruing to companies which offer sabbaticals. Not only does an employee return refreshed and refueled, but sabbaticals are a major attraction for recruiting new people. "Among the bright young people looking for jobs in today's job market," says Helm, "there is a general fear of retirement, a sometimes-justified backlash against the pension system, and a skepticism about the cycle of dependence and affluence which comes with an executive position. The possibility of a sabbatical without strings could become a powerful inducement to join a certain company in the years ahead."

Needless to say, Helm feels his experience was well worth the effort, the risk involved, and the cost (he had to sell off a significant amount of his company stock to finance the family's trek West). Helm's enthusiasm is admittedly buoyed by the fact that he was able to claim his old job when his sabbatical was over; he points out that others in the company interested in taking sabbaticals held back to see what his fate would be when his school year ended. With Helm back on the job, interest by others in the sabbatical began to perk again, but Helm believes that there will always be risks involved in taking time off from a key job. "A company is not like a college where a certain course can be easily canceled for one year because a professor is taking his sabbatical, it must continue to do things like pay its taxes, issue annual reports, and make a profit," says Helm, adding, "The potential for disruption is much greater."

A good many months after my first conversation with Helm, I talked with him a second time to see whether he had come up with any intervening second thoughts on his year off. In the interim, he had been promoted to a vice-presidency. He was still as positive about the experience, stating categorically that it had not set him back and had, in fact, made him qualified to take on new responsibilities.

The experiences of Helm and President Goldston were so positive, and the negative reaction so minor—only three of Eastern's nine thousand stockholders complained when it was announced in the company's annual report that the President was taking off for six months—that these two men had become spokesmen for the idea. Goldston, shortly before he died, wrote a glowing review of the sabbatical idea for the *Harvard Business Review*, in which he asserted that the result of his time off in London was ". . . not a recharged battery, but a new motor."

Today, the exact future plan for the sabbatical as an institution at Eastern Gas has not yet been set, but it clearly does have a future. One proposal now undergoing serious consideration is a plan under which a person would be eligible for up to three long work breaks depending on his or her length of service. The first would come when the person is in his or her thirties or forties, and would be an educational program geared to training the person to take greater responsibilities within the company. For this first break, an engineer might be given a year off to broaden himself through a course in finance or labor relations. This first departure would be for a year at full pay plus expenses. The second time off would be much less formal than the first, and not job-related—a clear break from the business world. The person on this second sabbatical might opt to do social work, teach, or play on all the tough golf courses in North America. This break would be for six months at half pay. The last sabbatical would come at age sixty-two and be a compulsory six months off. The idea here would be to let the person retire on a trial basis, presumably to spend the six months doing what he or she would do during retirement, thereby learning how to deal with that forthcoming and often jarring event. In addition, it would let the company give the person who is being groomed to take over the sixty-two-year-old's job a chance to be tested in that position. The future of this idea at Eastern Gas bears watching. If it takes hold, Eastern Gas would then serve as an important model for the career life of the future.

All of this prompts the question of how many others have begun to experiment with, or think about, instituting sabbaticals. Interestingly, at the time that Helm and Goldston took their sabbaticals, they assumed that what they were doing was unique. However, as news of their sabbaticals spread, they were contacted by others who were toying with the same idea, so they decided to find out how much interest there was in the sabbatical as a business institution by conducting a simple poll of the five hundred largest companies in America. Of the companies contacted, 266 responded, and, of those, 24 percent had some form of program they considered to be a sabbatical, while another 41 percent had no program but considered the idea to be a good one (with the rest being noncommittal about the concept). Only a lowly 4 percent termed it a bad idea which leads to the conclusion that the idea has a foothold in some places and is attracting interest elsewhere.

While the vast majority of the companies with sabbaticals in the survey had very limited programs, allowing, at best, a few middle managers a chance to go into structured four- to ten-month executive development programs (such as the Advanced Management Program at Harvard), there are some who have either gone into more extensive programs or are planning to.

Time, Inc., grants a sabbatical as a reward for its executives and writers, giving them each a year off with pay when they attain fifteen years with the company. Chase Manhattan Bank President David Rockefeller recently came out in favor of his managers taking off one year in seven to go back to college to ". . . deepen their insights with regard to social relationships." One of the older extended-break programs in the country is a plan which was negotiated in 1963 by the United Steelworkers, who obtained contracts providing its senior production workers a period of thirteen weeks off for every five years worked. This is one of the very few programs, if not the only program, which extends a long break to working people other than executives and highly trained technical staff members. In another area, the Danforth Foundation has been financing sabbaticals for college deans, administrators, and others who are not included in the near-universal system which gives the pure academician time off every seven years. In government, the recently established Executive Exchange Program sets up a mechanism which allows corporate and Federal employees to switch jobs for the period of a year, essentially a sabbatical of sorts in which each gets a year off to work in a completely different atmosphere.

Meanwhile, as examples of sabbatical programs and pilot projects come to light, there has also been an increase in public advocacy of the idea. Paul Armer, the director of Stanford University's Computation Center, has used his "Paul Principle" as an argument for the need for sabbaticals in a highly technological age. A companion to the "Peter Principle" (which dictates that, in a hierarchy, every employee tends to rise to his level of incompetence), Armer's Paul Principle holds that ". . . individuals often become, over time, uneducated and therefore incompetent at a level at which they once performed quite adequately." Armer contends that change is occurring at a rate which is very fast in comparison to man's life, and that, therefore, the answer to encroaching incompetence is continuing education. He advocates broad application of both smaller excursions—such as evening classes and short, intensive, full-time courses—and full-fledged sabbaticals of six months to two years. Armer also sees the need for a new mechanism, in the nature of the Social Security system, to make the sabbatical a national institution. In this regard, it is interesting that, lately, informal proposals have been made both inside and outside government for an amendment to the Social Security Act so that a person might be allowed to take a year or two's worth of retirement benefits during one or two preretirement-age sabbaticals. Under such a system, the person would continue working until sixty-six or sixty-seven (instead of sixty-five), depending on whether he or she had to pay back one or two years off. Such an amendment to the rules would not only foster sabbaticals but also help subsidize those who wanted to go off to prepare for a second career.

Without a doubt, the most ambitious idea which has been seriously suggested for the United States is the Universal Worker Self-Renewal Program offered in *Work in America*. This system would allow each working American the option of taking one six-month educational sabbatical every seven years, or a one-year educational sabbatical every fourteen years. In the words of its authors, this training-oriented scheme would ". . . make lifelong education a reality." By their estimate, it would cost about $22 billion a year to support. This fantastic amount would be offset, they argue, by such factors as the increased productivity of retrained workers, the reduction in unemployment and its costs (as the out-of-work people are used to fill in for those on sabbatical), and the savings which could be made as the billions spent annually on industry training and government manpower training are cut back. In addition to being economically efficient, it is also claimed, it would lead to much greater social efficiency, as a new environment would be created in which there would be constant education and training, great job mobility, and widespread career-changing possibilities.

This proposal is not the only broad societal change based on educational sabbaticals which has been advanced recently. A variation on the *Work in America* theme was proposed by Gösta Rehn, director of manpower and social affairs for the Organization for Economic Cooperation and Development (OECD), at that group's 1972 conference on "New Patterns for Working Time." His idea is a "study credit" which would be given out by the government to everyone who has passed the end of their compulsory education. The credit would cover tuition and living costs for a specified number of years, and could be used anytime during the person's life, either as a block or in pieces. Rehn believes that this would reduce the pressures on young people to complete all of their education at an early stage, and enable them to take education when they feel they really need it.

What this suggests to Rehn is a situation in which ". . . the difference between high-status and low-status jobs could then be, to a much greater extent, a matter of different stages in an individual's life rather than early and definitive class distinctions." He believes that even greater flexibility could be added to the credit system if the person who did not want to study could apply the credit to leisure pursuits or to a pension. He suggests, though, that it would be advisable to give the credits a lower value when put to uses other than study, so that the system would remain primarily educational.

While neither Rehn's proposal nor that of the *Work in America* task force were advanced with the anticipation that they might come quickly to reality, the early momentum needed to get sabbatical systems of this scope into the area of serious discussion and consideration may not be that far away. As more and more employees ask for long periods of time off for various reasons, and as more employers grant these requests, the notion of sabbaticals for all will seem less far-fetched.

6
Time Off for Good Works

The first cousin of the educational sabbatical is the similarly promising custom of letting people off for extended leaves of absence, or for some time each week, to do social or political work. A growing number of companies not only allow, but actively encourage, their employees to take time off for such actiyities, with some companies offering full time off with pay for periods of a year or more.

Underscoring the extent to which the practice has taken hold are the results of a 1972 survey conducted by Grace J. Finley of the Conference Board, a nonprofit New York business research organization. Finley queried eight hundred of the companies in the *Fortune* listing of the one thousand largest in the country to see what political- and social-leave policies are current. While only 34 percent responded to her questionnaire, of those that did, 28 percent have formal social leave policies and another 17 percent have informal (unwritten) policies. An additional 10 percent did not have a policy at the time of the survey but were considering the adoption of one, whereas only 6 percent reported that they were opposed to such leaves.

Among those companies offering formal leave policies, the policies and rules in force are diverse, but most of them have these features in common: the active encouragement of employee involvement in socially relevant work; the proviso that work done on leave cannot involve conflict of interest; leave without pay but counting as uninterrupted service for purposes of seniority and benefits; continuation of group life and medical insurance at the employee's expense; and reinstatement at the end of the leave conditional on there being an opening. For leave granted for elected political office, most companies terminate the leave after one term in office, as reelection is considered to amount to a career change. Generally speaking, the longest leave periods granted are for election or appointment to political office and VISTA and Peace Corps enlistments. A number of companies contacted offered a plan of "shared time," or giving employees free time off each week in equal proportion to that which they give of their own time. For instance, a person giving his Saturday to work with community programs would also be given one workday with pay by the company.

As for the corporate rationale for granting such leave, Finley concludes,

> Respondents give a variety of reasons, but all center on a feeling of corporate responsibility. Some say the company wants to be a good neighbor; others, that they recognize the necessity of employee involvement in a democratic system. . . . Respondents also say they know that the success of their own business enterprises depends in large part on the social and economic health of the community and the nation. A growing number of companies see increased corporate support of employee political and social action as a form of job enrichment.

While the Finley survey reveals a growing and important movement toward freeing people from a single form of work without their having to make the big break from the security, benefits, and seniority of regular employment, it also shows the limitations of the practice of social leave-taking thus far. One major inequity uncovered is that policies are usually different for salaried, managerial employees than for hourly workers. A typical case cited is that of a company whose stated policy is to give salaried help part-time off with pay for civic work and to encourage its managers to take longer periods off without pay for larger missions such as elected political office. However, they restrict hourly employees to brief periods off *without* pay (except for United Fund drive work and service as election officials) and actively discourage absences of longer duration without pay. Attempting to justify this position, the company states, "As a practical matter, we are more liberal in allowing time off to our . . . managerial employees since their work schedules are more flexible and, usually, they represent the company as well as their own interest." *

Another limitation which crops up in the study is the difficulty that companies have in determining exactly what constitutes legitimate political and social action worthy of their sponsorship, or, simply, at what level does outside work become too partisan or too close to conflict of interest for the comfort of the company? This inability to define limits seems legitimate to a point but also seems to provide an easy out for those wanting to avoid starting or extending the practice.

Beyond the subject of leaves itself, the survey spotted a positive portent, which was that many of the companies contacted seemed to be groping for new ways to integrate with the world around them. For instance, several companies were looking beyond their normal leave-of-absence mechanisms to a policy which would allow social action to become an integral part of the job responsibility—perhaps by relegating so many hours of the job per week to civic work. One executive went so far as to suggest a needed change in the way we view such works: "As long as we still use the words 'leave of *absence*' and 'time *off*,' we

* As is true of Conference Board studies in many areas, the names of companies quoted and used as examples are not given, hence the anonymity of this one and the one that follows.

implicitly relegate community involvement to a role somewhat less important than 'real work.' This relates to how we define 'work.'"

While most social-leave programs in operation today are small and not very visible, some are programs of significance and illustrate the movement's potential. Two of the best known and most ambitious social-leave programs are those at Xerox and IBM. Of the two, Xerox's is the smaller and newer. Under the motto, "Xerox is offering what it can spare least: You," a formal program began there at the beginning of 1972. In the first year, twenty-one people were selected by a special board of employees from a field of over two hundred applicants. The eighteen men and three women picked took jobs as diverse as teaching at a maximum-security prison, helping Palestinian refugees, and counseling Puerto Rican college students. The Xerox rules require three years of service with the company before one can apply. The company will pay the person's salary if the job is unpaid, or make up the difference between the pay of the outside job if the person's regular pay is more.

IBM's record as a pioneer in the field is impressive. The company has been granting time off for civic action on an informal basis since the 1950s. The practice took on added importance in 1970 when then-Chairman Thomas J. Watson, Jr., declared that the company had to take on additional responsibilities in the community at large. At that point, local managers were told to pay particular attention to requests for social leave. As a low-key practice in the past, the granting of such leave had worked out well, so, since the company sought new expressions of social responsibility, its expansion seemed natural. To cite one of many pre-1970 leaves with a long-range impact: An IBM marketing man, in 1967, had asked for, and gotten, the time off, the equipment, and the use of other IBM people as teachers to set up a computer programing course for prisoners at the Arizona State Prison. The course was developed and succeeded, thereby providing a programing pool which has been used by state agencies and, most important, a highly usable skill for the men involved on their release from prison.

Since the Watson declaration, well over three hundred employees have been granted leave, many of them with full pay and benefits, with about eighty out on social leave at any given moment. IBM's Director of Employee Benefits, H. P. Kneen, Jr., explains that the system is flexible. "Leaves are granted on a case-by-case basis. We have no rules on how short or long the period is to be, and we have no exact quota of how many people are to be out at once. Just at the point we might start to think that we've got a maximum number out, we get a request that is so good we can't turn it down."

Of the people out at any given time, Kneen estimates that about half are working on projects which were initiated by the individual and the other half are initiated by IBM, often in response to the request of an outside group which could use IBM expertise. An example of an IBM-initiated effort was the thirty-four employees who were on voluntary teaching assignment at colleges with large enrollments of minority and economically disadvantaged students at the time of our conversation. At IBM, people on social leave are given their old jobs (or equivalent) on returning. "All it takes is management interest and careful planning," says Kneen. For their part, employees are expected to return, and most of them have. "The number we've lost through social leave has been quite small," says Kneen, who adds, "But if we do lose people this way, it is probably the most satisfying kind of separation you can have, because presumably the person has made an important career change and is planning to continue the work he started on leave."

Running through a list of people on social leave, Kneen reads off a long set of examples to show the diversity and scope of jobs undertaken. One employee was working to set up a new hospital wing and another was starting a Braille library in Atlanta. Others lined up with established charitable and social-action groups such as the Urban League, the Legal Aid Society, and the

National Alliance of Businessmen. A smattering chose to set up new programs such as a model alcoholic treatment center and a drug research program. Several found themselves in locations as far-flung as Lebanon (helping orphans) and Rumania (teaching in a UNESCO program). One employee had left to help an integrated community in Colorado stay on top of its economic and social problems; another, who is part Indian himself, had taken a year off to attempt to improve the economic status of the residents of the Flathead Indian Reservation in Montana; and another, who, for a long time had spent much of his spare time helping to find college applicants among poor blacks, had taken a leave to serve as a recruiter for Harvard. The list goes on and on, and is truly diverse. While going through examples, Kneen said, "Here is one working with the Junior Chamber of Commerce, the next is working with Model Cities, and this one is working with minority entrepreneurs in Texas."

7

OTHER TIMELY OPTIONS

Once one starts hunting for new time patterns, it becomes apparent that the ideas covered so far are just a beginning. Still newer ideas, variations on existing ones, combinations of ideas, and unusual time customs established by employers here and there offer still more opportunity to break down time barriers and replace fixed worktime with a menu of à la carte options. Consider further both some other real innovations and imagined possibilities for assaulting rigid worktime:

The Hand-picked Holiday. In recent years, a small but growing number of companies has started giving a specified number of fixed holidays along with "open holidays." Commonly, six or seven major holidays are assigned for all employees along with four or five open holidays which the employee selects in advance for whatever celebration seems appropriate. No questions are asked, so the custom-made day off might be a religious observation, a birthday, an anniversary, a chance to climb a mountain, or to get drunk. Employees are thereby given an extra degree of freedom, and the employer does not have to close down his plant or office quite as often to accommodate holidays which everybody takes at once. In the same vein, the Labor Department has noticed that there is a growing trend to give an employee his or her birthday off as a regular holiday.

The Two-hour Module. Einar O. Mohn, vice-president of the International Brotherhood of Teamsters, has framed an interesting alternative to the forty-hour week, which he presented at the 1972 White House Conference on the Industrial World Ahead. He points out that the basic module of work in America is forty hours. Until the advent of the computer, it was hard for employers to handle deviations from that basic module, but it is now possible to deal with new, smaller, and more flexible modules. Mohn advocates changing the basic module from forty to two hours. Under this system, workers would be able to bid on the collection of two-hour modules they wanted, thereby creating a tailor-made workweek. Priority would be given to those with seniority, and new bidding would take place at periodic intervals to allow people to retailor their week to suit changing needs. Some people would choose to work less than forty hours, and others more. As Mohn puts it, ". . . the forty-hour week, whether it be completed in five or four days, is not sacrosanct. Nor is there anything right or wrong with a forty-two-, or forty-six-, or even a sixty-hour week—as long as the worker wants to put in these hours and as long as he can perform effectively on the job. Nor is there anything right or wrong with a thirty-seven and one-half-, thirty-five-, thirty-two-, or even a ten-hour week performed under the same considerations." The system would accommodate permanent part-timers as well as those who wanted to, say, work full time for a while and then go to part time to get additional education. The worker coming up on retirement could easily opt to drop modules at his or her own pace, thereby easing the transition. Mohn believes that such a flexible system will be an inevitable response to growing worker demand for the opportunity to build their own lives.

The Time Bonus. An interesting variation on the four-day week is in effect at Bonne Belle Cosmetics in Cleveland. Twice the company has changed its workweek for a specific period of time from five eight-hour days to four nine-hour days—paying workers for forty hours of work even though they only work thirty-six. Introduced in 1971 for the period from Thanksgiving to New Year's Day and repeated again for the months of July and August 1972, it amounts to a free bonus in time. Joe Sunseri, the company's vice-president for manufacturing, says, "It's a way of thanking our employees for good work while, at the same time, serving as an incentive for good work in the future." The company was so pleased with the morale boosts from the Christmas and summer four-day weeks that it gave the employees an even greater time bonus at Christmas 1972—four days off between Christmas and New Year's at full pay.

The Variable Shift. Dr. Thomas M. Calero, an Illinois Institute of Technology business and economics professor who is an advocate of varied and flexible workweeks, has called for a variety of tests and experiments. One intriguing idea he would like to see explored is the varied workshift in places like hospitals and heavy industry, where shifts are required. He says, "There's not much reason to run three eight-hour shifts when two nine-hour shifts and a shorter six-hour shift might be far better. People could be rotated back from short to long shifts, then back again, giving them variety and leisure in some periods, then more work in alternative periods."

The Monthly Option. Not all companies which have moved in the direction of the flexible workday have chosen to approach it the same way. A relatively timid, but nonetheless interesting, variation, suited for certain operations, has been adopted by the H. P. Hood Company, the large Boston dairy mentioned in the previous chapter. It has offered its office staff a choice of a variety of schedules from which to choose, but they must stay with their choices for a month at a time. For example, one can, say, opt for an 8:00 A.M. to 4:00 P.M. day with a half-hour lunch for January, and then move to an 8:30 A.M. to 4:45 P.M. day with a three-quarters-of-an-hour lunch in February. According to Frank MacDonald, assistant office manager, the system has the built-in advantages of the staggered day, with its ability to let people better contend with traffic as well as giving people the sense of participation in establishing work patterns.

The Six-month Workyear. At the National Broadcasting Company's New York television affiliate, WNBC–TV, a group of senior technicians over age fifty-five with more than twenty years of service has been granted the right to work for half a year and then take the rest of the year off. This enables those in the program to phase themselves into retirement at half pay, and enables the employer to phase younger workers into the system more effectively.

The Six-month Workyear (Version II). The practice of working intensely for a given period of time and then having a vacation of the same length of time is not new. For years, many American riverboat and barge crews have worked for thirty consecutive twelve-hour days and then had thirty days off. During their six working months, these people put in about two thousand hours, which is about what one person working a traditional forty-hour week puts in in a year. Today, there are proposals to extend this form of equal work and vacation periods to others. One which has gotten much attention is a week-on, week-off plan advanced in a paper by M. David Keefe, a labor arbitrator from Michigan. Keefe's plan would be to have people work seven consecutive ten-hour days, for which they would get the equivalent of two weeks' pay, and then be given seven days off. Keefe insists that his plan would offer true leisure time away from the routine and thwart absenteeism (because there would always be a vacation just around the corner and because the loss of ten hours' pay would be more costly than the loss of eight hours' pay), and points out that the plants would never have to close for vacations or weekends. He insists that the gain in productivity which would result would offset the fact that people would get eighty hours' pay for seventy hours' work

The Vacation Bank. The large majority of employers clear the boards of vacation time when the year is over, thereby forcing an employee to take his two or three weeks during the space of a calendar or fiscal year. A growing number of small firms and a few large ones (the Aluminium Company of America, for instance) allow people to bank vacation time from one year to the next. Under such a system, a person with three weeks a year might want to take one week the first year and five the second, creating what may seem more like a mini-sabbatical than just another vacation.

The $4\frac{1}{2}$-day Week. Pioneered in 1969 by McDonald's, the hamburger people, for its headquarters staff, the $4\frac{1}{2}$-day week is introduced each year for the span of Daylight Savings Time in order to let people off for a $2\frac{1}{2}$-day weekend which starts midday on Friday. People switch from winter to summer hours by coming in an hour earlier during the $4\frac{1}{2}$-day weeks in order to free Friday afternoons. It is one of the few time innovations which acknowledges that there is a difference between the warm and the cold months and that people want an early shot at the weekend when it is mild outside.

Second Career Mechanisms. Not too long ago, the number of people beginning second careers in their middle years was few, and most of those few had been forced to switch as the demand for the skills associated with the first career dwindled. Today, there are still those being forced into new careers, such as those specialists who found themselves no longer needed after the great aerospace boom of the 1960s; however, by all accounts, there is also an increasing number of those who are choosing on their own, for a variety of reasons, to leave the security of one world for a new start in another. Career switching, whether forced or by choice, is a tricky business which could be made easier by new centers (perhaps located in colleges and universities) which would offer counseling and training for those making the switch.

One of the clearest indications of the desire for a mechanism to help in career switching comes out of the experiences of Alan Entine, who ran an experiment at Columbia University called the New Careers Program. It ran from 1963 until 1969, when the Ford Foundation funds which had supported it ran out and were not renewed. (Ford had adjudged the program a success—often the kiss of death in foundationland—and for that reason felt it should be able to attract support elsewhere. It got plenty of vocal support but no funds.) The idea behind the program was to see if the university could enable individuals to make the career shift from business into nonprofit work such as hospital administration and social work. Preference was given to those in the forty- to fifty-five-year age group who already had a bachelor's degree. It provided counseling and one thousand dollars a year in tuition aid, and required those enrolled to spend full time in school. In all, the program took care of over fifty individuals—with no dropouts.

What is most interesting about the program, however, is not the small number of people which it was able to handle on its limited budget, but the number of inquiries and calls for help it got from outside. At the 1971 Upjohn Institute "Conference on New Directions in the World of Work," Entine recalled, "Thousands phoned and wrote asking about what they could do. The inquiries are still coming in, even though the program had to be discontinued two years ago." He added, "The number of calls rose during the week, reaching a peak on Friday afternoon as the work frustrations built up." Entine reports that over four thousand letters alone had come in by the end of 1965. In a chapter he wrote for the book *Where Have All the Robots Gone?*, he points out, "With the deluge of correspondence and telephone calls came the knowledge that the desire to change careers was not limited to businessmen seeking the nonprofit sector. Teachers asked to become stock brokers, social workers desired to become accountants, and farmers wanted to be salesmen."

The Departmental Option. In 1971, the government of San Diego County authorized its department heads to set up whatever schedules they and their workers felt were best. The provisos were that each person still had to put in eighty hours every two weeks, that no additional manpower needs might result, and that nobody could be forced to adopt the system. Some departments offered four-day weeks, others a seven-days-on, seven-days-off schedule, and a few a nine-hour-per-day biweekly schedule, with a three-day weekend every other week. A 1973 report by the Urban Institute, looking at new ideas in local government, said that the San Diego system led to an ". . . apparent increase in the output of some agencies" (due largely to fewer interruptions during longer morning and evening hours) as well as providing employees with additional usable leisure time, relieving traffic and parking problems, and cutting child-care costs. At the time of the Urban Institute survey, over fifteen hundred employees had voluntarily adopted their department's nonstandard workweek.

In short, as far as time is concerned, there are still many realms to be explored. The situation is much the same when it comes to another working dimension: physical space.

VII

The Democratic Office, the Do-it-yourself Factory

1
THE ENVIRONMENTAL PREROGATIVE

There are vast differences among individual workspaces in today's highly organized world. A stroll in Manhattan from the gleaming offices of corporate country around Madison and Park in midtown to the warrens of the garment district drives the point home quite nicely. Yet, paradoxically, there is an amazing sameness to the offices and factories where we work. From the dingiest, greasiest, noisiest, and most ill-lit factory in New Jersey's industrial outback to the clean, bright, quiet, Muzak-sweetened atmosphere of a firm manufacturing scientific instruments in Palo Alto, most factories and offices have one thing in common. They are designed and tended by others, and it is up to the person who comes there to work to fit in, not the reverse.

Interior designers, plant managers, time-study specialists, architects, office managers, and all the others who have a hand in the process of laying out workspace may have little or no later occasion to revisit their handiwork, but the people who actually inhabit these spaces on a daily basis seldom if ever have a say. The reasons this is so are many, but most of them pretty much boil down to the thought that the layout of work stations is a management tool and prerogative. So a machinest finds that because an outside efficiency consultant came through his shop in 1957 and concluded that it would be most productive to have all lathes exactly six inches from all workbenches, his own request to have the lathe moved to a more convenient distance is denied. In a much different context, there is the case of the executive I met with (to discuss some very real innovations in the way people were treated in his company) who pointed to a large product of the abstract expressionist school which had been hung on his wall despite his objections. To him, it was ". . . a

Godawful imposition and a rude shock each morning," and not at all in line with his taste, which runs to paintings of New England villages and seascapes. The painting, like the immovable lathe, is a management prerogative and tool. In this case, the need for a corporate image of progress, advanced thinking, and art patronage had been conceived in the head of the president; to fulfill this goal, he brought in a truckload of paintings and ultramodern furniture. This uneasy executive and the inconvenienced mechanic are not rarities, unfortunately, but are part of a large population which must live with the daily frustration of ill-fitting, dispiriting environments. The range of bad fits is tremendous, and travels a long way from an objectionable painting. Office workers get penned in lonely cubicles from which they can only emerge "on business" or to go to the rest room, while others get lined up at desks in long, regimented rows like soldiers in formation. Factory workers must live with noises and smells which are offensive and often dangerous.

At its most serious and sobering level, there are those working environments so bad as to be unfit for human habitation. The repertoire of facts which led Congress to pass the Occupational Health and Safety Act of 1970 underscores the grimness of the situation. An average of fourteen thousand five hundred American workers are killed each year on the job, 2.2. million are injured, and three hundred thousand suffer from job-related diseases. Some 250 million days of work are lost each year because of this—amounting to ten times the number of days lost from strikes. Although it is not yet clear to what degree this recent law and its stiff penalties will stop this carnage, it is apparent that health and safety on the job will continue to be an issue of increasing concern, especially as new hazards become evident in much the same way that black-lung-producing coal dust and carcinogenic asbestos fibers have already become issues of major concern. The passage of the 1970 Act signals the beginning of a new period in American industrial history, in

The Democratic Office, the Do-it-yourself Factory 283

which it is no longer the legal prerogative of an employer to ignore ear-damaging and nerve-jangling noise, foul air, life-shortening exposure to pollutants, and blatantly unsafe machinery.

It is becoming more and more apparent that the job itself and the physical environment in which work on it is to be done are complementary elements in the quality of work. Though many of the apostles of job enrichment consider the environment a secondary matter of hygiene which can produce *dis*satisfaction but not long-range satisfaction, it would seem that such singular emphasis on the task itself may be dangerously misleading. No matter how enriched a person's job is made, if it is located in a bad environment, it will still be a bad job. The efforts of the Chrysler Corporation—which is going through what one official there told *The New York Times* was a "small revolution" in job enrichment, job rotation, and worker-management brainstorming sessions to improve job content—did not prevent three Chrysler plants from closing by wildcat strikes in as many weeks during the summer of 1973. The major reason for the walkout in two of the three locations was conditions at the plant, not the job itself, as at Lordstown.

When bad jobs and a bad environment combine, the results can be sensational. A telling case in point was a situation studied by three scholars from the University of Michigan's Survey Research Center and presented in a 1972 paper entitled "The Multimillion Dollar Misunderstanding." In the authors' words, their efforts document a company's ". . . very ambitious, very expensive, and very unsuccessful attempt to solve a problem confronting an increasing number of companies in urban areas—the problem of reducing turnover among economically disadvantaged workers."

The company studied was a heavy manufacturer which was hiring a large number of men officially classified as "hard-core unemployed" to fill assembly jobs. The pay for these jobs averaged well over three dollars an hour, but even with this fairly high starting wage, the turnover was extremely high: 42 percent of the recruits were leaving the company within the first six weeks of their employment. In line with conventional wisdom, the company took this to mean that the problem was one of unskilled people without familiarity for the ways of industry, people who, furthermore, lacked the "right attitude" toward work. The company, which had publicly pledged to help the disadvantaged find jobs, got help from the United States Department of Labor's Manpower Administration to develop a massive training program to ready the poor for blue-collar futures. Several grants worth millions of dollars were allotted for the program, amounting to the highest monetary aid ever given to a single company for this purpose.

Under the new training system, men were given six weeks of training, ranging in scope from basic job-skills lessons to such matters as developing self-esteem in a job, learning to deal with foremen, and the advantages of punctuality—all matters which assumed that the basic cause of the high turnover was inherent in the men, not in the working situation. It was expected that this six weeks' intensive "vestibule training," for which the men were paid two dollars and fifty cents an hour, would bring the turnover rate to an acceptable level. It did not. According to the researchers, "Although the company's training program graduated many men who kept their subsequent company jobs, *precisely the same effect would have been achieved, and a few million dollars saved, had each disadvantaged worker been placed directly on the job without any vestibule training.*"

After a series of in-depth interviews with sixty-six men who had come to the company (twenty-seven who had left, thirty-nine who had stayed), the team concluded that the major reason why men were leaving in such numbers, regardless of whether they were trained or not, was the poor quality of their working lives. Most reported that they were moved from work station to work station without reason, many (48 percent) felt that they had more than one foreman and—most devastating of all—35 percent of the sixty-six men interviewed had been injured on the job during the first six weeks. From this, the researchers concluded that no amount of employee training can make working conditions "objectively less noxious."

In this case, a dangerous and ugly environment plus monotonous jobs with no inherent meaning had combined to make a situation so bad that the research team added with unscholarly bluntness at the end of their report, "Perhaps this study should have asked not why many disadvantaged workers *left* the company, but why any of these men *remained* at all." Needless to say, the government and industry are still very much tied to the idea of job training as the answer to turnover and hard-core unemployment. Far too few of the well-intentioned people involved in such programs are questioning the structure or physical environment of the world for which they are preparing people.

The health and safety of the worker must be the primary consideration in creating a better physical working environment for working people. Once safety is achieved, however, other factors such as aesthetics and convenience can be considered. Many workplaces have reached the point where they are not just safe but are attractive as well. A very few have gone further and are now beyond simply providing for the natural desire to work in pleasant surroundings and are using terms like "democratic," "user-oriented," and "participative design" to describe what they are doing. Three detailed examples of the most progressive edge of workplace design follow. Two are offices and one is a factory. They are, respectively, a hot-shot company in the fast-food business, an out-of-the-way corner of government, and a small European multinational corporation. In each case, the people in charge have given up old authoritarian ideas for new democratic ones and have either found or are expecting to find that their operations improve as a result.

2
McDonald's: The Unwalled Corporation

McDonald's Plaza is an eight-story office complex located in the Chicago suburb of Oak Brook. The top three floors house the international headquarters of the McDonald's Corporation, purveyor of hamburgers to the millions—5 million a day, to be precise. From the outside, it is nothing special to look at—a white, boxy affair with rounded, oblong, Boeing-747-style windows. Yet, the public's demand to get inside has been such that the company has assigned some of its employees to tour-guide duty. The McDonald's spread has become what must be the first three floors of office space to emerge as a tourist attraction of some proportion.

One reason for the outside interest is that these offices are a total break with the office concept of the past, and are actually not really offices in the traditional sense at all. There are a minimum of doors and walls (the major exception being rest rooms), with each floor so open and free of cubicles that if you stand on a chair you can look from one end of the building to the other.

This openness and rejection of the walled corporation is only a part of what draws crowds. What really gets people to tell their friends to go over for a peek is the combination of ideas and deviations from the norm which, when taken together, add up to something unique: a pleasant vision of the landscape of work in the future, or, more simply, what now appears to be a great place to work. If the dream of the small businessman is to have picked up a few McDonald's franchises some years back before they turned to gold, the dream of the deskbound worker who has seen the headquarters may be to work there.

The Democratic Office, the Do-it-yourself Factory

The genesis of this place was the discovery that the old McDonald's headquarters in the downtown Chicago Loop area was fast becoming too cramped, with no room for expansion. The decision was made to create a new place nearer O'Hare Airport than downtown because of the constant motion of the company's executive corps; on any given day, up to 80 percent of the high command is liable to be off in the hinterlands tending to the business of some two thousand McDonald's restaurants.

Rather than just create a conventional corporate nerve center, President Fred Turner felt that the company should aim to tailor it to psychological objectives instead of—as is normal—operational objectives. The assignment that Turner gave to Tom Waterson, the man appointed project leader for the move, was to develop a place which fostered high spirits and low turnover, and which would be configured to engender a feeling of constancy and security even though there would always be some degree of flux and department shuffling as the McDonald's plan for world conquest unfolded.

The company hired Associated Space Designs, Inc. of Atlanta, Georgia, to plan the interior spaces with the aid of Waterson's planning group. One technique used to determine what best suited the needs and desires of the people who would work at the headquarters was the use of a series of questionnaires and in-depth interviews with department heads. In case after case, the resulting department plan differed from the traditional. Rather than put the accounting department into the classic regimented rows of close desks, a roomy accounting area was designed in which the desks were placed at irregular angles. Switchboard operators, who are traditionally assigned to lonely, out-of-the-way niches, were placed out on the floor in low, upholstered bunkers where there could be privacy and quiet while sitting down and a full view of what is going on—and others to talk with—while standing up. To get a basic furniture unit that exuded permanence yet could be moved in minutes, a special item was designed for the job given the somewhat pretentious NASA-like name of "Task Response Module." This sleek contraption is a low wooden partition which doubles as a room divider and fold-open work area. Tucked into a typical module are its own desk, table, phone, drawers, coat closet, bulletin board, bookcase, and electrical and phone wiring. The operating principle behind the module, as with other appointments, was to offer privacy and openness at the same time. Like the switchboard operators, you are alone while seated at your module but, by turning around or standing up, you open onto the whole floor.

After a three-and-a-half-month period of intense planning, the headquarters was blueprinted, built, and finally opened in March of 1971. Hailed by McDonald's as a new departure in "open planning"—and as a manifestation of the company's open attitude—it also got rave reviews from the outside. The magazine *Building Design and Construction* characterized the 110,000 square feet of workspace as "order without rigidity, vigor without frenzy, freedom without chaos, continuity without monotony." *Interiors* magazine saw it as "a breakthrough" in the open-plan corporate environment, and went on to praise its "status-free" atmosphere, in which those at all levels of the hierarchy shared 3,050 windows and got furnishings of the same top quality.

If there is a style to the place it would have to be called democratic plush. Without cells and cubicles, everybody but the denizens of the computer room, who must be shut into temperature-controlled spaces with their temperamental machines, share the same space, air, and light. Moreover, everybody has a window with a view and an equal chance to take a break gazing out the window. The spaces marked off for the chairman of the board and president are as open as that of the lowest clerk, and they share the same gargantuan wall-to-wall carpet. As you saunter through the "office" of Ray Kroc, board chairman and the man who parlayed one 1955 hamburger stand into an empire, you fully realize that the description "open offices" is no

The Democratic Office, the Do-it-yourself Factory 289

bit of public-relations puffery. Like many other companies, this one boasts of easy employee access to the highest level of management. But here they mean business. It would be hard for a protective secretary to say that the boss was out or too busy to see you if you could easily see for yourself that it was not true.

Despite the openness, the noise level is very low. For one thing, it was designed to be quiet. The deep carpeting, acoustical ceilings, chamoislike vinyl covering on the perimeter walls, and the foam cushioning on the back of the wood modules and filing cabinets all trap sound. Even the four hundred-odd large, rented tropical plants trucked in from Florida are intended to serve as sound absorbers (and double duty as spirit lifters). In addition, the design and openness seems to discourage loud talking; one immediately finds himself lowering his street voice. By design or not, the only sound that seems to carry across the floor is laughter.

Except for the orange carpeting throughout, the color scheme is deliberately neutral, with beiges and browns predominating. This neutrality was the designer's notion, a way to encourage people to supply the color through the way they dress and the way they embellish their workspaces with posters, pictures, mementos, and other expressions of personal taste. The desired effect has been achieved; people have individualized their work-spaces. In most cases, a glance will tell you a lot about the person who lives there. Another nice individualistic touch was the decision to invite each employee to a special showroom to choose his or her own optional equipment. For instance, each person was given the choice of four different chair styles.

Still another out-of-the-ordinary feature is that the terrain of the three floors is varied. Padded circular conference rooms are strewn about each, and there is a soundproofed audio-visual center, a large meeting room, and a roomy employee lounge replete with kitchenette, lunch tables, lounge chairs, and a place to buy a nickel Coke on the honor system. Great hunks of modern abstract sculpture are strewn about, mingling with such corporate memorabilia as plaster mock-ups of the McDonald's double cheeseburgers and a bronze likeness of Ronald McDonald.

By far the most remarkable amenity in the place is the company "think tank," a 2001-ish compound which one enters by way of an unobtrusive hatch in a wall on the seventh floor. Next to the hatch is a buzzer one pushes to enter, and three status lights. If you buzz and the green light comes on the place is free; an amber light means someone is in there who does not mind sharing it; red indicates that someone has set the "do not disturb" switch. Beyond the hatch is a padded labyrinth which meanders to two equally plush but distinct domains. One is the workroom, a large, soundproofed oval area entirely covered with a beige, suedelike fabric. It features dimmable lights, a hydraulically operated stand-up, sit-down writing desk, a large bean-bag chair, and a deep-pile runway which has been designated "the pacing area." Nearby is the meditation capsule, which is a round, elevated enclosure which one boards by climbing up a short flight of stairs and pushing a button that brings on a hydraulic hum and opens a panel in the side of the capsule, leaving enough room to tumble into it. The floor of the capsule is a seven-hundred-gallon, nine-foot-in-diameter water bed, which is covered in a soft, deep, furry fabric. The suede-lined sides taper away from the bed to meet the white dome at the top of the capsule. A small environmental control panel sunk in the wall features an array of buttons and knobs with which to open and close the entry panel, manipulate the lights, run a tape deck, or pipe in stereo music.

The think tank is not meant to be a tacked-on gimmick or an executive toy, but rather a legitimate refuge open to all employees who are free to reserve it by making an appointment. It is there to be used for whatever reason seems appropriate—to

The Democratic Office, the Do-it-yourself Factory

puzzle out a problem, to cool off after a bad encounter, or to pace determinedly without onlookers. The idea has been well thought out. It was placed on the floor below where the president and other top officers work so that it would not appear to be an executive preserve. As an antidote to the open, linear world outside, it is cocoonlike and all curves and swells, a conscious attempt to put people in a different frame of mind than would be natural outside.

Tom Waterson, McDonald's director of Facilities and New Projects, says that the company has not attempted to make quantitative measurements of what the new environment has meant to people working there—although he does point out that turnover among clerical and administrative workers has dropped to a quarter of what it was in the old location. "However, we do know that it has done a lot for morale and spirit. We can feel this every day," he says. "Communications have become more direct and there is a lot less factionalism in terms of my department versus your department. Another benefit has been that the openness of the plan has served to remove some of the fear that people normally have for the highest level of management, as the design has made them a lot less aloof." Waterson believes that the environment that has been created at McDonald's is the environment of the future, and describes it as ". . . just the kind of atmosphere which is very appealing to the generation now entering the labor market."

The McDonald spread advances along the line of a recent trend in interior design toward open planning. This trend includes various schools of thought, one of which is the currently popular one of office landscaping. It is generally agreed that this trend is the product of two modern imperatives. The first was the economic condition of Europe right after the Second World War. When European business was being put back on its feet, offices tended to be fitted out in the simplest, most economic manner possible, which meant that the costly trappings of prewar offices were out. This, over the years, helped lead to an appreciation of functionalism and a new feeling that an office devoid of the barriers and traditions of status and hierarchy was inherently more democratic and pleasant.

On the heels of this imposed postwar leanness came a second and more dramatic force, the proliferation of the computer as a piece of standard office equipment and all the implications of this new tool. Data was being processed at fantastic new speeds, which prompted the redesign of offices so that the people in them could better interact with the high-speed machines around them. The free flow of information was beginning to be seen by some as more important than maintaining the regimentation and hierarchy of the office. Common sense dictated that the automation-age office should be flexible (able to be rearranged over a weekend if need be), open, and responsive to new lines of communication—which were not necessarily those shown on the organizational chart.

The first group to translate these developments into a school of design was Germany's Quickborner Team—so called because the designers were located in the Hamburg suburb of Quickborn. Their approach was dubbed *Bürolandshaft* (literally, "office landscaping"), and developed as a hybrid of management consulting and interior design. At the core of the Quickborner approach is a team of specialists which comes in and works with the client to map out the organization's flow of work and communications. From charts and the stated needs and goals of the organization comes a design which often bears no resemblance to the old lines of individual disciplines, departments, and office hierarchy. Visually, the solution most often results in a clean, open design with maximum flexibility and visibility. Doors, walls, and cubicles are swept away and portable screens, desks, filing cabinets, bookcases, and large potted plants serve as the markers which delineate individual work stations. Managers in such situations frequently find themselves placed out on the floor as part of the team. Essentially, the approach is one which borrows more from computer programming and operations research than traditional design, and amounts to the first breakaway from the typewriter age which, with the introduction of that machine, helped put large numbers of people in the linear, hierarchical offices which are still, in most places, the order of the day.

Besides being its prime innovator, Quickborner has also been a seminal influence in moving office landscaping internationally. It now has an American team working out of Millburn, New Jersey, and it is generally credited with having given office landscaping its first major American showcase, in 1968, when it redesigned the offices of Eastman Kodak in Rochester. Other large companies have adopted the idea, and to service them, there are today about a dozen firms in architecture and design selling a variation of the approach. Some are loath to call it "office landscaping" because this is the Quickborner term, so other terms, such as "open landscaping," are used. Others have chosen to work with a less specific approach, called "open planning," which takes in some of the same considerations as office landscaping but is less formal in the way detailed operations plans are made. All of this gets a bit confusing, as the terms are used synonymously outside the design field, and are the subject of considerable debate within it.

The proselytizers and most of those who have converted to the landscaping-open-approach view are able to recite many advantages. R. E. Planos, president of the United States Quickborner Team, claims that the approach commonly proves itself by giving a 10 percent boost in efficiency. There is no questioning the fact that this system provides substantial savings for companies where things tend regularly to get moved around. At Kodak, where 10 to 20 percent of the office space is reconfigured each year, the per-square-foot cost of moving has gone from between two dollars and fifty cents to seventeen dollars down to about thirty-five cents with the open approach. Another economic benefit: *Business Week* has pointed out that, for tax purposes, a movable partition is a piece of furniture, and, unlike a wall, can be depreciated at tax time. As for worker attitudes, the general consensus is that the open plan is more democratic, tends to deter arrogance on the part of any given group, helps foster a team spirit, and gives people a sense of not being left out of things. A Kodak poll revealed that four out of five workers preferred it; in the newly "landscaped" portions of the Weyerhauser Corporation, a survey showed that 35 percent of all people in the new environment felt that they were now able to make faster and better decisions.

Although the landscaping–open-concepts ideas have created an important new alternative for office working and have begun to break the old mold, most of them do not go nearly far enough. People are still treated as part of a machine, and for all the implied democracy of openness, what such conversions often amount to is the replacement of an office set out along mechanical lines (the typewriter age) to one set out along electronic ones (the computer age). What is fundamentally important here, however, is the length to which these new ideas can be carried along humanistic lines. McDonald's headquarters is an important example because its objective went beyond the Quickborner goal of improving operations to a stated objective of psychological improvement. For this reason, its designer has said that his work was not office landscaping but rather a new form of human-oriented open planning. The McDonald's scheme can be seen as an important step in creating a modern, humane environment. But, as we shall now see, the idea can be taken further in involving the individual in designing his or her custom environment, something more directly democratic.

3
"The Social Waterhole": An Office Built Around Individual Needs

Perhaps the last place one would expect to find a radical approach to the way people spend their workdays is in the United States Government. For anyone who has spent any time in Federal corridors, the notion of a fresh idea in this generally bleak, bureaucratic terrain seems doubly amazing.

With the exception of some of the newer offices and the lairs of those in top slots, government offices are marked with a singular dreariness and sterility, designed in line with a strict hierarchical code. The mentality of "A title on the door rates a Bigelow on the floor" has been worked out to the degree that, in some bureaus, one has to be at a certain Civil Service grade level before he can have a plant from a government greenhouse on his desk. Even at the visible core of powerful agencies, one finds the same drabness. Adjoining the seventeen and five-tenths miles of corridors in the Pentagon are large, ugly work pens without a hint of natural light to soften *that* color—the wretched, greasy, light-green wall paint that anyone who has been in the armed forces recalls with pain. The innards of the State Department are so sunless, colorless, and impersonal that one can't help wondering whether there is a correlation between this environment and the conduct of foreign affairs. Things can get even worse out of the mainstream; the military still has a few people working in buildings which were thrown up as temporary quarters during World War I.

Of more than symbolic importance is the business of what

office managers in and out of government call "personal effects." In quite a few government offices, there are rules against visible personal effects; photographs, trophies, post cards, mottos, and what-have-you must be confined to the insides of desks. In some of the slightly more liberal niches of the bureaucracy, personal effects may be in sight but they must be in frames.

In this domain, the desk takes on a meaning all its own. So structured is the desk-allotting system that, with a little experience, one can learn to tell the annual earnings and hierarchical level of a person to a fair degree of accuracy by looking at the desk at which he or she is sitting. The size and material of the desk are the keys. The common, small, gray steel job is for your lower grades; simulated wood paint is seen at the next notch, after which come the veneers and on up to the solid woods of the government executive. At the cabinet rank, one finds a great wooden windjammer of a desk, with an expansive working surface, for which the government pays $1,073.10. The list of status points and demarkation items is long, and probably the proper subject only for a team of anthropologists versed in esoteric tribal ways and symbols.

In charge of managing the physical plant of government is the Government Services Administration, a definitely unglamorous agency which plugs along as the building contractor, landlord, desk procurer, and resident manager for the rest of government. About the only time in a decade the GSA made news was in 1973, when it kept coming out with different sums on what it had spent on the Nixon manses at Key Biscayne and San Clemente. However, in the last few years, under the direction of Administrator Arthur Sampson, the agency has begun to show some signs of life. One departure has been what it has termed its "Office Excellence" program, which has involved getting into formerly heretical things such as brightly colored furniture, open planning, and carpeting whole offices to be used by those whose civil service ratings would formerly have called for linoleum.

Part of this turn of events has been to allow a heightened

The Democratic Office, the Do-it-yourself Factory 297

degree of experimentation. The most interesting new idea has come from a young architect and designer named Dennis Green who, while working for GSA in the Pacific Northwest, began developing new thoughts about office design—which led him to a major project in which the employees themselves guided the design of their new offices. The idea was initially an extension and refinement of work that Green had been building up to in some of his other projects in which he had introduced the idea of user-oriented design—getting the people who would be using the office to tell him what they needed and wanted. The GSA project was undertaken for the Federal Aviation Administration at their new facilities at Boeing Field in Seattle, Washington. As it developed, Green was taking many of the elements of office landscaping—plants, free-standing acoustical screens, open space, and close attention paid to sound levels—and letting the office workers guide him in how they would be arranged, rather than having a plan imposed by his design team and the people who ran the office. He admits that this came about only after he began to reject the prevalent concept, which was to design offices as aesthetically pleasing machines in which people were just another part of the machine. He was part of the "no-personal-effects school." However, this was not prompted by the authoritarian stuffiness which is often *de rigueur* in government, but derived from what he terms "the German approach": the lean, clean, open Quickborner functionalism that decreed a sweeping harmony not to be disturbed by personal memorabilia and clutter.

Green now sees the large office primarily as a creature of the twentieth century, one which has seen its most dramatic growth in the last thirty years. To him, the development of the office has directly paralleled that of the factory. Both are dominated by the same concern for productivity, efficiency, and speed; both partake of fragmentation, division of labor, and assembly-line techniques. What has been created is the white-collar replica of the factory, in which the product is information instead of something tangible—like a car. Green points out that, in the modern office, a worker is not seen as a social animal but rather as "an information link," in much the same way that a factory worker is seen as "a production link." To challenge this, he has been developing his work along the lines of what he terms "the social waterhole" concept, which acknowledges that the office is a human gathering place where social and behavioral considerations should be taken into account in the design process. He says, "The 'social waterhole' concept doesn't deny the value of functional criteria in design; rather, it extends that rational basis to include the aspects of interpersonal relationships, motivation and other human needs as prime forces shaping the activities of working people."

For the Seattle FAA project, Green worked out a rough plan to be tried as a full experiment. The idea, accepted by the GSA as well as to the FAA, included an extra allotment of funds for behavioral research—an unprecedented extra for an interior-design project. The team contracted to work on the project included Green, a psychologist, and two architects from the People Space Architecture Company of Seattle. The man put in charge of the design team was Sam Sloan, the president of People Space, who has specialized in the application of behavioral research to office design. Sloan, like Green, had been working to apply individual needs to the design process. Earlier, while on a Fulbright study grant in Australia, Sloan had studied the working lives of clerks in an insurance company office in order to come up with an antidote to long, regimented lines of desks, one that would take into account the personal preferences and social requirements of each clerk.

The five men met for four days in Seattle in October 1972 to set up their plan in order to have the new office space ready for occupancy in the summer of 1973, when the new building would be opened. Their immediate clients were three hundred forty office workers, who were then located in temporary quarters. A plan was outlined and approved by the FAA.

The Democratic Office, the Do-it-yourself Factory

The first step was to poll the workers to find what they liked and did not like about their present location in order to get a general idea about the group's feelings and to have some before-and-after comparisons. Generally, the people felt their offices were pretty grim, with poor to bad acoustical qualities and fair to poor equipment and furnishings.

Next on the agenda was letting the office people know what was happening and what their alternatives were. A special brochure, at once a primer on the various ways offices are laid out (office landscaping, conventional, open plan, and so on) and a vehicle to tell people how they would be involved in the design process, was prepared. It said, in part,

> The program we are attempting to implement . . . will provide the opportunity for each and every person to participate in the design of his or her place, . . . determining the extent of privacy or conversely the ability for others to comfortably enter into the work station space to interact. When cost will not allow a person to have everything he or she wants, it will become the prerogative of the person as to what is given up . . . not an arbitrary decision by management or a designer who neither cares nor understands what the needs of each person are.

Requesting everyone's cooperation, Sloan's group then moved into the existing offices to administer a questionnaire, conduct a personal interview with each worker, and observe the operations and social relations of the office. The questions ranged from overt ones of preference and practice (Whom do you most enjoy working with? Do smokers bother you? How much of your job is done seated at your desk?) to hypothetical questions posed to reveal deeper character traits. For instance, each person was asked to mark on a diagram where he or she would choose to sit in a given situation. By indicating a series of seats with specific relations to doors, other people, and corners, the person would show the degree to which he or she had a "territorial requirement." The interviews were designed to further refine the needs and preferences of groups and individuals by attempting to get beyond the questionnaire. In one case, interviews with a group of office workers indicated an intense desire to be situated near windows. All of those in the group were aircraft pilots as well as office workers and, naturally, had a much greater interest in the weather than their co-workers.

From all the data gathered and processed from both questionnaires and the interview came two major design tools. The first was a synthesis sheet for each individual, which summarized his or her wants and needs. In all, seventy-four issues were addressed, ranging from special physical needs, as in the case of the handicapped worker, through personal preferences in colors, to the need for specific tools and storage requirements. In a special section on each person's sheet were eight possible acute needs which could be checked off. In most cases, the person was liable to have revealed two or three such needs from a list of categories which included privacy, environment, communications, and social needs. If, for example, an acute need for privacy showed up, this would alert the designer to go back to items 41–45 on the longer list to get a more refined reading of this need, in order to find out whether the need was based on a personal urge for visual or audio privacy, or both, or was a need based on the security requirements of the job being done. The second tool was a series of profiles of the groups of people who would be working together in a division or department. These profiles aimed at showing a consensus of needs and preferences.

To illustrate how a group was profiled from all the data, here are the researched needs of two typical divisions:

Manpower Division (thirteen men and twelve women)
- ¶ Severe requirement for group and individual social interaction.
- ¶ Group expression of privacy requirement from smokers.
- ¶ Bright color preference.

- ¶ High incidence of outside visitors.
- ¶ Moderate to severe expression of individual privacy requirement.
- ¶ Expressed need for visitor guest chairs.
- ¶ Manpower information system computer equipment in the office of the chief.
- ¶ Moderate requirement for exterior orientation (i.e., windows) in the Personnel Operations Branch.
- ¶ Severe requirement for privacy in the Labor Relations Branch.
- ¶ Major volume of storage required in the Labor Relations Branch.

Budget Division (four men and two women)
- ¶ High intensity of visitors.
- ¶ Expressed need for guest chairs.
- ¶ Severe requirement for group and individual social interaction.
- ¶ Unusually low expression for privacy.

The group profiles and the individual synthesis sheets were then used in laying out the office. While divisions and departments were basically modeled around the group needs, the individual sheets were used to make sure that individual needs were not slighted. "If three people in a group of twenty expressed a severe need for visual privacy," says Green, "we made sure that the proper screens and barriers were put in front of them so that they could be alone and private when they needed to be." Similarly, people with a strong aversion to cigarette smoke were either put out of the range of smokers or placed where ventilation and air conditioning would cut the smoke dramatically.

Once the design of the office was roughed out by Sloan's firm, it was again time for its future inhabitants to take part in the design process. An aircraft hangar was borrowed (no problem for the FAA), and there a series of workspaces were mocked-up to display different furnishings. Among other options presented were some ten desks, a variety of desk tops of different materials, fifteen different chairs, a selection of chair fabrics, and telephones in different colors. Each person got an order blank and was able to order the furniture of his or her choice after testing out the various chairs and desks. While most picked equipment that was close to what they would have been given in a traditional situation, with secretaries tending to take secretarial desks and managers picking larger "status" desks, the choices were entirely free.

One element of the new office which did not lend itself to individual choice was the color of the carpet which would be laid throughout. Nevertheless, a democratic compromise was developed. A committee of fifteen employees was appointed and presented with a choice of five colors provided by the building's architect. All five were rejected, and the panel asked instead for three new colors, blends taken from the first five. All eight samples were taken around the office by the committee for additional reaction, and one of the custom blends was finally chosen.

What emerged from all of this when the new offices opened in August 1973? Green says,

> The look is very heterogeneous, something like coming into a party and seeing a bunch of people dressed in different clothes in different styles and colors. The only real trend in the place is that there are a large number of desks with teak tops because this was by far the most popular choice when people picked their own equipment. It's a very open place, with no enclosed spaces, not even for top management. We've used a lot of potted plants, and personal effects have been encouraged. . . . Although it's not obvious unless you are looking for it, you can see by the places where they are working which people desire to be in open surroundings and which ones need privacy. Each departmental grouping has its own distinct identity. For

The Democratic Office, the Do-it-yourself Factory

instance, you are liable to walk into one where the boss is sitting right in the middle of his or her group and then move on to the next where he is in the corner.

Commenting on the design process itself, Green says, "What we did was to transfer the self-satisfaction of the designer to the people through a democratic process. As it worked out, this is highly satisfying to both the designer and the individual he is designing for because the designer no longer has doubts about the decisions he is making and the people know that they have had a firm hand in operating their own workspaces."

There are some immediately apparent benefits, according to Green. For one thing, the actual design process is shortened; there need not be the debating over what is most appropriate for Department X, because it is all specified by the people in Department X themselves. He adds that future applications of the approach would actually take less time now that a procedure has been developed. Moreover, the cost of the project finally amounted to about the same price as similar-sized projects in which there was no participation—suggesting that perhaps, with greater refinement, the democratic process might be more economical than established authoritarian ones.

It will be some time before the final results of this experiment can be determined. There will be considerable follow-up. Sloan's firm and another not associated with the original plan will be brought in to evaluate the plan's effect on the people in the office after they have worked there for a year, and the results will then be compared to another recent GSA installation of similar size (in Los Angeles) which was also designed on the open plan but with no employee participation—"A very nice, light, and open place," says Green, "but one in which people are expected to fit in like cogs in a machine." *

---

* Formal evaluation of the project had not yet begun when I last checked on it in late 1974, but a member of the staff close to it said that it was running well and the subjective results were good. Green,

If the results are as good as Green and the others on the team hope they will be, the results in government could be far-reaching, not only as a model for government offices of the future but as a foot in the door for other participative ideas.

Meanwhile, in Europe, a similarly important step in factory design has proven itself. Like the GSA work, it has gotten very little publicity but is highly important.

4

The Place Where They Let the Workers Design a Factory

The idea of letting those who will work in a new factory design it themselves is simplicity itself, yet not one example of its actually having happened on a large scale could be found by the venturesome management of Sadolin and Holmblad, a large Danish paint and lacquer company, when it decided to give the idea a try.

In 1969, the company concluded that its aging printing ink manufacturing operation in Copenhagen had to be modernized and expanded, and that this would require a new plant. According to Kaj Poulsen, the experiment-minded managing director of the company, the yet-to-be-designed plant offered the perfect opportunity for Sadolin to push its program in worker participation to a new and higher plane, or as another manager in the company puts it, presented ". . . a chance to collaborate with the workers on something really big, not just something like

---

incidentally, left for a job with a private architectural firm in Denver before the evaluation was completed.

The Democratic Office, the Do-it-yourself Factory

how do we clean the floors or improve ventilation in a particular shop."

A site was chosen in an industrial park in the suburb of Glostrup, and Poulsen invited all the workers from the printing ink group out to see it on a Saturday afternoon in November 1969, and, afterward, to attend a luncheon where they would hear the pitch. All but one of the eighty-five invited employees showed up. The proposal was quite simple: If the workers wanted to set up groups to design the new plant, the company would supply them with the architects and technical help and would then, within reason, abide by their plans. After a little initial confusion at the meeting as to what was actually expected of them, the workers decided that they wanted to go ahead with the job. Groups were assigned by intrinsic categories to plan parts of the new factory. For example, the premixing department worked to set up the new premixing department. Each of these groups was given a rough outline of the floor space they were to be allotted in the new plant, and each was to come up with a detailed plan which was to be forwarded to an overall employee steering group, which, in turn, was to work out the final plan with the architects. After a few alterations and compromises required by architectual reality, a final plan was presented to, and accepted by, the company's directors. In late 1970, bids from building contractors were solicited.

Sadolin's corporate sincerity was well tested when just before the eighty-five workers were to come out to the site for a groundbreaking ceremony, the management was given an opportunity to buy another factory perfectly suited to the printing ink operation at a bargain price by a firm that was going out of business. It passed the test when the economically seductive option was ruled out of the question for the simple reason that such a move would break the spirit of the workers involved.

The new plant went into operation in January 1972, a little more than two years after the workers had been given a chance to do it themselves. The company readily admits that it took longer to get the plant into operation than would normally be expected. Part of the delay resulted from problems encountered when the first contractor went out of business before the plant was complete, but the cost in time of worker design was about two extra months—what Poulsen calls the only major extra cost of the experiment.

In truth, there is nothing particularly distinguished looking about the large, sprawling, printing ink complex of three buildings connected by covered passageways. It is clean, well-lit, and spacious—rather nice as factories go but nothing special. Any unique aspects of the place must be explained to the layman. The vice-president in charge of the plant is E. L. C. Smith-Petersen, who says, "The differences between it and the plant which management would have created are subtle and by no stretch of the imagination radical. It is, perhaps, 80 percent like the factory which the bosses would have created on their own." On a tour of the factory, he points to something typical of the workers' planning. In this case, it is the arrangement of the vats in which the inks are mixed. In the old factory and in most operations of this type, the vats sit on the floor and the workers have to climb up on scaffolding to work with them. The overwhelming consensus of those concerned was that this climbing around was a waste of time and effort, and so they insisted on having the vats placed in long trenches, enabling them to work and move with ease at ground level. Most of the other innovations pointed out were similarly mundane but, nonetheless, significant to the workers. In addition to determining the placement of machinery and equipment, new procedures were developed and incorporated into the design by the workers. These procedures were largely aimed at easing the flow of materials, waste, and paperwork, and providing greater decision making on the floor.

Besides the functional groups which created the new departments, there were two special groups established to plan the

The Democratic Office, the Do-it-yourself Factory

landscaping of the plant and design the cafeteria. After drawing in a line through the cafeteria to indicate the wall for the traditional separation between white-collar and ink-spattered blue-collar diners, the committee reconsidered and removed that line in deference to the growing feeling among the workers that such a wall violated the spirit of the experiment.

Just as the place where the wall would have gone is pointed to with considerable pride, so, too, is the employee swimming pool, visible from the glass doors at one end of the cafeteria. Due to the high flammability of the chemicals used in the plant, Sadolin's insurers insisted on two sprinkler systems, which, in turn, required a large storage area for water. As the plant was being designed, it became apparent to both management and the workers that for about a thousand dollars extra, the storage tank could be made to double as a swimming pool—an idea that was leaped upon and executed. "If the attitude and atmosphere had not been what it was," says the plant manager, "I doubt the idea would have ever come up, and if it had, I don't think it would have been taken seriously."

According to the company's management, the experiment has been an overwhelming success, a conclusion attested to by the fact that the process will be repeated with Sadolin's planned research and development laboratory and, thereafter, with other new facilities. As of early May following the January opening, not one worker had quit, and, more significantly, in the two-year period during which the plant was being designed and built, the only worker of the original eighty-five the company lost was a man who died. Before the planning scheme was introduced, the turnover rate among the group in the old factory had been running over 15 percent a year. The introduction of worker planning also contributed to a halving of the absenteeism rate in the group from about 10 percent to 5 percent on the average day. During the first weeks in which the new plant was in operation, the productivity of the group rose 15 percent; that gain was still holding four months later. As is always true with such things, the rise was hard to attribute to specific factors, but it is Poulsen's contention that the factors of the new design, coupled with the consequent high morale of a group that had designed its own workplace, were responsible.

Plant manager Smith-Petersen says that the process has not only been important in that it gave each worker a chance to change those things which may have bothered him or her about a job for years, but gave each a chance to make his or her own mistakes. He cites the case of a man—whose collateral duties include making the labels for different batches of inks—who had neglected to ask for a place to make the labels and store his equipment. "He really couldn't complain to management, because he had made the mistake himself, and it was up to him to work out a solution," he says, adding, "The concept of self-determination at work in the planning of the factory was meant to be carried into its day-to-day operations." In the first months in the new factory, examples began to show up; for instance, when the plant opened, it had a contract with an outside firm to clean up the particularly messy residue of printing ink manufacturing. The work was found unsatisfactory by the workers, who got permission to cancel the contract and keep the place clean themselves.

As for the instigator's view of the new factory project, Poulsen feels that it has worked out better than he expected—he had been sure that there would be more squabbles and interminable rounds of meetings than there were—and that it has changed the company in a very fundamental way. Although he will not attempt to predict how the new plant will develop in the years ahead, the effect of the experiment has been such that he predicts "there will never be another major project in this company without the direct involvement of the workers concerned." He adds, "We think we are on the way to a whole new form of industrial life, and this factory was the turning point. We can't go back. The attitudes of the workers throughout the company have changed to the point where if today I were to go to a group

The Democratic Office, the Do-it-yourself Factory 309

of workers and ask them to solve a problem and they came up with a solution which required a new piece of equipment that cost ten thousand dollars, I'd be obliged to get it. This is as it should be."

The ultimate importance of what is happening at Sadolin transcends the idea of the worker-designed factory itself, which simply served as the most ambitious of a series of experiments in worker participation at the company. Poulsen believes that workers should be allowed to create their own working environments both physically and in terms of atmosphere and day-to-day conditions. The factory presented him with the perfect opportunity to demonstrate the sincerity of this belief.

Like many other Scandinavian firms with an experimental outlook, Sadolin is no upstart hole-in-the-wall outfit willing to recklessly gamble its future on backfire-prone experiments. On the contrary, it has been in operation since 1777 and has seen some of its most dramatic growth in recent years. Its printing ink operations are an example: It exports to fifty-five countries and has established printing ink plants in five of the fifteen nations where it now has factories. Nor has its willingness to experiment been born of the desperation of a company with deep-seated labor problems, but rather a willingness prompted by a management which decided that it was time to improve on what most companies would see as an adequate situation.

Taken together, the new environments which have been created at McDonald's, the FAA in Seattle, and Sadolin and Holmblad mark the beginning of a new appreciation for the worker as one deserving more than just good lighting and a clean, safe place to work. Although the three examples cited are quite different—the ink factory, for instance, being more radical than McDonald's—they all embody the realization that the working environment should not be an alien one. With all of the talk about worker alienation, too little attention has been paid to the physical side of the workplace as a source of that alienation. Thus far, most of the attention has gone to the job itself, but as these illustrations point out, there is much creative opportunity also available in reshaping the place where people work. Meanwhile, too much of the working world is still represented by environments which are closer to the one in the Michigan study than those reported on in Seattle, Oak Brook, and suburban Copenhagen. This state of affairs keeps current a classic description of the workplace: "Dead matter leaves the factory ennobled and transformed, whereas men are corrupted and degraded." This was written in 1931 by Pope Pius XI.

VIII
To Thine Own Self Be Boss

1
THE SELF-EMPLOYMENT ALTERNATIVE

Much of the hope for changing the way we work is still dependent on the good-natured, imaginative, and thoughtful response of others above us. With some notable exceptions, even the most innovative companies and institutions are moving with deliberation; experimenting, taking and implementing one thing at a time so as not to unsettle the status quo. Below the most progressive organizations in the changing workplace come the timid corporate innovators with their task forces and feasibility studies, then come the companies that dabble, and last is the innovative wasteland—where an awful lot of people work. Prospects for change in the near to mid-range future look, at best, to be based on gradual evolution.

If one is so inclined, an alternative to waiting for a new world of work to be brought to you by the same folks who created the job you now have is to split. That is, chuck it, strike out on your own, buck the tide! Become your own boss and create your own job along the freest, most personal, flexible, and enriching lines and rather than be paid by the hour or salaried by others to do their work, do your own work in an enterprise of your own.

Even for those without such an inclination, this alternative is worth examining, because it is a valuable model from which many corporate innovators have begun to borrow ideas, starting from the simple premise that independence in workstyle tends to promote higher satisfaction and productivity. Time and again, those managers implementing the ideas already discussed in this book have mentioned such borrowing. An excellent case in point is flex-time, which consciously attempts to give the employed-by-others a freedom that the self-employed have long cherished.

Self-employment describes a wide range of activities and a diverse lot of people ranging from heart surgeons to drug peddlers. For this reason, the species has to be separated into two subspecies. First, there are those who have purposefully opted for independence in their work and life: farmers, doctors, small business men, writers, accountants, carpenters, architects, gardeners, and too many others to mention. The second and much smaller category is made up of those who, for the most part, are self-employed because there is little else available to them: street vendors, migrant farm workers, and women who take in laundry. As this second category of workers represents mostly people who have accepted marginal self-employment, the fact that it is generally getting smaller (though it swells during recession) is fortunate, but so is the first category getting smaller, and this is unfortunate, as shrinkage in the first represents the closing down of an important option in the American working landscape.

It is this first category of the self-employed which will be explored in this chapter as a working alternative for the 1970s. Unlike the other chapters of the book, the present chapter draws heavily on the day-to-day working experiences of the author, who is self-employed, and attempts to give the positive as well as the negative side of this option while admitting that there is here a clear authorial bias in favor of the working freedom which accrues to those who boss themselves. The underlying premise at play is that, even with definite drawbacks, self-employment is a far more satisfying and free form of work than can be found in organizations—especially appropriate for those who do not want or need supervision and cannot identify with hierarchies. This conclusion has been suggested elsewhere. In *Where Have All the Robots Gone?*, the large-scale study of worker dissatisfaction, it was determined that work dissatisfaction [life dissatisfaction] was practically nonexistent among the self-employed, and the HEW *Work in America* study not only described it as the most satisfying form of work but called for new mechanisms to support it.

Discussing self-employment as an alternative for the future has

To Thine Own Self Be Boss

a certain whiff of futility about it, given the trend of society. Americans are herding themselves into dependent work situations in overwhelmingly increasing numbers. A century ago, less than half of all working people worked for wages or salaries, but the shift in the other direction has been going on ever since. By 1950, 75 percent of the nation's nonagricultural workforce labored for an employer, and by 1971, that number had jumped to 88 percent, leaving a scant 6.7 percent of the total nonfarm working population self-employed. With the notable exception of farming, which is still a stronghold for the self-employed, most other professions which have been most closely associated with autonomy and self-employment have been steadily jumping aboard the corporate bandwagon. According to government statistics, most photographers (66 percent) and most writers (62 percent) are now being bossed by others.

Behind such statistics are examples galore of a societal shift *accompli,* which tells us much about the degree to which society has become bureaucratic and corporate. For instance, one of the most cherished pieces of American folklore is that of the independent inventor tinkering his way to the next Xerox machine, laser ray, or Polaroid camera. Yet that revered tradition of Bell, Edison, and the brothers Wright is dying fast—just one of a number of dying independent traditions.

Beginning immediately after the Second World War, the independent self-employed inventor began to go into eclipse. Based on the total number of patents granted, by 1950, only 45 percent of all patents were granted to individuals, with the rest going to corporations, universities, foundations, and government agencies. In 1971, the number given to individuals had dropped to 21 percent, while the corporate share had leapt to 76 percent. What is more, of the decreasing number of individual inventors taking out patents today, most hold regular jobs and invent on the side, meaning that the number of full-time independent inventors is quite small.

The reasons for this turn of events are several. For one thing, the cost and red tape associated with getting a patent has increased to the point where just getting the patent requires a minimum of one thousand dollars in registry and attorney's fees, and may cost ten times that in the case of a sophisticated invention. Beyond this initial outlay, the inventor must pay to market his invention. Another factor working to make the lone inventor an anachronism is the great emphasis now placed on large-scale innovation, represented by the average of $17 billion that the government has been spending annually on research and development, and the fact that individual companies sink vast sums into their own research programs. Big industry and big government have become increasingly reluctant to take a chance on the small inventor's ideas. Significantly, the people who invented the devices and techniques needed for the Apollo program were, in the vast majority, faceless specialists on research and development teams in the government and in the laboratories of the big aerospace and electronics firms.

Understandably, today's unaffiliated inventors feel oppressed by industry, government, and even the press, despite the abstract homage we pay to the inventive urge and the spirits of Edison and Bell. In March 1973, I visited the International Patenting and Licensing Exposition at the New York Hilton Hotel, at which over six hundred inventors were showing their new ideas. Inventors from all over the United States and twenty-six foreign countries had come to show off an array of mostly serious ideas, with a smattering of bizarre items whose time has probably not come. What several inventors told me was that they resented the fact that the local press was treating them like so many Gyro Gearlooses. The complaint was valid; accounts of the show on TV and in the papers tended to emphasize the kinky, offbeat, and silly ideas, giving the exposition the aura of a freak show. *The New York Times* review of the show, entitled "Inventors Display Latest Gizmos and Widgets," featured items like doggie johns, self-lighting cigarettes, and zipper pullers, with little attention to such things as sophisticated electronics, new processes, new industrial tools, and important new devices such as one to monitor the heartbeat of an unborn child. An earnest young inventor from Oregon summed up his feelings this way: "You'll notice that when a big company like IBM or RCA comes out with a press release to announce a new invention of theirs the press treats it with respect, but when we try to show off our ideas, the tendency is to laugh at us." The fact that independent inventors feel this way is sad—but justified.

If the inventor is a convenient metaphor for the passing of the self-employed, so too is the small "mom and pop" grocery-store owner, the independent service-station operator (who has been trying to prove in court that the major oil companies are out to bury him), the single-lawyer law firm, the very small farmer, and others.

What is happening is that one of the most cherished pieces of the American Dream—the part that goes: "When things get too bad at work, I can always take off and do it on my own, on my own terms, as my own boss"—is in miserable shape but still doing quite nicely as a daydream.

2
STRIKING OUT ON YOUR OWN— A PERSONAL OBSERVATION

Self-employment is the daydream of the 1970s. The same wistful look of those of the 1950s and early 1960s who envied the professionals in their offices can now be seen on the faces of those inside the offices, their eyes fixed on the seaside loft where sails are rigged, on the writer's garret, the custom car shop, the ski instructor's billet, the rural antiques shop, the studio of a freelance photographer, the small farm, or even the beach-umbrella rental outlet—toward one of a thousand places where a body can become not a better part of a whole but rather a whole unto him- or herself. To everyone ranging from the lay-off prone, sick-of-it-all missile designer to the skilled factory hand or to the memo-and-regulation-crazed bureaucrat, the aspiration to break away is gaining in popularity.

Ironically, the boom in the self-employment aspiration parallels and equals the boom in office construction. Perhaps, it is always this way—the dream of going back to the farm came alive at the very moment when the family farm began to decline. This dream captivated minds in the 1930s, and some people actually followed through with it, but, more generally, the fantasies merely mesmerized the others, permitting them an easier way of denying that the day of the small American farmer was over. So it is that thoughts of entrepreneurship rise in proportion to the heights of buildings and spread along with new office contracts.

For many, then, self-employment is a countercurrent that permits the heavier flow of traffic in the other direction—toward institutional work. The exaggerated belief in the glory of going it alone is the greatest obstacle to the *possibility* of going it alone. More and more people envelop their aspirations in an impossible-dream trap which becomes, thereby, an effective component of the nine-to-five job trap. The bait for this trap is some unattainable goal, one that in your heart you know cannot be realized except at reincarnation in the next life.

This trap comes in many shapes and sizes, but three varieties are the most common. The first is the Big Moment Trap, in which the subject waits for Opportunity to come crashing through his or her door. Like the eager starlets of yore, the subject is mentally perched on the drugstore stool at Hollywood and Vine awaiting discovery. The second variation is the Great American Novel Trap, which is largely self-explanatory, tailor-made for those who need a goal so big that it precludes starting. Finally, there is the Weekly Newspaper in Vermont Trap, best described as an aspiration for those who need a convenient,

To Thine Own Self Be Boss

nice-sounding rustic dream that flies in the face of reality. It is usually held by those who don't know—or don't choose to know—that the back pages of *Editor and Publisher*, show that country weeklies in Vermont (and Oregon, Maine, and other parts of Pepperidge Farm Country) are folding, not being created. These schemers never make demographic sense, and consider it heresy to talk about ventures in booming areas such as Northern Virginia, Long Island, and suburban Atlanta because these *might* be able to support a folksy, muckraking weekly newspaper. Of course, there are Vermont weeklies that prosper. And there are people that get discovered, but these are long shots and, to put it crudely, long shots seldom pay the rent.

Beyond the impossible-dream traps, for those who get that far, there are other, more formidable obstacles to independent work: employee benefits. As the urge to be self-employed grows, these are usually also growing. They may not be deterrents to making the decision to break out—most employees do not notice their dependence on the company for cradle-to-grave security—but once the decision is made to cut away, the security gap suddenly widens frighteningly. At one time, the advantage in benefits the corporate types enjoyed over the self-employed could quickly and easily be equaled by any person who had the will to go out on his or her own. But as the advantages of institutional life have grown, so, too, has the corresponding insecurity of the outside world. As more and more people expect the needs of existence to be filled through the office, it is becoming more and more difficult to fill those needs outside. People who break with organizations have to cope with "benefit shock."

Perhaps the best description of benefit shock is contained in a fairly recent report from the Institute for the Future, a futurist think tank, projecting changes in employment and employee benefits in America in the near future, and describing what working conditions will probably be in 1985. The three-volume study, resulting from over a year's effort by a score of experts from fields in which benefit patterns are a prime concern, foresees broadly expanded advantages, and predicts that benefits will render self-employment even more of a rarity than it is today. One description of conditions in 1985 goes like this:

> Employee benefits have merged with compensation, social welfare, and on-the-job amenities; it is difficult to tell where one ends and the others begin. They are integrated in the minds of employers, employees, and the government. In effect, the environment created by the integration of social welfare programs and benefit programs required by legislation and existing as a result of agreements between labor and management has guaranteed all employees reasonable wages, more education and leisure, safer and more pleasant working places, and the avoidance of most of the fiscal hazards associated with accidents, ill health, and old age. The programs mesh together: we have translated at least part of our capacity for economic production into *security*. The "rugged" individual who wants to take his wages in cash instead of guarantees against adversity has almost passed from the scene.

The Institute's report is just one of many voices telling us that as corporate and government employee benefits increase and on-the-job sweeteners get sweeter, self-employment will appear ever more anachronistic and self-defeating. If you are self-employed, you can be assured that it will be almost impossible to keep up with those benefits generally available to the employed Joneses.

Some of the specific upcoming benefits that your co-workers may presently lay on you as reasons for not leaving might include an odds-on-shot at a four-day workweek, improved health benefits, and periodic raises, but these are peanuts compared to the cornucopia of benefits predicted by the Institute. Assuming that the Institute is basically correct, in your bout with benefit shock you must not only consider the weight of benefits now

To Thine Own Self Be Boss

provided but add to them those which will be commonplace by 1985:

¶ Employers will pay about 50 percent of payroll in benefits.

¶ Benefits will generally reflect cost of living. For example, cost-of-living escalators will be built into most pension plans, effectively guaranteeing the pensioner a standard of living rather than a dollar amount.

¶ The thirty-five-hour week and flexible working hours will be common, and more holidays and longer vacations the norm.

¶ Corporate-owned leisure facilities will be available to most employees, along with many more leisure-oriented benefits.

¶ It will be common to find on-site education programs and facilities, and some firms will provide educational leaves and even paid sabbaticals for employees.

¶ Subsidized housing and company cars will be available to many employees, along with savings plans in which the employer matches the employee's deposits.

¶ Expansive employee-counseling programs on matters as diverse as taxes, investments, and retirement will be widespread.

¶ Psychiatric and dental-care provisions will be part of the standard package of medical benefits.

¶ Since individual automobile insurance costs will have zoomed out of sight, group car insurance offered through the company will become the norm.

¶ Interconglomerate pension plans will have been established nationally, ushering in the day of the truly movable pension.

Alvin Toffler, author of *Future Shock*, predicted in a 1967 essay entitled "The Concept of Post-economic Work" a world in which ". . . want ads would seek employees on the basis of the kind of experience the employing company would supply. Instead of merely offering hospitalization, sabbaticals, and on-the-job·training, the employer might offer the best educational facilities, the most progressive psychologists and the best sensory gratification chambers in the country." Addressing itself to Toffler's vision, the

Institute report offered this comment, "Today, in 1985, we are still far from the world which Toffler painted, and yet the direction in which we seem to be moving is quite consistent with his image of our future society."

Benefit shock is, at best, a difficult reaction with which to contend. Such visions of the future have their effect on the currently self-employed, who project the disadvantages of their situation and conclude that they will be relatively much worse off later than now. Such despair can be countered, depending on one's love for "benefit freedom," the funny and insecure set of feelings not far removed from those held by the unsomatized Mr. Savage at the end of *Brave New World*. Benefit freedom includes not having to do what one is doing now until 1985, being unbossed and unbossing, and relying on ingenuity to make up for security (for instance, forming an independent group to buy car insurance as it becomes increasingly difficult to purchase alone). The value of such freedoms may continue to inflate as the price each individual must pay for his or her benefits (in terms of decreasing autonomy) becomes greater.

The prophecies of the Institute for the Future are already beginning to be fulfilled. The men from Hartford, for instance, are not all that excited anymore about what they term "non-group individuals." They may be eager to sell you life insurance, but they are less eager to sell medical coverage to the self-employed. In most cases, the independent must employ some razzle-dazzle consumer salesmanship to get such coverage, one area in which the burden of Willie Loman falls not on the seller, but on the buyer. Group health and hospitalization insurance, the only kind people can afford these days, is increasingly bought in large blocks by employers, and when one seeks single-person or single-family coverage, one can expect physicals and anticipate "exemptions" that relieve the insurance company of any responsibility for past ailments or illnesses. Maternity coverage is virtually unheard of outside group plans, and one can also forget about disability insurance or any policy that pays for working days lost, because such things are almost never sold to the unsalaried. In short, in the eyes of the insurance computers and tables, the self-employed person becomes a random, unloved digit.

To lenders and merchants, the self-employed are generally relegated to the untouchable status of those who carry cash. (Since nobody trusts anybody with hard money anymore, it is, as Marshall McLuhan puts it, a "poor man's credit card.") Credit, loans, little plastic cards, and other amenities do not come easily to those who have no salary to proclaim and to have garnished and no work telephone number where creditors can call for a quick financial history. The self-employed person is advised to sharpen up the traditional American ability to persuade others to "run up a tab" or "hang on for a few days." Generally, little stores, dentists, and others with some kinship to self-employment are pretty easy to deal with on this basis. Such is definitely not the case with big institutions, those same ones that proclaim their love for the entrepreneurial spirit.

The day-to-day realities of getting along on less-than-adequate health insurance and other self-purchased benefits can be dispiriting, and so can the demands for payment made by institutions upon those self-employed. The hospital is a good case in point. The self-employed person without full coverage commonly has to pay at the door in cash, while those on corporate or government insurance plans flash a little card which guarantees that Blue Cross or some other insuring agency will ante up some weeks later. Outside of a group, it is all but impossible to come up with maternity coverage, so, for example, when the author's wife entered a large Washington hospital to have our baby the hospital demanded five hundred dollars cash in advance; a little checking proved that this is now common practice elsewhere. Not only does this not happen to most employed persons, but their Blue Cross or whatever does not pay the hospital for several months.

Another financial problem: Our material well-being is becoming more and more a function of being able to meet timed payments and to plan ahead financially. The only thing that the self-employed can bank on today is the inability to time his finances and plan financially. Once freed from wages and a salary, one is no longer paid on every second Tuesday or Friday. One's new enterprise will most likely be supplying goods or services to others, and having "sold" something is often a far cry from getting paid for it. For instance, writers find a veritable payment-policy jungle in their realm: Some of their outlets give money in advance, others pay on acceptance, and still others when the article or book is on sale. It is, therefore, not unusual for the self-employed to be owed relatively vast sums for their labors without having any money in pocket. Meanwhile, as we all know, the clearly established trend is for large institutions to demand payments from the individual on exact schedules. To cite one of many, the person on his own payroll has nobody to withhold his income taxes in small doses, so it must be paid in jarring quarterly lumps which come straight from the pocket. Then there is the business of Social Security payments. Not only do the self-employed pay them out of pocket, but they have to pay more than their employed peers. What is often forgotten is that employers pay a part of Social Security; as his own employer, the whole amount must be paid by the self-employed individual. As a result, to the person leaving a job, Social Security deductions become, in truth, what is very appropriately but unwittingly called *Self-employment Tax*. If, in 1974, a person made $12,600 as an employed worker, he had $737.10 deducted for Social Security, but if he made the same amount on his own his Self-employment Tax came to $1,008.00. Perhaps $261.10 is not too much to manage, but Social Security is going up—and it is by no means the only tax on self-employment.

The major offsetting consideration in these matters of finance and benefits is that as a self-employed person you are now in control, being the owner of the enterprise in question. If it makes it financially, so do you, in which case it is easier for you to buy your own benefits and provide for the needs of your family. This is unabashedly capitalistic, the ultimate in profit sharing. You take your vacations without any pay, but you can take them when *you* want them, and for the amount of time you deem fit; you can take none, or a lot, or none for a few years, and then take off for a really long one. If the folks at the corporation you have left wake up to a new benefit package which adds three days' vacation, you can add four to your own.

Harder to offset are some of the societal and statutory factors working to discourage the lone worker. For example, the burgeoning proclivity to zone communities is actually making it illegal to work at home in many areas. More and more so-called "nice" neighborhoods, fearing backyard rendering operations and cottage industries that might mushroom, have zoned out all home-based businesses (although doctors, dentists, and veterinarians are often exempted). For the same reason, more and more apartment and house leases specify that no business is to be conducted on the premises of the rental unit. Clearly, many residential areas have become exclusively so in order to serve only as centers for working people to come home to. Moreover, several jurisdictions now have special taxes on the income of the self-employed. In the waning days of the Lindsay Administration in New York, for example, a special 2 percent tax on income became a new liability for the self-employed.

On another level, there is overwhelming evidence that we are entering an age of instantaneous computerized procedures, in which such things as international computer links for routine commercial and governmental transactions will hum away, generally freeing us from dreaded clerkships and nagging detail. In contrast to this marvelous world of cybernation stands the self-employed individual, who, of economic necessity, must languish in an unautomated state, wallowing in his own details. Often the margin between success and failure for the self-employed is the ability to note every dime and detail of every transaction in crummy little notebooks. Clear, comprehensive records are required by what the tax men call "unincorporated small businesses," and if one does not want to be taxed into insolvency, he must prove that he, like multinational corporations, has incurred business expenses. As with big companies, certain tax breaks are offered to the self-employed, such as being able to deduct part of the rent as a business expense. Such things are worth knowing about, but they require some heavy reading in tax guides.

Generally, the self-employed are thought to be pursuing a specialization such as writing or mechanics, but they must devote sizable chunks of time to playing the many roles of an institution. As jobs and roles in society have become increasingly specialized, the self-employed person must buck the trend by becoming not only his own tax consultant but also his own promoter, salesman, accountant, bill collector, treasurer, secretary, janitor, coffee shop, building maintenance staff, and trash removal service.

Despite all of these adverse trends, ranging from increasingly traumatic benefit shock to the need to fill a variety of detail-laden commercial roles, the picture is not all bleak. Even lumped together, the disadvantages to self-employment do not as yet add up to an insurmountable hurdle. The simple fact that many thriving self-employed people are roaming about is testament to the surmountability of the odds. To be sure, the aforementioned list of disadvantages suggests that, unless things take a radically new direction, the odds against realizing the aspiration to becoming self-employed will grow to a long-shot. But there is clearly still time to squeeze through the door; it is as if society is telling us the same thing we hear from the department store P.A.-system voice, "Attention shoppers: this is your last chance. . . ."

While the logistics of breaking away from the job trap may become more of a hurdle, the reasons for resistance are strong and will remain so as long as bureaucracies and organizations retain their present dominant character. Those major desires that define the dream—happiness, freedom, and asserting one's integrity—are still very real. Beyond these major considerations there is yet another lure: the indefinite but promising new quality of life awaiting those freeing themselves from captivity. One's days will change, taking on an entirely new complexion. Some aspects of these days are good, some bad—but almost all are of one's own doing, and, as many who are self-employed will testify, become habit-forming.

For openers, there are a host of things which strike one's fancy in the new incarnation, but which may also give pause. First, there is the mild jolt upon realizing that the phrase "striking out on one's own" has a double meaning, and the realization that one is too small a business to qualify for Small Business loans and other Small Business Administration goodies.

On a more upbeat level, there are the incidents which serve to revitalize one's enthusiasm. For example, there is the phone report from one's former place of employment in which the quavering voice of a former coworker says that the office politics have degenerated to their meanest level in history. "Not so," you are liable to tell him or her with cruel glee, "just as bad when I left." Then there is the blissful business of listening to the morning and/or evening reports of traffic snafus on the radio—just as one imagines the President and other work-at-homes do.

Finally, there are the meaningful little rituals that the self-employed create to celebrate their freedom. Such a ritual can be as simple as creating a sign that reads, "I know things are slow, but you're going to have to find some way of LOOKING BUSY anyhow," or some other endearing slogan commemorating the bad old times and hanging it in a place where you will see it each morning. One may even opt to tuck in his shirt for the hell of it to show that he really does care about corporate image. Or one may decide that it would be nice to hold an "office Christmas party" with you, your spouse, a friend of the small business, and a six-pack.

Being your own boss, you encounter new and sometimes contradictory concepts of time. Normally, the self-employed person finds himself or herself plagued by recurring questions such as "When one is on one's own, is every day Saturday, or Monday, or is every day a little of each?" Then there are a host of purely pleasurable encounters with time: having the exhilarating experience of, say, decreeing Wednesday and Thursday the weekend (and then working on everyone else's weekend); learning anew, like a kid let out for the summer, to see time as one's own and to feel the heady burden of contending with its promises and limitations; realizing that 9:00 A.M. and 5:00 P.M. are just two relatively lackluster digits on the old wall clock; remembering that you can take time off without having "earned" it and without having asked for it; or, after four days of ten-minute lunches, taking a three-hour lunch and finding that there is really nobody to ask you where you have been. The newly freed can be prepared for the first time in years to find out what eight hours means in terms of what really can or cannot be done when one is liberated from meetings, bossing and being bossed, office politics, baseball pools, telephone marathons, collections for the about-to-be-wed lady in the accounting department, and all the rest of the things that people who use terms such as "counterproductive" in their memos must face every day.

On the other hand, there are unpleasant discoveries, such as one's first encounter with the pressures of an unproductive day or days. One recalls wistfully that as a foreman, junior executive, or government worker, such days meant much less because somebody paid your way through them.

A selfish outlook on time is indeed a natural outgrowth of living in the new free-time dimension. One can work the four-day week (or the six-day week); flex-time is there for the doing, and experimenting with time can be the new order of the day, so protecting your time from outside encroachment means protecting your right to be free and to make your own rules.

Consider one of many examples of why this protective attitude is called for. Many companies today require that a pregnant worker leave work months before she feels she needs to. Commonly, policy also dictates that, in addition to an early departure, she must leave without re-employment rights and no pay. Few jurisdictions have laws protecting the expectant mother, and some even have laws which aggravate the corporate picture; the State of Washington, for example, requires women to be off their jobs in the fifth month of pregnancy (although the law doesn't cover housework). Much of this attitude can be traced back to an ugly nineteenth-century mind-set which held that public pregnancy was somehow obscene (although child labor wasn't). The self-employed woman can, of course, overthrow these arcane practices. For that matter, there is nothing to stop the self-employed male from taking some days off as his own paternity leave, to help the mother and to enjoy the new child.

Not to be overlooked, either, are some unexpected little adjustments to time which are often quite fun. For instance, there is a certain glee—if such things appeal to one—in observing the old body clock go bonkers as it realizes that the person it is inside of is no longer observing programed wake-ups, appointed coffee breaks, ritual lunch hours, and corporate-subsidized (and sometimes monitored) midmorning bowel movements. Thus freed from this clock which was set by others, one is given the creative do-it-yourself option of adjusting it to one's own specifications.

No less dramatic than the new sense of time are those crises of identity which occur to the newly self-employed when others find that they have encountered a *bona fide* weirdo without a boss. Examples:

¶ You are stopped by a traffic policeman to be given a ticket and he asks the name of your employer. You say that you work for yourself. Next he asks, "Come on, where do you work, or are you employed or not?" You say "self-employed" with the pride of a robber baron, but you know that he thinks that you are an able-bodied welfare loafer. He, among others you meet, "knows" that "self-employed" is a tired euphemism for being out of work.

¶ If you are self-employed at home, neighbors become curious and somehow nervous about the fact that you are around the house a lot and not tying up traffic. To those busybodies who demand to know your business, you are torn between answering the prideful "self-employed" offered to the cop and "I've decided to take up mugging and now work nights."

¶ Your alumni group or a similar group sends you a computer-readable form to fill out, in which you are asked to check the box that describes your occupation. You find that there is no box for you so you scribble something in the margin describing what you do. The machine sends you another form and a note saying that the first form was incomplete. You pencil in another box and write "other" next to it and then check it off. The alumni computer accepts that, as will other data and dossier-gathering devices which, as a group, consider you as undigestible as anything besides "other."

Also encountered under the heading of identity are other situations of mixed blessing. One is the discovery—both limiting and liberating—made by all newly self-employed people that suddenly one is bereft of title and credentials for the first time since he or she was eleven years old and elevated to the position of corresponding secretary for the stamp collector's club. One feels nude. For example, reporters who have become freelance writers are stripped of press passes; former government people are numbed by the plunge from GS–12 to GS–00. (This situation can be easily simulated in advance by taking your wallet and pulling out one at a time all of those identity cards, passes, business credit cards, credit union memberships, and the like until you are left with only your driver's license and library card.)

Still another typical identity-reckoning problem occurs when, despite other political proclivities, one finds oneself thinking in the most starkly capitalistic terms on certain issues. As an unincorporated, unsubsidized small business, one finds one's attitudes bent to the point that it is not rare to find oneself watching some jowly fat-cat industry spokesman on the tube

To Thine Own Self Be Boss 331

pleading for some new subsidy, Congressional bailout, depletion allowance, or other taxpayer-supplied amenity, and mumbling things like "socialist creep." In another version of the same attitude, one dreams of addressing the board of Exxon, Lockheed, or GE to brief them on the thrills and realities of operating in a rigorous free-market economy.

But these identity crises have a short life and disappear with time. One's identity as a Lone Ranger in the land of the herded is a refreshing one. No longer is your identity defined by a salary, a title, or a job level assigned to you by others. Your vocation and avocation are allowed to merge. Your job is you and what you want to make of it, and there is nobody there to tell you that you are getting in over your head, that you are not part of the game plan, or whatever. These things are now your business. If the work situation you have created for yourself is not exactly right, you are the dictator who can change it. While there are many new problems to be faced, a large share of them is immediately traceable to yourself and are not to be blamed on others, so the chance to solve them is paradoxically both easy (because they are yours and you are in control) and tough (because the convenience of blaming "them" is removed, and you stand in the nakedness of your own mistakes). Of course, this way of worklife is one person's desire and another's hell; there are many who are not suited for it.

Not to be overlooked in this discussion are the many revelations that come to the self-employed about costs, which are liable to change one's habits of consumption radically. Up, one quickly realizes, is the cost of paper clips and other consumables which used to be "borrowed" from your employer. So, too, are utility bills (if one works at home). On the other hand, many things come down. In most cases, commuting costs, clothing costs, and lunch allotments are sharply reduced. Often, the most dramatic decrease is in what the corporate-employed person writes off as "walking-around money," or that spent for the bag of M&M's for extra midmorning energy, the beers after work, overpriced bitter coffee in plastic cups, and the twenty-five-cent chances taken on the St. Somethingorother's raffle for a new Pinto. Best yet, somewhere along the line, you may lose such vices as the costly—not to mention fattening—lust for those ubiquitous, doughy, morning Danish pastries.

The best is saved for last: those triumphs which mean so much to the self-employed, those things that carry little importance for those employed by others but are totally and thrillingly relevant to the self-employed. Among them: paying a bill on time, getting paid for one of your goods or services on time, getting paid (period), noting offhandedly that one might be able to make it through the year financially, and finishing one project and launching another without getting five people to okay the completion of the first and another five to approve starting the second. One also learns to avoid new traps, such as the easing-back-to-the-old-job-in-pieces trap and the big-deal trap. The first trap is commonly baited with the offer of fee for going back to one's old job for a few days to help them out of a jam. No matter how tempting, one learns to avoid it with a polite "no." The big-deal trap is an occupational hazard of the self-employed, because, for reasons that are not altogether clear, people working on their own act as magnets for those who are in perpetual possession of seldom-executed big deals. This trap is rendered harmless, when one is presented with a big deal, by noting it, filing it in the "big deal" file, and plowing ahead with one's own little deals.

Once such triumphs begin to occur with any frequency, the habit is formed, and one concludes that, despite a paucity of benefits and the trends of contemporary life, one has passed the mental point of no return. You ask: Is all of this just a new trap with its own constraints, limitations, and demands on freedom? Perhaps so, but if it is, at least, it is a trap of your own design and, for that reason, not at all a bad place to live—and a great place to work.

3
Rescuing
an Anachronism

Having determined that self-employment is on the decline as an American option and having argued that with all of its advantages and disadvantages, it is worth saving as a sanctuary from the organized and bureaucratized world, we turn now to the question of how the option can be held open and widened.

Despite the steady decline in the self-employed population, there are some encouraging developments which deserve aid and comfort. None is, in itself, a cure-all, but all have something going for them. Most respond to the needs of the unincorporated self-employed and the incorporated small businessperson—two breeds whose fates are intertwined.

One recent important call for new encouragement of self-employment appears in the HEW *Work in America* study, which has concluded that this form of work is ". . . the most satisfactory of all kinds of employment." It suggests that we might consider leveling some of the hurdles which are making self-employment an increasingly difficult road to job satisfaction and job creation. To this end, it suggests that tax laws and other regulations be re-examined and revised to give the self-employed and small business owner a better chance for survival among the giant institutions which have their own galaxy of breaks and considerations. Such a course, the report says:

> . . . might require the exemption of certain categories of the self-employed and the smallest businesses . . . from certain licensing, insurance regulations, and expensive and time-consuming reporting to government agencies. Also we might make more risk capital available through the Economic Development Administration and through the Small Business Administration and through incentives to private

investors. . . . Many other ideas, no doubt, can be developed to support self-employment and small business.

Such suggestions are not entirely new, having been pushed for some time by professional and trade groups representing small enterprise, and by certain Congressmen who have identified with the little entrepreneur rather than the companies in the *Fortune* "500." One of the strongest-felt injustices against which these people are fighting is the tax system, which favors big business. Leading this fight has been the Small Business Association (a lobbying group not to be confused with the Small Business Administration), whose major premise in this area is that, by hook, crook, loophole, and subsidy, the big companies have been able to create a system where they are taxed at a much lower rate than small businesses. This assertion is not just lobbyist's blather, but has been confirmed by several Congressional committees investigating the situation. One finding was that, in 1969, the nation's one hundred biggest companies paid corporate taxes of 26.9 percent, while the small companies averaged 44 percent—a gap in favor of big boys to the tune of 17.1 percent. Representative Charles Vanick (D.-Ohio), one of the voices for small business on the Hill, stated flatly before the Joint Economic Committee recently, "Our tax laws operate to suppress the small business." A significant movement is underway for small-business tax reform at this point, and has already garnered an amazing degree of support—ranging from some of the most liberal Senators to some of the most conservative House members—making the chances for a slate of reforms in the near future seem good.

In the same vein, another *Work in America* suggestion for which small businesses and self-employed individuals are pushing is relief from the paperwork and form-filing forced upon them from government at all levels. This may sound like a small problem, but it is not. A 1973 study by the Senate Small Business

Committee revealed that over five thousand different forms are routinely filed by businesses to the government—*exclusive* of Internal Revenue Service forms and those required by state and local governments—a revelation which prompted Senator Thomas McIntire (D.-N.H.) to say that small business is drowning in a sea of red ink imposed by a mountain of red tape. Volume is not the only problem. Many of the forms themselves have built-in irritations. For instance, in mid-January 1973, the Census Bureau sent out a packet of forms for its 1972 Economic Census that had to be completed and mailed back by February 15. The catch was that the forms required information on 1972 taxes which did not have to be completed until April 15, meaning that, in order to comply with the census, the dozens of tax forms which a firm must complete had to be done on a rush basis well before the tax people needed them.

While the paperwork problem is immense for the incorporated self-employed person and the small businessperson, even the simplest unincorporated one-person operation is liable to be buried in paper by zealots from government paper mills. In an article in *Writer's Yearbook,* a freelance writer from New Mexico recently wrote about the Kafkaesque series of events which happened to him. It began with a threatening phone call from his state's Bureau of Revenue to the effect that he was in violation of the law because he had not registered as a business. On top of this he found that he was not supplying monthly reports of earnings to the state as required, and was not paying a special tax of 4 percent on his gross receipts. Later, he also found that he was in violation of city law to boot, as he did not have a city license to work, was not paying a special "occupation tax" of one dollar per one thousand dollars earned, and had not appealed to the zoning board for a permit granting him the right to operate a "home business." Forms begat forms, and at the end of the narrative, this lone, unincorporated individual working out of his den at home had finally become licensed with all the appropriate forms, but was still fighting the monumental paper load which had been imposed on him.

Although relief is not really in sight as yet—and one can bet that the situation will get worse before it gets better—some members of Congress have begun to listen to the legitimate protests of the paper-burdened, and this may someday lead to some letup at the Federal level. An added sweetener for reform in this area has been pointed out by John Lewis, executive vice-president of the National Small Business Association, who says, "One of the most logical ways to reduce government spending is to first determine which reports are essential to the efficient functioning of government. By eliminating unnecessary reports, unnecessary administrative costs are also eliminated."

Besides these practical points of tax reform and paperwork relief, which were also raised by the HEW task force, its *Work in America* went on to make the seldom-heard recommendation of developing courses in entrepreneurial skills in the schools. The report viewed our schools as institutions concentrating on training us for employment by others, and which have kept the practical knowledge needed for self-employment in the realm of a "well-kept secret." It goes on to say, ". . . this knowledge is usually transmitted from father to son in middle-class families, and is thus difficult for women or the poor to obtain."

This image of the educational system as a corporate training ground has been seen by others. Alvin Toffler, in *Future Shock*, argues that mass education was the ingenious machine constructed by industrialists to serve their needs. He says, ". . . the whole idea of assembling masses of students [raw material] to be processed by teachers [workers] in a centrally located school [factory] was a stroke of industrial genius. . . . The inner life of the school thus became an anticipatory mirror, a perfect introduction to industrial society." On a more mundane, less metaphoric level, one can see the modern customs of education which drive this home. They range from the common practice of taking elementary school children to see people at work in factories and offices to the role which colleges and universities play as recruiting centers for government and industry. There are few colleges which do not offer their seniors long lists of recruiters to meet; yet few—if any—set up any formal situation where students can consider the option of self-employment.

This lack of preparation in entrepreneurial skills is, no doubt, partially responsible for the very high rate of failure which attends those striking out on their own today. There are no figures on failure among the unincorporated self-starters, but the rate is probably not too far out of line with the grim statistics for those who do start their own companies. The Department of Commerce has determined that only one out of five new businesses is likely to last for ten years, and a mere half make it past the first year and a half. In going over the 10,326 firms that went under during 1971, Dun and Bradstreet concluded that 93 percent of them died because of such owner-oriented reasons as lack of experience, incompetence, and the inability to collect monies owed. The risk is, of course, fantastic, and that cannot be altered, but one must wonder how much lower the failure rate would be if there were greater opportunity to learn about these risks and how to live with them.

Admittedly, the suggestion that such counter-*Organization-Man* training be introduced to the world of education is something far from implementation or even serious consideration. But the idea does deserve serious consideration for the simple reason that the next generation of Americans deserve more than solely being directed into careers with the ITTs of the world whether or not they want to be. Such a change would break with the assumption that all but the few who will become doctors or take over their father's stores are relegated to work for others for wages or salaries.

If educational change in the direction of self-employment is far off and, perhaps, never destined to be implemented, other institutional changes have begun to occur. For instance, the historically small and lackluster United States Small Business Administration has begun developing some new ideas which go beyond its traditional role as an agent which obtains and guarantees loans. Such items as lease guarantees, revolving lines of credit for small contractors, and management consulting services to borrowers are coming to the fore. Although only time will tell if its actions are as good as its stated intentions, the SBA is now stressing its role as an advocate for small business, and is working to make sure that other government agencies treat small business fairly. On another institutional front, more and more self-employed people have begun to organize themselves into associations to obtain group hospitalization and other benefit plans and to advocate their positions nationally. While some groups—most notably doctors and farmers—have long been associated formally, others have only lately begun to, ranging from black merchants to writers and inventors.

Even in some of the bleakest corners of the self-employed world, new institutional arrangements show promise. Even for the dying breed of the independent inventor mentioned earlier, there are some positive trends which could breathe new life into the patient. One is the idea of a loose banding together to get ideas marketed on a national scale. One of the few existing examples in this area is the Oregon Inventors Council, run by the College of Business Administration at the University of Oregon, which has been formed to help local inventors get themselves and their ideas into the marketplace. Another source of relief is beginning belatedly to emerge from the same Federal Government which, over the years, has stacked the deck against the independent inventor with its costly rigamarole for patent-granting and its overwhelming proclivity for corporate innovators. A little-known group called the Office of Invention and Innovation at the National Bureau of Standards is now beginning to show that at least some people in government see the independent inventor as a species worth saving. One service provided by the group is a free invention-referral service by

To Thine Own Self Be Boss 339

which an idea is forwarded to them and they, in turn, determine what Federal agency or agencies might have use for it and forward it accordingly. This service is intended to help the small inventor get an idea into channels where it is most likely to find a buyer or an agency which will help develop it. Another service is the group's program of expositions for inventors held periodically in various parts of the country. For a token ten-dollar fee, an invention can be shown in the hope that it will be scouted and bought by an industrialist out looking for a new product. All of this is not to say that the number of lone inventors will rise, but it may help keep a good number afloat and create a climate that will induce others to enter the field. Lowering the cost of getting a patent through patent reform would also help considerably.

Still another movement which has begun to gather some momentum is one leading to the mechanism by which self-employed persons will be better able to provide their own self-designed benefits. The most notable accomplishment to date in this area has been a bill sponsored by former Rep. Eugene Keogh (D.-N.J.) which was passed in 1962, allowing the self-employed to set aside in a tax-file shelter as much as 10 percent of their yearly income (up to a maximum of twenty-five hundred dollars), thereby allowing them to set up their own pension plans with some of the same tax breaks which accrue to employers who set up pensions for their workers. Once retired, the individual can begin taking back the money he has invested, paying taxes on his pension as retirement income. Although the plan displeased both the Kennedy and Johnson Administrations, which felt that it was a drain on tax revenues, it has become increasingly popular, and the push for its liberalization has come from forces ranging from the insurance industry (which set up many of the Keogh plans for individuals) to professional associations (whose members have felt that they should be able to squirrel away more). In April 1973, President Nixon sent Congress his bill on pension reform which revised the Keogh level to 15 percent of one's income or seventy-five hundred dollars, whichever is less. The bill passed both houses by an overwhelming majority as part of a pension-reform package, and was signed into law by President Ford on Labor Day 1974.

Despite these advances, the fact of the matter is that too few of those in power—who dearly love to pay abstract homage to the entrepreneurial spirit—have seriously questioned the narrowing of the option to be self-employed and small. For all the rhetoric which the Nixon Administration and much of Congress has expended on the idea of boosting minority small enterprise in America, relatively little has actually been done. In 1971, the year the push to help develop small business with minority owners got going, the amount loaned to 8,387 new and existing minority enterprises was $231 million. This was laughably small compared to the goodies that government had in store for big business. One 1971 loan in and of itself—the $250 million to bail out Lockheed—was much larger than the entire much-touted loan plan for minority business.*

All of this leads to the conclusion that self-employment is an important option that must be kept open for some, although it is, of course, impractical for the majority. It is inconceivable that the United States or any industrialized nation will ever again be dominated by freelance operators. Perhaps their number will

---

* Overlooking the small operator is common to both sides of the political aisle. During the 1972 campaign, for example, George McGovern continually made an unthinking gaff which was inconsistent with his something-for-the-little-guy philosophy. In explaining the tax reforms which would take place when he took office, he stressed again and again that reform would not increase the tax burden of those who ". . . depend on wages or salaries for their income." He probably meant that he intended to sock the coupon-clippers and the idle rich, but he never made that clear. As a result, the impression he gave was that Harold Geneen, whose salary as ITT Chairman hit $812,494 recently, or Henry Ford II, whose job pays him $702,000, were not to be touched, but that a nonsalaried, independent cabbie making $10,000 or the capitalist owner of a barber shop making $15,500 were in for a shellacking.

To Thine Own Self Be Boss

never go above 10 percent of the American working population. This brings us again to the world of organizations, where most people work, after all, and where some employers are groping toward ways to grant their employees greater authority, flexibility, and freedom—the very things that people head off on their own to find.

❋IX❋
Brave New Work

1
PORTENTS OF THE FUTURE

By late 1974, when this book was nearing completion, two important phenomena were manifesting themselves in the area of workplace reform which, taken together, add much extra weight to the contention that innovations of the type reported in preceding chapters are not just curiosities randomly popping up here and there, but harbingers of things to come.

The first of these is that the process of job restructuring, reform, and general tinkering with the old principles is going out of public view at many companies. Increasingly, the situation in which a company like Volvo, General Foods, or Bankers Trust proudly lets the world know about its experiments is giving way to a situation in which companies are telling little, if anything, about their experiences. In fact, some of those who were eager to tell about their initial experiments—mostly small-scale—are now granting very little information as the lessons of those experiments are applied throughout the organization.

At first glance, it would seem that this silence is a reflection of the fear of letting the world know about something which may fail. While this is certainly a factor in some situations, the major reason is that change is proving to be such a windfall to those implementing it that the change process is beginning to be seen as an important proprietary development—akin to the discovery of a new product or industrial process. For many companies, finding a path to employee satisfaction, lower turnover, and higher productivity is looked upon as a highly valued discovery not to be shared with competitors. Some see little sense in giving away what they have pioneered at any price, while others have gone into the unlikely business of job consulting with others for a fee. Among those who have hung out shingles as job consultants are The Travelers, American Airlines, Lockheed, and Ralston Purina.

In practice, this trend toward keeping such things under wraps is frustrating to those trying to keep posted. An example of this—and there are many—occurred when an independent consultant, bursting with pride, gave me the outline of a major restructuring on which he was working at a major insurance company. The account he gave was that the company was in the throes of completely changing its organization and the way individuals worked. The conditions he insisted on before he gave me the information were that I could not use it unless I got it firsthand from the company, and that I couldn't use his name when contacting them, as he was not supposed to be talking about it. I called the man running the program inside the organization, asked him about it, and was told that he wasn't sure what I was talking about. When I came back with a fuller description of what I knew was going on, he said, "Oh, that. We won't be able to talk about it for a couple of years."

So it is that job reform has now begun to emerge as a valued commodity rather than just something for the daring to experiment with. Or, put more dramatically: The humanization of work is becoming an element of the profit motive. Utopian thinking aside, this seems to be the best thing that could happen. It not only makes change acceptable at the most capitalistic level, but it should also provide what can be termed "antifad insurance." If the move to an improved and humanized workplace solely rested on idealism and "being nice," it might develop nicely during flush periods and then be the first item thrown overboard in an economic slowdown. This is precisely what happened with the highly touted industrial application of sensitivity training, which flowered in the salad days of the mid- to late 1960s and all but disappeared when profits slipped. Job reform, on the other hand, flourished in the recessionary-inflationary atmosphere of 1974-1975, the kind of years that kill mere fads.

Brave New Work

The second observed phenomenon is that experiments which are currently beginning, soon to get underway, or even just being seriously considered are, compared with those of only a few years ago, bigger, more ambitious, greater in number, and involve a greater variety of participants—including trade unions, government employers, and those who previously sat on the sidelines wearing jerseys marked "academic theorist." It seems appropriate to say that the scattered early pioneering, which has been the source of most of the material in this book, is beginning to spread to the extent that it is taking on the character of a fuller *exploratory movement.*

Despite the recent tendency of many companies to take their efforts underground, there exists ample evidence to support the assertion that much development is taking place. The following examples—taken from organizations where secrecy is *not* the rule—are only a sampling, but sufficient to demonstrate this development.

The Ohio Project. For the first time, leaders in a highly industrialized state have recognized that work restructuring on a broad scale will improve the state's competitive position. The idea goes back to 1972, when former Governor John J. Gilligan of Ohio set up a Council to dig into the problems affecting the business and employment health of the state. This Council, made up of leaders from business, education, and labor, quickly concluded that one of the most pressing problems was the loss of jobs to the South and overseas, and that efforts must begin to improve—and ultimately to save—jobs in the state. As a first step toward job improvement, the Council set up a Quality of Work Project (which was eventually to turn itself into the permanent, not-for-profit Quality of Work Institute) to assist labor and management in efforts toward restructuring work. The Project, as well as the subsequent Institute, has been jointly led by labor and management, which, in this case, includes such people as the chairman of the B. F. Goodrich Company and the president of the Ohio AFL–CIO.

The immediate purpose of the Committee was to help initiate a series of joint management-labor demonstration projects in the area of job restructuring, hopefully to become useful models for other Ohio companies. As for the role it will play, a statement put out by the group says, "It is not the purpose of the Quality of Work Project to impose any solutions. The function of the Project is to work with labor and management to define what the problems are in a specific plant, and, at the request of the parties involved, to arrange for the assistance of the country's top experts in dealing with these problems." The first project began in mid-February at a plant of a major corporation in Northeastern Ohio, in collaboration with a major union. Other projects were underway by the end of 1974 in a second manufacturing facility, a service industry, and a portion of the public sector. The Project also offers such assistance as in-company seminars, tours of plants where new working structures are being introduced, and a central clearing house where data on work experiments is being collected.

Institutes. One of the surest signs that an idea has gathered a good amount of momentum is when it prompts individuals to stick their necks out to form new, hopefully permanent, organizations to further it. Such is the case with work reform, which has occasioned two new outfits bidding to have national impact on the way we work. One is the Quality of Working Life Program in Los Angeles and the other is the Quality of Work Center in Washington, D.C.*

The Los Angeles operation is the brainchild of Louis E. Davis,

---

* As these and the Ohio operation show, "quality of work" is becoming a popular phrase which looks as if it might emerge as the dominant term to describe workplace reform. While it has been used by those in the field since at least 1970, it appears to have been first given wide circulation in a speech by Richard Nixon on September 13, 1972, in which he said, "In a quest for a better environment, we must always remember that the most important part of the quality of life is the quality of work."

Brave New Work

a professor at the UCLA School of Management and a well-known expert in the field of job redesign. In the fall of 1971, Davis founded his Quality of Working Life Program as a small university research and study program with limited goals. Shortly thereafter, Davis was instrumental in putting together the First International Conference on the Quality of Working Life which, in 1972, brought together experimenters and theorists from all over the world to share information and insights. Largely because of the interest generated by this conference, the UCLA program began getting—and accepting—requests for assistance in job redesign efforts. As these requests continued to roll in, it became apparent that a decision had to be made: The program would either have to limit itself or expand into a permanent, independent institute operating on a national scale with long-range plans and funding. In 1973, with the help of the Ford Foundation, a planning group composed of managers, union leaders, and professional researchers was established, with the goal of developing the Institute's functions, strategies and programs.

By late 1974, the program was ready to turn itself into the Institute for the Quality of Working Life, a feat that will probably have been completed by the time this book appears. The list of the Institute's planned output includes the first scholarly journal in the field, a series of Quality of Working Life books, training conferences, new indicators for measuring the effectiveness of change, and, most important, an action-research program in which new concepts are tested. If, in the next few years, it can attract sufficient grants, contracts, and fees, it will become the first full-fledged, multifaceted American think tank for work.

The second organization, the Quality of Work Center, was formed by Ted Mills, who had left the National Commission on Productivity when its research funds petered out in the spring of 1974. Mills' Center began as a follow-up (called, not surprisingly, the Quality of Work Program) to a program which had started in the Federal Price Commission and moved to the Productivity Commission.

When it began, in 1972, the government version of the program was envisioned as a major effort geared to national workplace improvement, better use of the nation's human and technological resources, and increased national productivity. It was a bold idea, and its sponsors were frank about their intention to make American economic history by speeding up the process of workplace evolution. There were to have been between ten and twenty major demonstrations at worksites in manufacturing, service, and government, involving employers, trade unions, and workers themselves. The planned role of the government in this was to be the "seeder"—the agent that got the parties together and then found, recommended and funded consultants to help with the transformations. Later it was to broadcast the findings to the nation at large, using conferences, papers, books, and films. The demonstrations were to run through into the second half of the decade, by which time it was hoped that many of the lessons learned would be widely adopted. The Productivity Commission stated that it felt these lessons might concern:

¶ Innovation in work restructure.
¶ Innovation in organization restructure.
¶ Increased employee involvement in work improvement.
¶ Decreased workplace (and product) costs.
¶ Increased workplace (employee and technological) productivity.
¶ Improved workplace communications.
¶ Increased labor-management interdependence and collaboration.
¶ Increased employee motivation and allegiance to union and company.
¶ Innovation in the distribution of productivity gains.
¶ Increased organizational responsiveness to change.

This grand plan did not work out. Congress let it run out of money on March 1, 1974, before it really achieved any momentum. It seems that the Productivity Commission, which housed the program, got into difficulty because of general Congressional disenchantment with the Nixon Administration and specific disenchantment with its economic game plan.

However, a group of experiments had been lined up before the money gave out. A few had begun and several others, which had gotten underway on their own but which fit the Commission's criteria, were being helped. For example, the Commission supported the start of an effort in coal mining run by Rushton Mining, Inc., the United Mine Workers, and Eric Trist, a leader in the field of work restructuring from England. Two other important programs which had already been underway but attracted support, were the Bolivar Project, to be discussed shortly and a unique experiment going on in Jamestown, New York, where a committee with representatives from fourteen companies and eleven unions had been formed to lead the local economy out of the doldrums, to restore jobs, and to boost productivity. This panel has had early success in such areas as negotiating production-incentive systems and, in one case, bringing in outside experts to help bring back a large employer from the brink of bankruptcy into the black. It has now begun to move into the area of job redesign.

With all of this underway, Mills, who had directed the program in government, decided to try to keep it alive on his own as a private citizen when the Federal funds stopped. Mills' background would not seem to qualify him in this area at all, let alone to set up his own institution to keep that work going. The bulk of his working life had been spent as a documentary film producer and a network television executive. The made-for-TV films he produced included an Emmy-winning feature on the Bolshoi Ballet and a special entitled *Assignment India*, which won both Polk and Peabody awards. But Mills sees no contradiction in the switch from film producing to running a work-reform program. "Both involve bringing a lot of elements together in a single package. In the case of what I'm doing now, I'm trying to apply this ability to the public weal."

In May 1974, Mills' efforts to keep the program alive paid off when his Quality of Work Center was established in conjunction with the University of Michigan's Institute for Social Research as a nonprofit institute, beginning with funding from the Department of Commerce and the Economic Development Administration. With funding assured, Mills was able to reveal that by that summer three projects would be underway at the Bemis Corporation (formerly the Bemis Bag Company), the Mount Sinai Medical Center in New York City, and the Tennessee Valley Authority. The managements and unions at each institution had agreed to go forward under a plan in which a central labor-management council would begin the process of examining their respective operations for suitable reforms to be implemented with the aid of consultants paid for by the Center. Still other projects were being prepared to begin in 1975 and 1976.

Ironically, within a few weeks of the opening of the Center, the Productivity Commission which had been given up for dead, revived. A bill to keep it going, which had been bottled up in a Congressional committee, was unexpectedly reported out, and passed by a comfortable margin without the Congressional opposition that had been expected. In the process, Congress tacked on the words "and Work Quality" to the Commission's name, and gave it firm instructions to pay greater attention to innovative experiments. Mills, by the way, was quite happy with the decision, because it now appeared that the Commission would not start its own new in-house program but would, instead, fund the work of the Center it had spawned.

In line with the outline first set up in the Productivity Commission, the new Center will move through periods of experimentation, detailed measurement (Mills says that this will be the first attempt to do this scientifically and on a large scale), and dissemination. Beyond the time it takes to complete this plan—six years or more—Mills envisions the Center as a permanent technical assistance bureau and research center serving a broad range of clients. Mills, by the way, feels that the project now has a better chance of succeeding as a private effort, albeit with a government grant of money, than as an element of the government. He explains, "The mistrust of government is such at this point that more than a hundred people in business and the unions have told me that they're happy that this program is now outside of government."

In addition to what Mills took with him, there was yet another element in the original Quality of Work Program that did not die when the money stopped. This brings us to the next item.

Into the Bureaucracy. Until very recently, the least venturesome employer in terms of exploring new work arrangements has been the Federal Government, which has lagged far behind state and local government, not to mention private employers. Outside of a few departures, such as the office-planning experiment discussed earlier and a half-hearted and unsuccessful attempt to enrich jobs at the Internal Revenue Service, it has been hard to find anything worth noting as innovative in the whole Federal landscape. This situation is quietly beginning to change.

Starting about 1970, a group of key officials involved in running the Federal system began asking themselves hard questions about the system's ability to produce and the government's role as an employer. This concern more or less led to a 1972 report followed by a 1973 conference, which, in turn, led to action, including demonstration projects, within government. The plan involved making selected changes in the operations of certain agencies to see what effect that would have on their performance and organizational health. With initial funds and technical assistance from the National Commission on Productivity, and with the Civil Service Commission as the focal point, a program was launched in mid-1973. The method agreed upon was first to perform a diagnostic survey of the people in the organization to see what route seemed most appropriate. When the indicated course of action was approved by the agency and the unions concerned, the demonstration would begin. From the outset, it was made clear that the changes made would be applications of ideas already tested successfully in private industry, rather than anything highly experimental.

A half-dozen locales were picked for diagnosis and action. As of this writing, several of them have developed to the point where a course of action has been suggested and approved. The Social Security Administration's 519-employee Bureau of Disability Insurance is the process of job enrichment, and two military supply depots, with a total of 4,700 employees, are moving in the same direction. In another case, special dispensation has been arranged through the Civil Service Commission to let a Social Security payment center in Alabama begin testing flexible working hours.

Most interesting of all, however, is the action being taken with the 3,200 employees of the Bureau of Printing and Engraving, where a profit-sharing plan is being introduced. The diagnostic survey revealed that the people in this organization had the capacity and desire for greater productivity, but that it was being held in check by the lack of financial incentive and the widespread feeling of being underpaid. As the Bureau is unlike most government agencies in that it is a manufacturing operation with a foot in the market system (it competes with such private entities as the American Banknote Company to get contracts for jobs such as printing food stamps), profit sharing seemed to be the best answer. The trial got underway when funds were found within the system to create a "pot" to be divided as productivity rose.

When the Commission got its reprieve and new funds were on their way, Terence G. Jackson, Jr., who had started the government program, said that there would be more Commission-sponsored Federal demonstration projects as well as new starts in local government and the private sector. Meanwhile, the outlook for continued government work reform outside the

Brave New Work 355

Commission's jurisdiction is anything but bleak. The original demonstrations have continued with support from their respective host agencies and several others—the IRS and the Equal Employment Opportunities Commission, to name two—have started demonstrations on their own with their own funds.

Beyond these detailed examples, there are other developments indicating momentum:

¶ The Ford Foundation, which has been supporting study in this area for several years, is moving into a more active role as a seeder of ideas. One Ford-backed project on tap is to exchange teams of workers and union leaders between the United States and Europe as a means of fostering cross-pollination.

¶ Several new groups, such as the Society of Humanistic Management, have cropped up, and are now sharing progressive ideas by means of luncheon meetings and periodic conferences.

¶ Under the direction of the nonprofit National Training and Development Service, a series of job-overhaul demonstrations are getting underway in state and local governments across the country.

¶ A British National job reform effort called "The Working Together Campaign" recently got underway in London. In addition the Tripartite Steering Committee on the Quality of Working Life has become active in England and the European Foundation for the Improvement of Working Life has begun attracting international attention. Similar efforts have been proposed or are on the drawing boards in other nations impressed with the results of such national programs in Norway and Sweden.

However, the most ambitious and important experimental attempt to restructure work in an American company began in 1973. Even if all goes well, the job will not be complete until about 1980—which is another way of saying that the following report will have a beginning, but no middle or end. Incomplete this experiment may be, but it has tremendous potential impact for the future of the American workplace.

2
THE BOLIVAR PROJECT

In early 1972, the Department of Labor held a series of seminars on the topic of the humanization of work at Airlie House, a conference center in a rustic setting in Virginia outside of Washington, D.C. It was a get-together for people from business, labor, government, and the academic world, intended to foster a new creative atmosphere, but which often yields little more than crates of yellowing position papers, transcripts, and notes. In this case, however, the hoped-for spark was generated, because of the diverse crew which just happened to be brought together. The academic members included Michael Maccoby, a psychologist and student of Erich Fromm who heads the Harvard Project on Technology, Work and Character, and Harold L. Sheppard, a researcher at the W. E. Upjohn Institute for Employment Research. On the union side were three key officials of the United Automobile Workers: Irving Bluestone, Douglas Fraser, and Don Ephlin. Capital was represented by Sidney Harman, president of Harman Industries International. Finally there was Neal Herrick, then with the Department of Labor, who had organized the conference and who now directs the aforementioned Ohio Quality of Work Program.

The mix was a fortunate one. Sheppard, Herrick, and Maccoby were all deeply concerned with problems of worker alienation and interested in applying their ideas and skills to a real situation. In fact, earlier that year, Sheppard and Herrick had published the results of their highly regarded investigation of worker dissatisfaction, *Where Have All the Robots Gone?*, and Maccoby and Herrick had produced a paper outlining the principles on which a humanized workplace could be constructed. The UAW, which was on record as being opposed to industrial experimentation which excluded union participation, had let it be known that it was more than willing to participate in a project if it had a role of equal importance to that of management.

Harman himself was the perfect individual to complete the circle. Through his diversified company of two thousand employees, whose products include Harman-Kardon high-fidelity equipment, JBL loudspeakers, turbine parts, and automotive accessories, he had already been testing a number of ideas. At the Harman plant in Los Angeles, experiments had begun in which small groups were responsible for their own decisions on product quality. And, based on his belief that a worker's individual sense of self-esteem was directly related to his or her satisfaction and to the quality of work, he had instituted a series of weekend open houses in the various divisions of the company for which the rest of the worker's family was invited to see the plant, the product it made, and to be shown the family member's role in making that product.* Because these early efforts were proving successful, and because he was clearly concerned about the national problem of worker alienation (he was one of three representatives from private industry to testify at the 1972 Senate hearings on the subject), Harman was ripe for the role of voluntary host for a major experiment. And since the resident union at the Harman Automotive Division in Bolivar, Tennessee, was the UAW—which was represented at the seminar—Bolivar was the obvious locale for such a project.

After the meeting in mid-1972, a series of conversations was held between the interested parties and the outlines of a major

---

* Of this program, Harman has reported, "We have found that families who had no awareness whatsoever of what father was doing would come away . . . with a reasonable understanding of the business engagement and with a rather clear conception of the importance of his contribution to the final results. Without doubt, that has often resulted in the enhancement of the father within the family and with it significant enhancement of his self-esteem."

experiment began to take shape. As the year wore on, other bridges were crossed. Harman and E. T. Michael, the UAW's regional director for the area encompassing Bolivar, held a general meeting of the workers in the plant, told them about the experiment, and won their approval. Harman and Michael next went to Maccoby to tap him as director of the project, following which all parties agreed to a "treaty," outlining the roles and rights that each would have. Early in 1973, funding for the early part of the project was lined up—from the National Commission on Productivity, the Sloan Foundation, the Harman Corporation, and the UAW. A small staff was recruited, and the project was underway.

From the outset, the project has been clearly set apart in several important aspects from other experiments in the United States and from all but a few in Europe. Of central importance is the fact that it was created jointly by a major trade union and a large corporation, with each party having equal rights throughout the course of the project. For instance, should something go awry, both the union and company have an equal right as part of their treaty to halt the project. Maccoby has asserted in an early report on the project that what eventually comes forth is as much intended to provide a model for trade unions as for industry, and pointed out, "It is the hope of all of us participating in this project that the workers and managers of Harman International Industries will develop practices which will be adopted by unions as goals for collective bargaining." Moreover, the stated goal at Bolivar from the beginning has been to make it a national model which will have become widely copied by the time the 1980s roll around. For this reason alone, the project must be regarded as a most ambitious departure.

Equally important: The company and the UAW have agreed upon an imposing set of principles to guide the project. As a group, these principles (originally outlined by Herrick and Maccoby) point toward a total package of reforms in areas ranging from plant safety to new forms of compensation. Specifically, the four principles or goals are these:

Security, or the creation of conditions which give all employees who are doing their jobs freedom from the fear of losing those jobs. The term also refers to the creation of a system in which there are healthy working conditions with optimal financial security, based on the next principle.

Equity, or fair rules, regulations, and compensation. Also included in this principle are such specifics as the end to discrimination based on age, race, and sex, and the sharing of profits based on higher productivity.

Individuation, or the concept that each worker is to be treated as a unique human being rather than as an interchangeable cog. This principle dictates giving each worker the maximum opportunity for learning and for practicing craftsmanship. And, where possible, the job should be designed to maximize the jobholder's control so that the job can be performed at the person's own best pace and style.

Democracy, or that state in which individuals have a say in decisions affecting them—starting with their own jobs—and in which the rights of free speech and due process are part of the industrial experience.

Finally, this project is both unusual and ambitious in its methodology, which follows none of the established paths in job restructuring. Developed by Sheppard, Herrick, and Maccoby and given the cumbersome name of "the educative method of determining change," this methodology consists of making the people in the plant the architects of their own new job and their working environment. Rather than to hire outsiders to come in and change things by imposing some formula of their own or to let change get ordered down from the top, the goal here is to use the outsiders to educate the plant's management and workforce only so that they can decide on the changes they want. For this reason, the outsiders in this case refer to themselves as "instructors" rather than as "consultants."

There are two elements to this educative process. The first, completed at Harman by mid-1974, is a large study of the situation at the factory encompassing employee attitudes toward things ranging from the company and union to the general idea of work; differences among workers in regard to age, sex and race; problems in specific departments; and management attitudes as well as such things as economic and cultural background on the company, the town it is in, and the workforce itself. The report weighs in at a hefty 429 pages and is forthright and readable, as typified by this statement about the main production area in the factory:

> . . . this is inside on one floor under one roof encompassed by three large Quonset huts which were left over from World War II. The production floor is dirty and disorderly, compared to many large factories belonging to richer companies. Like most engaged in this kind of work, it is noisy. A shortage of storage space and the pace of production which overworks the luggers and towmotor operators results in parts and materials being pushed into every available corner and sometimes strewing out into the aisles. No time is allowed for anyone to keep his work area clean and orderly. Many machines are kept in poor repair due to lack of replacement parts and a lot of ad hoc repairs with wire and roughly cut pieces of metal. The atmosphere is stuffy and irritating to some because of fumes from die cast, plating and paint, and the towmotors, even though efforts have been made to blow away the most noxious fumes. There are holes in the roof, and pools of water on the floor. In winter, there is inadequate heating; in the summer no air conditioning. Comfort and sometimes safety have been ignored in the all-out effort to maximize production and profits. Only recently has management started to improve the physical conditions of the plant.

Even with this forthright sample, it is difficult to appreciate the total frankness and comprehensiveness of this document without reading all of it. It is devoid of platitudes and apologies about work, working people, and those who manage them, and is free of confusing sociological jargon. Instead, it pinpoints sources of unhappiness, physical discomfort, and inequality. One reads, for instance, that most hourly workers do not trust the company (55 percent), do not find management responsive or communicative (77 percent), and view the company as more concerned with profits than with human beings (77 percent). Such scrutiny does not end with the hourly employees; management and the relationships between groups in the plant are also explored. For example, while the majority of salaried employees feel that those under them are not creative, those same underlings report that they have many good ideas but they are not listened to; for this reason 34 percent of the hourly employees do not bother to make suggestions. The survey also revealed that a large percentage of salaried employees wanted a union to represent them.

The no-holds-barred frankness of this report is significant, because it is meant to be used by *everyone* in the plant to educate them about themselves and to provide a baseline for comparison during the years the overhaul is taking place. In addition, another report, which will assay the health picture in the plant, is to follow. An industrial physician has been hired to collect data on the potential dangers of toxic materials in the plant, as well as to screen employees for illnesses. This integral concern for health is not only unique to job redesign efforts, but adds credence to the claim that the project aims at a total restructuring.

The second element of the educative process is giving the people in the plant schooling in the alternatives open to them, letting them decide on the changes they want, and then helping them implement them. Part of this involves exposing the participants to the raft of projects and ideas which have been carried out elsewhere: job enrichment, participative management schemes, worker-designed environments, autonomous work groups, new time arrangements (such as flex-time), Scandinavian-style industrial democracy, and more. Nor will this instruction be restricted to big ideas; basic ideas such as making a better fit between the worker and his or her tools and machines will also be covered. Speaking as one of the instructors, Sheppard says, "We are going to be presenting them with all the options we know about so they can create their own plan. We're determined not to push any philosophy or idea over another and we have no idea what will emerge. It is quite possible that different departments will react differently and that when it is all over there will be no uniform plant-wide change but versions of change."

By mid-1974, the restructuring work in the Bolivar Project was moving toward a beginning. Einar Thorsrud, head of the Norwegian project in industrial democracy, had been brought to Tennessee for two days as an instructor.

An internal organization for change was also beginning to take shape. During the early days of the project a joint union-management group was formed to work on air conditioning and ventilation problems, these having been immediately identified as major sources of discomfort. Over the months, this group broadened its mandate to become the "Working Committee," and it appeared that it would act as the reform-implementing body within the plant. In late 1973 and early 1974, the group was already in the process of setting up a credit union and addressing problems of health, safety, parking and rest room facilities. Meanwhile, workers in a few departments in the plant had set up their own committees to wrestle with problems and to outline changes they would like to test. Also, a "shelter" agreement had been prepared by the workforce—and approved by the company—to guarantee certain basic rights for the duration, including the promise that there would be no pay cuts or lost jobs because of the experiments.

The ambitious and open-ended nature of this project is such that it is sure to hit its share of snags and rough spots. In fact,

Thorsrud's seminar itself produced an early problem of sorts. His presentation on what had been done in his country sounded so inviting that many immediately wanted to begin doing the Bolivar Project his way rather than to wait and weigh other alternatives. And there is the very real possibility that the project may collapse at any point as either labor or management finds it becoming incompatible with its goals. However, should the Bolivar Project run its course, the lessons and ideas it generates will certainly become major sources for discussion. It is far too early to say whether it could become more than a conversation piece and have its intended impact as a model for national adoption, but it would seem to have that potential.

Ultimately, the importance of the Bolivar Project may not be that it succeeds or fails, but simply that it began. In terms of American industrial history, it is the first joint union-management collaboration on a project of its type. If and when the unfolding events at the project are discovered by the media and the growing body of scholars interested in the workplace, Bolivar could well become the metaphor for what can be done that Lordstown has become for what is wrong. That the Bolivar Project has moved past the first phase—particularly with the baseline report, where honesty prevailed over public relations—is a model in itself, suggesting the possibility of more Bolivars—and fewer Lordstowns.

3

THE BOTTOM LINE

In recent years, it has become quite the style for authors and self-appointed futurists to conjure up detailed descriptions of what the shape of something will be in the year 2000. Although it would have been fun to try, this writer will pass up the opportunity to construct a "Workplace 2000" scenario for the reasons that, one, such speculation is bound to be inaccurate, and, two, it is really beside the point. The important point is not the degree to which the workplace will have changed by a certain date, but, as all the evidence suggests, that the rate of change will increase substantially as old premises are replaced with new ones.

As this book has attempted to demonstrate through real-world examples, these new premises are hardly radical, but rather based on common sense, flexibility, humanism, and enlightened self-interest—the precise mix of what is good for the employee with what is good for the employer.

Meanwhile, during the months which have intervened since the initial research was completed for the earlier American edition of this book, developments in the American workplace have occurred at such a rate that it is safe to say that every concept which has been discussed has spread significantly. To single out just one example, flex-time has become a full-fledged national movement aided in great part by the fact that President Jimmy Carter is a strong advocate of the system and within days of taking office threw his support behind proposed legislation which would extend flex-time to many more organizations both within and outside government. What is more, many of the experiments which have been discussed were little-known when the author looked into them, but have since been "discovered" to the point where they are now commonly cited in the widespread quality of work debate going on in the United States and Canada. In sum, much of that which seemed experimental and futuristic in, say, early 1975 seems much less so now.

Acknowledgments

I would like to thank the many people who helped me with this book with very special thanks to Robert Skole of McGraw-Hill World News, Dr. Hal Sheppard of the Upjohn Institute for Employment Research, Lars Lönnback, and Lars Georgesson of the Swedish Government, my agent, Helen Brann, and, most important, my wife, Nancy Dickson.

Chapter Notes

The major thrust of this book has been to report on workplace experiments and reforms which are new and forward-looking. Because they are new, most have yet to appear in the standard literature of business administration. Some, in fact, have yet to be detailed for public consumption anywhere save for this book. As the whole idea of chapter notes in a book is to aid those who would like to probe deeper and keep abreast of developments after the book is published, I have chosen to give an informal briefing on sources in each experimental area (replete with names and addresses) rather than present a less useful set of formal footnotes.

I. Working Alternatives. The key experiments to appear in this chapter are those being conducted at SAAB and Volvo in Sweden. As the work of these two companies has attracted a great deal of attention in the business and general press, it should be rather easy to follow in the future if this interest continues. To date, *Business Week* and *The New York Times* have been particularly good sources. Both companies are very open about what they are doing and are continually issuing papers, reports, and press releases on their work, most of which is prepared in English as well as Swedish. Their addresses:

SAAB-Scania Information AB Volvo Information
S-15187 Södertälje 405 08 Göteborg
SWEDEN SWEDEN

II. Job Enrichment. Several approaches suggest themselves for the person wanting to get deeper into this subject. One is to read the full account of the initial AT&T experiments in *Motivation Through the Work Itself* by Robert N. Ford (The American

Chapter Notes 367

Management Association, New York, 1969). A second is to subscribe to the *Job Enrichment Newsletter* put out by Roy W. Walters and Associates, Inc., and/or attending one of Walters' workshops which are held several times a year in various locations. The address for Walters Associates is 60 Glen Avenue, Glen Rock, N.J. 07452. One might also want to make contact with an organization involved in the job-enrichment process. Outside of the general industrial grapevine as a source for names, a number of job-enrichment experimenters are mentioned in the chapter and consultants in the field can usually supply names. Walters would be a good source as would Drake-Beam and Associates (280 Park Avenue, New York, N.Y. 10019). As no group of organizations are as deeply into job enrichment as the companies in the Bell System, one might also want to talk with the local phone company.

III. Scandinavian Industrial Democracy. While it might seem difficult to follow Scandinavian workplace developments without going there, many companies in this part of the world are quite willing to share written information on their experiments. And as there is increasing American press attention to what is going on in workplaces in these countries, leads are not hard to find. In fact, as this book was going to press, *The Wall Street Journal* ("More Swedish Firms Attempt to 'Enrich' Production-Line Jobs" by Bowen Northrup, October 25, 1974) and *The New York Times* ("Work Democracy Tested at Scandinavian Plants" by-lined Agis Salpulkas, a series beginning on November 11, 1974) had major articles on the subject. *Business Week*'s man in Stockholm, Robert Skole, continually covers the subject for that magazine. Also, a good deal of information on experiments not covered in this book appear in the book *Job Power* by David Jenkins (Doubleday and Co., Garden City, N.Y., 1973). Finally, there are several central organizations which produce periodic reports in English on experimentation. One is the seminally important Norwegian Work Research Institute (Box 81, 49 Oslo

Dep., Norway), which monitors the major experiments in that country. In Sweden, both the employers (The Swedish Employers Federation, Södra Blasieholmshamnen 4A, Stockholm, Sweden) and the central trade union (Swedish Trade Union Confederation, S–105 33 Stockholm, Sweden) report on progress from their perspectives.

IV. Democratic Designs in America. Information about and papers from the Changing Work Ethic conferences in the first part of this chapter are available from the Urban Research Corporation (5464 South Shore Drive, Chicago, Ill. 60615). Little printed material is available from American Velvet and Donnelly Mirrors, although Donnelly does hold periodic seminars on its system (address inquiries to Donnelly Mirrors, 49 W. Third St., Holland, Mich. 49423). The best source for material on these and other systems based on profit sharing is from the Profit Sharing Research Foundation (1718 Sherman Avenue, Evanston, Ill. 60201). This organization offers a wealth of information on the subject and seems especially willing to help. Much information has been put out by General Foods on its Topeka experiment which can be obtained through the company's office of public relations (c/o General Foods, White Plains, N.Y. 10625) and there is also Richard Walton's detailed article in the *Harvard Business Review* (November–December 1972). A prime source of information on other companies mentioned in this article is the company itself; however, policies change on sharing such information, and one is cautioned that requests for more information are not always met.

V. Support Systems. Again, one is best served by contacting the companies mentioned directly. General Electric, incidentally, has a regular program of internal publication on its experiment results which are issued as "Personnel Research Bulletins" (put out by the Manager of Personnel Research Programs, General Electric Company, 570 Lexington Avenue, New York, N.Y.

10022). Meanwhile, two national organizations publish occasional research on the types of systems described in this and the previous chapter. They are The Conference Board (845 Third Avenue, New York, N.Y. 10022) and the American Management Association, Inc., 135 West 50th Street, New York, N.Y. 10020). Of particular interest are two Conference Board reports by Dr. Hal Rush: *Behavioral Science: Concepts and Management Application* and *Job Design for Motivation*.

VI. Breaking the Time Barriers. Much has been written on the compressed workweek, but the best sources to date are "The Four-Day Week" (a research report from the aforementioned American Management Association) and Riva Poor's *4 Days, 40 Hours* (Mentor Executive Library, New American Library, New York, 1973). The Department of Labor is actively monitoring four-day experiences and its findings appear regularly in *The Monthly Labor Review*. As of this writing, there were no major sources of information on flex-time; however, the subject is attracting increasing press attention. A detailed case history of the system at one company is available from that company, Sandoz-Wander, Inc. (Route 10, East Hanover, N.J. 07936). Catalyst (6 East 82nd Street, New York, N.Y. 10028) is by far the best repository of information pairing, sharing, and other part-time systems. It has an active publications program and is very eager to share what it knows. Few references exist on sabbaticals; however, anyone interested in the subject should not miss the article by the late Eli Goldston in the *Harvard Business Review* (September–October 1973). The most valuable reference on the subject of social leave is the Conference Board report, "Policies on Leaves for Political and Social Action" by Grace J. Finley.

VII. The Democratic Office, the Do-it-yourself Factory. Very little coverage has been given to the subject of this chapter—with what little that appears showing up in magazines and journals in the fields of interior design and architecture. Since the impact of the cases presented in this chapter are physical, a good way to get a better feel for them is to visit them.

VIII. To Thine Own Self Be Boss. Since this chapter is based primarily on personal reflection and observation, there is nothing further to note.

IX. Brave New Work. As this chapter is devoted to new starts, the best way for an individual to keep up with their progress is by direct contact. Therefore, addresses are again in order. The Ohio Quality of Work Project (8 East Long Street, 9th Floor, Columbus, Ohio 43215) issues its own newsletter which makes it easy to keep up with its activities. The address of the Quality of Working Life Program is the Graduate School of Management (Center for Organizational Studies, University of California, Los Angeles, Calif. 90024). And that of the Quality of Work Center is 1750 K St. NW, Room 1000, Washington, D.C. 20006. The National Commission on Productivity and Work Quality (2000 M St. NW, Washington, D.C. 20508) has a very active publications program and will send a free list of its research reports.

Index

Abel, I. W., 223
absenteeism, 19; and environment, 307; and flex-time, 213, 229–31, 236; and job enrichment, 49–50, 68; and industrial democracy, 26, 29–31, 96, 109, 117, 130, 143, 152, 160; and support systems, 204–5; and time variations, 219, 226, 251
Abzug, Bella, 254
AFL-CIO, 223, 347
Ainsworth, Frances, 145, 147
Alcan Aluminum, 172
Alcoa, 166, 275
Alexander Hamilton Institute, Inc., 240
American Airlines, 346
American Banknote Company, 354
American Management Association (AMA), 219–20, 237, 370
American Telephone and Telegraph Company (AT&T), 17, 47–52, 53–55, 72, 166
American Velvet Company, 141–49, 166
Arapahoe Chemicals, 168–69
Argyris, Chris, 35
Armer, Paul, 263–64
Arthur, Richard N., 150–52
Arvika experiment, 115–21
Askert, Bjorn, 112–14
assembly lines, 6, 13; elimination of, 25–27, 30–33, 167, 171; and flex-time, 239; and industrial democracy, 113–14, 150; modifications of, 27–29, 185; and turnover, 283–85; white-collar, 14–15
Associated Space Designs, Inc., 287
Association of Scientific, Technical, and Managerial Staffs (Scotland), 242
Atlas Copco (Sweden), 111–14
attitude, of workers: and Bolivar project, 360–61; and environment, 291, 294, 308; and flex-time, 230–31, 234, 236, 240; and industrial democracy, 27, 31, 94, 110, 117–20, 152, 161; and job enrichment, 43, 50, 60; and support systems, 180, 181, 188; and time variations, 219–20, 226
autonomy, and industrial democracy, 91, 94, 113, 153, 157, 160–61

Bank of New York, 62
Bankers Trust, 60, 62–68, 345
behavioral research, and office design, 298–304
Behavioral Science: Concepts and Management Application (Rush), 370
Bemis Corporation, 352

benefit packages, 11; for part-timers, 254–55; projected future of, 320–22; and self-employment, 319–23, 325, 338, 339–40. *See also* specific benefits
Bennis, Warren G., 36
Bethlehem Steel Company, 4–5
blacks, at Polaroid, 193–95, 198, 199
Blake, Robert, 36
Bluestone, Irving, 356
boards of directors, workers on, 85, 89, 99–100, 108
Boeing Field, 297–304
Bolivar Project, 351, 356–63; methodology of, 359–63; principles of, 358–59
Bölkow (German company), 228–29
Bonne Belle Cosmetics, 273
bonuses, 97, 150, 152–53, 154, 198–99; in time, 273
Borg-Warner Corporation, 60
Brosius, Bert, 78–79
Browne, Whitfield, Jr., 202, 204–5
Buisch, David, 231–32, 237
Bureau of Disability Insurance, 354
Bureau of Printing and Engraving, 354
business failure, rates of, 337

Calero, Thomas M., 273
Canada, 172, 223
Canadian Labor Congress, 223
career changing, 211, 212, 214, 256, 264, 270; mechanisms for, 275–77
"Career exposure" program (Polaroid), 196
Catalyst (career clearing-house), 243–44, 254–56, 370; part-time teaching project, 249–52; part-timer categories, 244–46; "Westchester Project," 252–53; work sharing project, 246–48
Central Organization for Salaried Employees (Sweden), 110
Central Trade Union Council (Norway), 88
Changing Work Ethic Conference (1973), 139–40, 369
Chase Manhattan Bank, 62, 263
Chesapeake and Potomac Telephone Companies, 78–81
Christenson, Eje, 117–20
Chrysler Corporation, 178, 211, 283
Civil Service Commission, 353–54
Classified Municipal Employees Association of Baltimore City, 242
Commerce Department, 337, 352
communication, internal, 177, 239, 291;

371

and corporate publications, 86, 196, 199–200
Communications Workers of America, 72
"Concept of Post-economic Work, The" (Toffler), 321
Conference Board, 70, 168, 266–68, 370
"Conference on New Directions in the World of Work" (1971), 276
Congress, 11, 213, 224, 282
Connecticut Department of Public Welfare, 248
Contract Work Hours and Safety Standards Act, 224
Corning Glass, 17, 18
cost benefits: environment and, 293–94, 303; and industrial democracy, 152, 160, 169–71; of job enrichment, 51, 64, 69, 168; of part-timers, 245–46, 250, 251; of self-employment, 331–32; of support systems, 181, 188; of time variations, 219, 240, 264–65
counseling, personal, 178, 196, 204, 276, 321

Danforth Foundation, 263
Danielsen, Bech, 125–27
Davis, Louis E., 166, 348–49
Denmark, 122–33, 304–9
Derenfeldt, Arne, 122
Detroit, Mich., 251, 252
Development Council for Collaboration Questions (Sweden), 110–11
disability insurance, 322–23
discrimination: age, 120, 359; race, 80, 162, 193–95, 359; sex, 80, 120–21, 162, 359
Doherty, Grant, 218–19
Donnelly Mirrors, 17–18, 149–52, 369
Drake-Beam and Associates, 368
Dun and Bradstreet, 337
DuPont, 200

Eastern Gas and Fuel Associates, 257–62
Eastman Kodak, 199, 200, 293, 294
Economic Development Administration, 333, 352
education, 11; and Bolivar project, 359–63; for career changes, 211, 265; in entrepreneurial skills, 336–37; sabbaticals for, 257–66. *See also* training
efficiency, 4, 6, 219, 231, 265, 293
8-hour day, 210–11, 223, 226–27
Eltang, Jørgen, 128–33
employee participation, 113, 157, 168, 169–71, 187–88, 197; in administration, 123–24, 129–33, 185, 186, 203–4; on boards of directors, 85, 89, 99–100, 108; in factory design, 304–9; and job enrichment, 73–77
Employer's Federation (Sweden), 86, 109, 110, 369
Energoinvest (Yugoslav company), 172–73
energy crisis, and time variations, 215–16, 237–38

Entine, Alan, 276–77
Ephlin, Don, 356
Epstein, Albert S., 71
Equal Employment Opportunities Commission (EEOC), 355
equipment selection, by workers, 146, 151, 197. *See also* responsibility
ex-convicts, at Polaroid, 191, 192
Executive Exchange Program, 263

factory design, 123, 304–9
Federal Aviation Administration, 297–304
Federal government: and self-employment, 338, 340; and time variations, 215–16, 224, 253–54; and work reform, 353–55; and workspace design, 295–304
Federal Price Commission, 350
feedback, 12, 46, 67, 157, 185
Fein, Michael, 153
finances, of self-employment, 323–24, 331–32, 339–40
Finland, 133–34
Finley, Grace J., 266–67, 370
firing, 72–73, 109, 123, 125, 130–31, 158, 203–4
First International Conference on the Quality of Working Life (1972), 349
5-day, 35-hour workweek, 223
5-day, 40-hour workweek, 209–10, 221, 223, 227, 272
flex-time, 59, 228–43, 313, 354; advantages of, 230–31, 234–35, 236, 242; disadvantages of, 237–40; monthly option plan, 273–74; and unions, 241–42; and working mothers, 230, 232
Flexible Hours Employment Act, 254
Flextime Corporation, 240–41, 242
Ford, Gerald, 340
Ford, Henry, 6, 24, 227
Ford, Henry, II, 340n
Ford, Robert N., 47, 52, 54–55, 75, 77, 367
Ford Foundation, 18, 100, 276, 349, 355
Ford Motor Company, 6, 24, 211
Forslund, Gerhard, 113–14
4-day, 36-hour workweek, 216–19
4-day, 40-hour workweek, 214–28; 272; unions and, 210–11, 221, 223–24
4-day workweek: advantages of, 219, 226; disadvantages of, 220, 226, 227–28; failures of, 220–21; in the media, 218–19, 224–25; police operations and, 222–23; variations on, 273, 275
4 Days, 40 Hours: Reporting a Revolution in Work and Leisure (Poor), 215, 221, 228, 370
4½-day workweek, 275
Framingham, Mass., 249–50, 252
France, 153–54
freedom of expression: as Bolivar goal, 359; at Polaroid, 192–96
fringe benefits. *See* benefit packages
Fromm, Erich, 356
furniture, 287–88, 289, 299, 301–2
Future Shock (Toffler), 321, 336

Gaines Pet Food, 156–63, 369
Gallatin, Albert, 135
Gallup, George, Jr., 139
Gencarella, Charlie, 147
General Electric, 17, 139, 150, 179–88, 369
General Foods, 17, 134, 139, 155–63, 166, 345, 369
General Motors, 14–15, 17, 139, 150, 200, 211
General Radio Company, 236
Germany, 228–32, 241
Gillette (Jules) Stores, 221
Gilligan, John J., 347
Goldston, Eli, 257–58, 259, 261, 370
Gooding, Judson, 13
Goodrich, (B. F.) Company, 347
government, local, 169, 222–23, 242, 277. *See also* Federal government
Government Services Administration (GSA), 296–304
"Grand Eight Hour Leagues," 226–27
Grängesberg Company (Sweden), 109
Green, Dennis, 297–304
Gyllenhammar, Pehr, 31

Haines, Lundberg and Waehler, 221
Hansen, Willie, 99
Hansen's Eftr. Inc. (Denmark), 124–27
Harman, Sidney, 356–58
Harman Automotive Division, 357–63
Harman Corporation, 358
Harman Industries International, 356–58
Hawthorne effect, 10 and n, 48, 75
Health, Education and Welfare Department (HEW), 13, 20–24, 76, 212, 246, 264–65, 314, 333–36
health benefits, 321, 361; for the self-employed, 322–23, 338
Hedges, Janice, 213, 220, 224, 237–38
Helm, William, 258–61
Hengstler AB (German company), 240, 242
Herbert, John R., 236
Herrick, Neal Q., 13, 356, 359
Herzberg, Frederick, 45–47, 52, 77
Hewlett-Packard Company, 154, 235–36
hiring, 109, 116, 120–21, 123, 125, 130–31, 148–49, 151, 157, 158–60, 183
Hodgson, James D., 22
holidays, 213; hand-picked, 271–72
honor system, 177; and flex-time, 232–35, 236, 241
Hood (H. P.) Inc. 202–5, 274
Hulin, Charles L., 76
human relations movement, 9–13, 37
Human Side of Enterprise, The (McGregor), 34
Human Values Where People Work (Spates), 9, 11
Hunsfos Fabrikker (Norwegian company), 91–92
Huntington Beach, Calif., 222
hygiene factors, 45–46, 52

IBM, 134, 200, 269–71
identity crises, and self-employment, 329–31
Incentive Management System (Lincoln Electric), 152–53
Indiana National Bank, 60
Industrial Conference Board, 70, 168, 266–68, 370
industrial democracy, 25; as Bolivar goal, 359; conditions for, 134; definitions of, 87 and n, 90, 121; in Denmark, 122–33; in Finland, 133–34; in Norway, 88–102, 368–69; publicity for, 114, 119; resistance to, 92, 119, 126; in Sweden, 85, 106–22, 363, 369; and unions, 99, 108–9, 141–42, 144–48; in U. S., 140–72, 369; and workplace design, 123, 297, 299–309
"Industrial Democracy Project" (Norway), 88, 98, 110
Industrial Management, 8
Industrial National Bank of Providence, 240
Institute for Social Research, 352
Institute for the Future, 319–22
Institute for the Quality of Working Life, 349
Institutes, for work reform, 348–53
insurance plans, 11, 321; for the self-employed, 322–23, 338
"Interact" system (Polaroid), 196, 199
Internal Revenue Service, 70–71, 353, 355
International Association of Machinists, 71
International Brotherhood of Teamsters, 272
International Patenting and Licensing Exposition (1973), 316–17
International Typographers' Union, 210
inventors, independent, 315–17, 338–39
Inventors Council (Oregon), 338
Iowa Beef Processors, 150

Jackson, Terence G., Jr., 354
Jamestown, N. Y., 351
Janetos, Peter, 226
Janson, Robert, 58
Jenkins, David, 368
job consulting, 345–46
job content, 43, 45–46, 52, 59
job denuding, 52–55
Job Design for Motivation (Rush), 70, 168, 370
job dissatisfaction, 13–16, 22–23, 41–42, 45, 76–77; and environment, 283–85
job enrichment, 41–81; criticisms of, 71–77; drawbacks of, 69–70; failures of, 70–71; in Federal government, 354; and R. Ford, 47–55; Herzberg on, 46–47; for managerial jobs, 78–81; and motivation, 43–47; resources on, 367–68; social-leaves as, 267; and unions, 71–72; Walters' method of, 58–68
Job Enrichment Newsletter, 368
job fragmentation, 4, 6, 53–54

373

job posting, at Polaroid, 196–97
Job Power (Jenkins), 368
job redesign, 17–20; Bolivar methodology in, 359–63; failures of, 171–72; premises of, 16–17; unions and, 165; in U. S., 166–68, 347–49
Job Revolution, The (Gooding), 13
job rotation, 25, 28, 29; and flex-time, 239; and industrial democracy, 91, 93, 94, 96, 112–13, 116, 158
job satisfaction, 45, 50, 313
job security, 12, 202–5, 359, 362
John Hancock Mutual Insurance Company, 225–26
Jørgensen (R. Bøg) (Danish company), 127–33
Joseph and Feiss Company, 8

Kael, Pauline, 41
Karlsson, Lars Erik, 121–22
Kay, Andrew F., 172
Keefe, M. David, 274–75
Kennecott Copper Corporation, 178
Kennedy, Edward M., 19, 139
Kent, Corita, 257
Keogh, Eugene, 339
Keogh Plan, 339–40
Ketchum, Lyman D., 155–56, 162–65
Kneen, H. P., Jr., 270–71
Kockums Shipyard (Sweden), 109
Kroc, Ray, 288
Kuhn, Donald, 235, 237, 238, 241, 242
Kyanize Paints, Inc., 216–19, 228
Kyanize Shop Association, 217

Labor Department, 224, 272, 284, 370; and Bolivar project, 356–57
labor-management collaboration, 154, 182; at American Velvet, 141–42, 144–48; on Bolivar project, 356–63; on Ohio Project, 347–48
Land, Edwin H., 188–90, 193–94, 198–99, 200–1
layoffs, 12; at Bolivar project, 362; industrial democracy and, 126, 131, 151–52, 157–58; and support systems, 198, 202–5
leaves of absence, 212, 214, 266–71; at IBM, 269–71. *See also* sabbaticals
Lenin, Nicolai, 6
Lewis, John, 336
Likert, Rensis, 36
Lilley, Robert D., 139
Lincoln, James F., 152
Lincoln Electric Company, 152–53
Lindsay, John, 325
Lockheed Aircraft, 170, 171, 340, 346
Lordstown strike, 14–15, 25
Lufthansa Airlines, 229–32
Lungen, Gary, 72

Maccoby, Michael, 356, 358, 359
McDonald, Frank, 274

McDonald's Corporation, 275, 286–91, 294
McFarland, James P., 214
McGregor, Douglas, 34–35
McIntire, Thomas, 335
McLuhan, Marshall, 323
Main, Harold, 145
Malero, Marie, 253–54
management: courses in, 7–8, 18; and job enrichment, 78–81, 156; and workspace design, 281–82; X style of, 34; Y style of, 34–35
management consulting, 6, 18, 56–59; Walters' procedures of, 59–68
management movement, 7–8
Manpower Administration, 284
Marquette, Hank, 145
Maslow, Abraham, 44–45
Massachusetts Department of Public Welfare, 246–48
maternity benefits, 322, 323
maternity leave, 328–29
Mayo, Elton, 10–11
Memphis, Tenn., 222
merit pay, 131–32
Merrill Lynch, Pierce, Fenner and Smith, Inc., 71–72
Meyer, Herbert H., 179
Miami, Florida, 251
Michael, E. T., 358
Midvale Iron Works, 3–4
Mills, Ted, 349, 351–53
Minnesota Mining and Manufacturing Company (3M), 170, 171
Möet and Chandon (French company), 153–54
Mohn, Einar O., 272–73
moonlighting, 218, 223
Moore, W. H., 66
Moreau, Jan Erik, 108
motivation, and job enrichment, 43–47
Motivation and Personality (Maslow), 44
Motivation and Productivity (Gellerman), 11
Motivation for Work (Fein), 153
Motivation Through the Work Itself (Ford), 52, 367
motivators, 45–46, 52
Motorola, Inc., 167–68, 178, 216
Motzkus, Larry, 235–36, 238
Mouton, Jane, 36
Moving Forward (Ford), 227
"Multimillion Dollar Misunderstanding, The" (Survey Research Center), 283–85
Murphy, Wilton, 179, 182–86
Myrdal, Alva, 104–6
Myrdal, Gunnar, 104

National Broadcasting Company, 274
National Commission on Productivity (and Work Quality), 349–51, 352, 353–55, 358, 371
National Confederation of Employers (Norway), 88

National Council on Participation in Industry (Norway), 98
National Science Foundation, 18
National Training and Development Service, 355
needs: hierarchy of, 44; individual vs. corporate, 35, 55; industrial democracy as, 90; and office design, 300-1
Nestlé Company, 236
Netherlands, 172, 255
New Careers Program, 276
New Patterns for Working Time Conference (1972), 100, 212, 213, 265
New Ways to Work (company), 253
Niskayuna, N. Y., 251
Nixon, Richard, 20, 22, 149, 296, 339-40, 348n, 351
Nobø Fabrikker A/S (Norwegian company), 92-95
Non-Linear Systems (company), 171-72
Norsk Hydro A/S (Norwegian company), 95-98, 99
Northern Electric (Canadian company), 172
Norway, industrial democracy in, 88-102, 368-69
Norwegian Work Research Institute, 368-69
Nylands Verkstad (Norwegian company), 98-99
Nystrom, Nils, 28-29

Occupational Health and Safety Act, 11, 282-83
office design: and behavioral research, 298-304; development of, 297-98
"Office Excellence" program (GSA), 296
office furniture, 287-88, 289, 299, 301-2
office landscaping, 291-94; at Boeing Field, 297-304
Office of Invention and Innovation, 338-39
Ohio Project, 347-48, 371
Oil, Chemical and Atomic Workers (OCAW), 223
Ombudsmen, 177
Omega Watches, 239
On the Line (Swados), 33
"128 Syndrome, The," 260
"open planning," in workspace design, 288, 291-94
"Operations Improvement Plan" (Ralston Purina), 170-71
Options for Women (company), 253
Organization for Economic Cooperation and Development (OECD), 100, 212, 213, 265
organizational development (OD), 36
organizations: irrelevance of, 33-34; reconceptualizations of, 34-37; of self-employed persons, 338
O'Toole, James, 20-21, 76
overtime, 11; compulsory, 211; and flex-time, 231; and 4-day workweek, 210-11, 220, 221, 223, 226

Palme, Olof, 32, 103
Palmer, Robert, 191-95, 199, 201
part-time work (permanent), 243-56; fringe benefits for, 254-55; paired, 244, 249-50; shared, 244, 246-48; specialist, 245, 251; split-level, 245; split-location, 244-45; and 2-hour modules, 272-73
partnership work, 244, 249-50, 256
patents, 315-16, 339
paternity leave, 329
Pathfinder program (Polaroid), 196
"Paul Principle," 263-64
pension plans, 11, 146, 147, 198, 265, 321; for the self-employed, 339-40
Pentagon, 295
People Space Architecture Company, 298
Percy, Charles H., 19, 73, 139
personal effects, and office design, 289, 296, 297, 302
personnel movement, 9-13, 37
personnel offices, 9, 11-12
personnel research, 178-79; at General Electric, 179-88
"Peter Principle," 263-64
Pfautz, Charles V., 72
Phillips Company (Netherlands), 172
Planos, R. E., 293
Polaroid Corporation, 17, 188-202
Polaroid Handbook, The, 200-1
Polaroid Newsletter, The, 196, 199-200
police forces, 169, 222-23
"Policies on Leaves for Political and Social Action" (Finley), 266-67, 370
Poor, Riva, 214-16, 220-21, 226-27, 370
Poor's Workweek Letter, 215
Poulsen, Kaj, 304-9
Proctor and Gamble, 134, 165
product identification, 179-80
productivity, 19; and environment, 307; and flex-time, 229, 231, 234, 236, 239, 240; and 4-day workweek, 218, 219, 221, 226; and industrial democracy, 29, 91, 93, 110, 113, 116, 150, 153, 157, 160; and job enrichment, 60, 64, 68, 72; and lighting, 10; of part-timers, 246, 247; and profit sharing, 354, 359; and sabbaticals, 264; and self-employment, 313; and support systems, 180, 181, 187, 205
profit motive, and work reform, 345-47
profit sharing, 18; in Denmark, 122; and Federal government, 354; in grocery store chains, 155n; industrial democracy, 17, 135, 142, 146-48, 152-53, 154-55, 196, 198-99; and productivity, 354, 359; resources on, 369
Profit Sharing Research Foundation, 154, 155n, 369
Project Eve (company), 253
Project for Careers (company), 253

promotions: and industrial democracy, 151, 153; and job enrichment, 50, 64, 65–66; and support systems, 183–85, 196–97
publications, corporate, 86, 196, 199–200
publicity: and flex-time, 231–32, 237; on 4-day workweek, 218–19, 224–25; on industrial democracy, 27, 114, 119, 191; and work reform, 345–47

quality (of products): and flex-time, 239; and industrial democracy, 26–27, 29, 31, 91, 150, 152, 154, 160; and job enrichment, 50, 60, 68; and support systems, 181, 187
quality of work, 19, 348n
Quality of Work Center (Washington, D. C.), 348, 349, 352–53, 371
Quality of Work Institute, 347
Quality of Work Program (Ohio), 349–51, 353, 356, 371
Quality of Work Project, 347–48
Quality of Working Life Program (Los Angeles), 348–49, 371
Quantification of Concern, The (Goldston), 257
Quickborner Team, 292–93, 297

Ralston Purina Company, 170–71, 346
RAND Institute, 355
recruiting, 27, 191, 219, 260; and flex-time, 230, 231, 236; of part-timers, 246, 249, 252–53. *See also* hiring
Rehn, Gösta, 265
resistance: to flex-time, 234, 239–40; to industrial democracy, 92, 119, 126; to self-employment, 326; to shared work, 248, 249n, 252; to workplace redesign, 164–65
responsibility, of workers: flex-time and, 231; industrial democracy and, 29, 92, 113, 116, 125, 129, 167; job enrichment and, 46, 67; and self-employment, 331; and support systems, 180, 188; upward movement of, 54–55
retirement, 11, 12, 213, 256, 262, 273, 274
Richardson, Elliot, 21–22
Rockefeller, David, 263
Rush, Harold M. F., 70, 168, 370
Rushton Mining Inc., 351
Ryan, A. H., 8

SAAB (Sweden), 25–29, 31–33, 367
sabbaticals, educational, 212, 257–63, 321; "Paul Principle," 263–64; "study credit" system, 265; Universal Worker Self-Renewal Program, 264–65
Sadolin and Holmblad (Danish company), 304–9
safety, 9, 12, 60, 282, 361; and 4-day workweek, 222, 223; and industrial democracy, 125, 160, 169; and workspace design, 282–85
salary: and industrial democracy, 150–52, 171, 177–78; for leaves of absence, 267–

68, 269, 270; on sabbatical, 258, 259, 262, 263, 264. *See also* wages
Sampson, Arthur, 296
San Diego County, Calif., 277
Sandoz-Wander, 232–35, 237, 370
satisfiers, 45–46, 52
Scanlon Plan, 150–51
Schell, Herbert, Jr., 144, 145–46
Schmid, John, 171
Schwartz, Felice, 243, 245–46, 253, 255, 256
scientific management movement, 3–8, 12, 164
Scotland, 241–42
Scoville Manufacturing Company, 8
Scripture Press, Inc., 150
Sears, 154
self-correction, 30, 64
self-employment, 256, 313–41; advantages of, 324–25, 327–32; and benefit packages, 319–23, 325, 338, 339–40; disadvantages of, 319–26; encouragement for, 333–41; finances of, 323–24, 331–32, 339–40; and identity crises, 329–31; and paperwork, 334–35; pension plans for, 339–40; statistics on, 315, 337; taxes on, 324, 325–26, 333–35; and time perspectives, 327–29
"shared time" plan, as social-leave time, 267
shared work, 244, 246–48, 253–54, 256
Shell Refining Company, Ltd., 172
Sheppard, Harold L., 13, 15, 356, 359, 362
6-day, 60-hour workweek, 210
6-month workyear, 274–75
Skole, Robert, 368
Sloan, Sam, 298–304
Sloan Foundation, 358
Small Business Administration (SBA), 333–34, 338
Small Business Association, 334
Smith-Petersen, E. L. C., 306–8
social-leaves, 266–71
social needs, and office design, 300–1
Social Security Act, 11, 264, 324
Social Security Administration, 71, 354
"social waterhole" concept of office design, 298
Society of Humanistic Management, 355
sociotechnical approach, 166
Sony Corporation, 177
Sørlie, B., 98
Southern Central Bell Telephone Company, 69
Spates, Thomas, 9, 11
specialist work, 245, 251
split-location work, 244–45
Sposato, Joe, 147
staggered workday, 229, 274
Stahlberg, Erik, 134
State Department, 295
Steiger, William A., 224
Steward, Ira, 226–27
stewardship training, 180–81

stock-ownership plans, 122, 153
strikes, 14–15, 25, 154, 187
"study credit" system, 265
suggestion boxes, 171
Sulzer Frères (Swiss company), 239
Sunseri, Joe, 273
supervisors: job enrichment for, 65, 78–81; selection of, 183–85; training of, 157, 158–60, 161, 162–63
supportive environments: examples of, 177–78; at General Electric, 178–88; at Hood Dairies, 202–5; at Polaroid, 188–202; resources on, 369–70
Survey Research Center, 283–85
Swados, Harvey, 33
Sweden: industrial democracy in, 85, 106–22, 368, 369; SAAB experiments, 25–29, 31–33; social equity in, 102–6; Volvo experiments in, 25, 29–33
Switzerland, 229, 232–33, 239
SX-70 camera, 198–99
Sylvania, 199

Tandberg (company), 239
tardiness, 152, 181; and time variations, 213, 226, 230
"Task Response Module," 288
Tavistock Institute of Human Relations, 89, 90, 101
taxes, and self-employment, 324, 325–26, 333–35
Taylor, Frederick Winslow, 3–8, 12–13
teaching: as paired work, 244, 249–50, 256; as specialist work, 245, 251, 252
TEAM (Total Effort at Motorola), 168
technology, and job denuding, 52–53
10-hour day, 210–22, 223, 274–75
"Ten Worst Jobs in America," 56–57
Tennessee Valley Authority, 352
Terkel, Studs, 13, 33, 41
"territorial requirements," and office design, 299–301
Texas Instruments, 154, 168
Textile Workers Union of America, 141–42, 144–48
theft, 60, 160, 192
Thorsrud, Einar, 88–96, 99–100, 134, 362–63
3-day, 36-hour workweek, 216
Time, Inc., 263
time-and-motion studies, 4, 6.
time clocks: elimination of, 151, 152, 157, 178, 232; and flex–time, 229, 240–41
time perspectives, changes in, 94, 118, 327–29
time restructuring, 130, 209–14, 321; flexible days, 228–43; part-time work, 243–56; resources on, 370; sabbaticals, 257–66; social-leaves, 266–71; suggestions for, 271–77; workweek variations, 214–28
Toffler, Alvin, 321, 336
tool standardization, 5
Towards Equality ("Alva Myrdal Report"), 104–7

Townsend, Robert, 35, 243
Trade Union Confederation (Sweden), 108–9, 110, 369
traffic, 209, 228, 229, 230, 231, 327
training, 25; and industrial democracy, 96, 109, 178, 196, 204; projected future of, 321; "right to learn" clause, 99; for self-employment, 336–37; of supervisors, 157, 158–60, 161, 162–63, 184–85; and turnover, 284–85
Travelers Insurance Company, 14–15, 60, 68, 346
Trist, Eric, 165, 166, 351
trust funds, corporate, 146, 147
TRW Systems, 165, 200
Tunney, John, 254
Turner, Fred, 287
turnover rates, 19, 213; and environment, 283–85, 291, 307; and industrial democracy, 26, 29–32, 91, 96, 109, 143, 152, 160; and job enrichment, 47–48, 49, 51, 60; of part-timers, 246, 247, 251; and support systems, 198, 204; and training, 284–85
2-hour modules, 272–73

U. N. Conference on the Human Environment (1972), 108
unions, 86; and flex-time, 241–42; and 4-day workweek, 210–11, 217, 221, 223–24; French, 154; and human relations movement, 9; and industrial democracy, 99, 108–9, 141–42, 144–48; and job enrichment, 71–72, 165; and scientific management, 6–7; and support systems, 186; Swedish, 32
United Automobile Workers (UAW), 139, 210; and Bolivar Project, 356–63
United Mine Workers, 351
United Steelworkers, 263
"Universal Worker Self-Renewal Program," 212, 264–65
Up the Organization (Townsend), 35
Upjohn Institute for Employment Research, 15, 22, 276, 356
Urban Institute, 169, 223, 277
Urban Research Corporation, 369

vacations, 11, 12, 275, 325
Vanick, Charles, 334
variable hours workday, 229
Volvo (Sweden), 25, 29–33, 345, 367

wages, 11; and industrial democracy, 91, 93, 97, 109, 124–26, 150, 161–62, 362; quarterly payment of, 127–29; and support systems, 177–78, 188, 198; worker-determined, 124–26, 131–32, 188
Walsh-Healey Public Contracts Act, 224
Walters, Roy, 56–68
Walters Associates, 56, 368
Walton, Richard, 156, 161–62, 166, 369
Washington, D. C., 222
Washington Opportunities for Women (WOW), 253–54

377

Waterson, Tom, 287, 291
Watson, Thomas J., Jr., 269
week-on, week-off plan, 274–75
welfare casework, as shared work, 244, 246–48
"Westchester Project," 252–53
Western Electric Company, 10
Weyerhauser Corporation, 70, 294
Where Have All the Robots Gone? (Sheppard and Herrick), 13, 15, 276–77, 314, 356
White House Conference on the Industrial World Ahead (1972), 272
Whitsett, David, 74, 75
Wilhelm Shaumans (Finnish company), 133–34
Williams, Kathleen, 66, 67
Wimpfheimer, Clarence, 141
Wimpfheimer, Jacques D., 141, 143–45, 148, 149
Windle, James, 76, 77
Winpisinger, William, 71
women: and industrial democracy, 26, 93, 120–21, 198, 199; maternity coverage for, 322, 323; maternity leave for, 328–29; as permanent part-timers, 243–56; and time variations, 213, 221
Women's Education and Industrial Union, 249
work groups, autonomous: French, 153–54; Scandinavian, 25, 26, 27–29, 91, 93, 113, 116–17, 129–33; U. S., 150, 157, 160–61, 171, 185
Work in America (HEW), 13, 22–24, 76, 166, 212, 264–65, 314, 333–36

Work Itself Program, 51
work reform: Bolivar principles of, 358–59; "educative method" of, 359–63; and Federal government, 353–55; institutes for, 348–53; and Productivity Commission, 349–51; and profit motive, 345–47. *See also* job redesign
Work Research Institute, 88, 99, 100–1
workdays. *See* flex-time; part-time work
Working (Terkel), 13, 33, 41
working mothers, 209–10, 220, 230, 232, 245, 255. *See also* women
"Working Together Campaign," 355
workshifts, variable, 273
workspace design, 123, 146, 178; at Boeing Field, 297–304; development of, 291–93; and Federal government, 295–97; at Gaines Pet Food, 156–60, 162–63; Ketchum on, 163–65; at McDonald's, 286–91, 294; as management tool, 281–82; at Sadolin and Holmblad, 304–9; and safety, 282–85; and "territorial requirements," 299–301; worker participation in, 304–9
worktime. *See* time restructuring
workweek variations, 11, 12, 59, 214–28, 272, 274–75

X style of management, 34
Xerox, 134, 154, 177, 200, 269

Y style of management, 34–35
Young, Richard, 161
Yugoslavia, 172–73